MW00678801

Praise for *HR's !*

"This book is a terrific primer on why HR is a critical component of strategy execution. Having a great strategy is not enough; you need to have the team to execute in order to win in the market. Understanding what your existing leaders need to succeed is as critical as the strategies to recruit new leaders, and this book knits together all these components in a straightforward fashion that reflects the realities of today. I would recommend this book to HR leaders who have a thirst to be 'in the game' with the business leaders they support."

—Byron Vielehr, President, D&B International
and Global Operations, Dun & Bradstreet®

"In most firms, labor is among the largest costs—in fact, often the biggest cost—but very few enterprises manage the people equation with the same effectiveness and precision that they handle production, supply chains, IT, sales, and finance. That is largely because HR departments lack the skills to make a difference in today's fast-changing, hyper-connected, global business environment. This book provides a proven path forward for a new type of high-performance HR leader—one who can bring a unique skill set to the top decision-making table by understanding how the business operates and how to find the right people, craft the best organizational design, and hone processes to make the firm's strategy successful."

—R. Gary Bridge, PhD, former senior vice president of the Cisco
Internet Business Solutions Group (IBSG), Cisco Systems, Inc.

"HR executives are entering a critical new era, charged with broader and more complex responsibilities while facing widespread talent and resource shortages. This timely book provides a blueprint for HR professionals looking to shift their skill set, take a more sophisticated approach to talent management, and, most important, expand their organizational influence in challenging times. It's a terrific resource of progressive concepts and best practices."

—Charles W. B. Wardell, III, President and CEO, Witt/Kieffer

"Now that I'm a CEO, I enjoyed the two parts of this book. The first portion centers on the higher-level, business partnering dialogue—how HR can solve business problems. The second part describes the practical talent acquisition and deployment tools that organizations' executives should embrace. I found the references powerful and contemporary in nature, and truly invaluable for senior business executives across the functional silos. The proprietary examples from the authors' corporate work are captivating. But here's what's most engaging about this book: Rather than best practices, this work captures, in so many ways, the next practices required to differentiate HR's future from HR's past."

—Mark Parrish, CEO, Stuart Dean Company, Inc.

"Wise investment in human capital can cause remarkably good results. But when a company gets it wrong, the costs can be staggering. This book absolutely nails the essentials of getting it right, from assessments and selection to talent growth and organizational development. A must for CEOs in enlightened companies that seek maximum success."

—Steve Townes, CEO, Ranger Aerospace

"In today's world, where things that were unique resources years ago, like access to capital, are now commodities, there is only one real battlefield: who has the best talent. It requires a new view of the integral role today's HR executive needs to play. This book helps lay out what it takes for companies and HR executives to raise their collective game to compete."

—John McKinley, founder, Great Falls Ventures; former president of AOL Digital Services and CTO, Merrill Lynch and News Corporation

"As the CEO of a fast-growing $140 million nonprofit, our number one concern is to ensure that the right talent is doing the right job at the right place at the right time. In the end, it is people that power the vision and mission of any organization; this is especially true for not-for-profits. I see many organizations fail because they don't understand the critical role played by developing and sustaining a strong organizational culture that promotes creativity and innovation—and one important component in this effort is thoughtfully deploying individual talent in all facets of the organization. This book is directly on point in encouraging HR executives to play a key role in building that culture—having the 'right' conversations with key executives and then finding and vetting essential talent for its workforce."

—Christine McMahon, CEO, FedCap

"Given the realities of the current executive talent market, this book provides a practical set of tools for talent, HR, and search consultants to use every day. CEOs', and their direct reports', time is limited; and if their go-to talent advisor can put themselves in their shoes and see what they see, it makes for a smarter and more involved relationship. The tools in this book will allow a top HR person to take a 20-minute meeting to another level and allow for a better business-focused relationship to develop between the CEO and the HR person now at the table. Personally, I was lucky to be mentored at a young age by a kind and merciful CEO who relied on me. I wish this book was available then, but I am thrilled it is here today. This will be a great resource for me and for our developing associates and researchers in our executive search firm as well."

—Conrad Lee, Managing Director,
Global Executive Search, The Judge Group

"This book is of great value to the customers (especially dissatisfied customers) of HR shops. Appearances to the contrary, nobody wants to see HR succeed more than HR's customers, if and only if that success is based on increasing enterprise value in appropriate ways. For many in HR, that enterprise success is based on HR stepping outside of its traditional comfort zones. HR will earn—and deserve—a seat at the table when its efforts clearly result in substantially growing enterprise value. This is a highly readable and actionable guide for any HR practitioner who wants to add considerable value to an organization of any type."

—Jack Flanagan, founder, Center for Nonprofit Governance
and Management; former SVP, Operations, USO and Giant Eagle

"The organizational challenges of today are not going to be addressed by reusing the approaches to talent acquisition and retention from previous decades. This book brilliantly highlights the salient issues and provides solid, actionable suggestions for both the leadership team and their HR organization to build a talent strategy partnership in a straightforward readable manner. I believe that HR executives would be well served to read, absorb and put together a pro-active execution plan aligned with the objectives of their organization based on this book's recommendations."

—Jerry J. Brennan, Chief Executive,
Security Management Resources Group of Companies

"We are in the midst of what I call 'The Era of Behavior'—a time when *how* we do what we do matters more than it ever has and in ways that it never has. Companies are emphatically proclaiming their humanity, with tag lines like 'The Human Network' (Cisco), 'Human Energy' (Chevron), and 'The Human Element' (Dow). So how could it be that a function like *Human Resources* can be sidelined, siloed, and *not* at the table for critical decisions? This book is full of reasons why and, more important, tangible steps HR executives can take to become relevant, powerful, and inspired stewards of the single most critical asset our companies have: their leaders at all levels."

—David I. Greenberg, Executive Vice President, LRN; former Senior Vice President and Member of the Corporate Management Committee, Altria Group, Inc.

HR'S SEAT
AT THE
TABLE

HR'S SEAT
AT THE
TABLE

HOW TO LEAD THE CONVERSATIONS
AND DELIVER THE TALENT
THAT DRIVES STRATEGIC RESULTS

Jack H. Cage, PhD,

and

Laura E. Larson

www.Leap4words.com

NEW YORK

Leap for Words
  A woman-owned business of Antigua Partners, Inc.
789 E. 17th Street
Brooklyn, NY 11230-2411
Phone: 917.538.9204 / E-mail: Leap4words@gmail.com / www.Leap4words.com

This publication is designed to provide accurate and authoritative information in regard to the subject matter covered. It is sold with the understanding that neither the author nor the publisher is engaged in rendering legal, accounting, or other professional service. If legal advice or other expert assistance is required, the services of a competent professional person should be sought.
— *From a Declaration of Principles Jointly Adopted by a Committee of the American Bar Association and a Committee of Publishers and Associations*

Printed in the United States of America.

Cover design: Jim Osborne
Book design and composition: Andrea Reider
Editor: Kathleen L. Florio

Ordering Information: Shop for Books and More Online at
www.HRs-Seat-at-the-Table.com
See back pages for an order form and information on how the sale of this book benefits UNICEF. Special discounts are available on quantity purchases of 10 or more books. This book is also available as an e-book, an audiobook, and e-reader-compatible files. For details, contact Laura Larson at the publisher address and phone number above.

Publisher's Cataloging-in-Publication Data
Cage, Jack Hays.
   HR's seat at the table : how to lead the conversations and deliver the talent that drives strategic results / Jack H. Cage and Laura E. Larson ; foreword by Andy Goodman.
      pages cm
   ISBN: 978-1-940687-53-7 (pbk.)
   ISBN: 978-1-940687-24-7 (e-book)
   Includes bibliographical references and index.
   1. Personnel management. 2. Organizational effectiveness. 3. Strategic planning.
4. Employees—Rating of. I. Larson, Laura E. II. Goodman, Andy. III. Title.
HF5549 .C23 2013
658.3—dc23   2013949904

To my amazing wife and partner, Laurie,
who showed me love and how to be a better man,
and who writes so powerfully that tears come to my eyes

—Jack

To the loving memory of my still-inspiring parents,
Ervin and Mary Larson,
two of the greatest "human resources" in my life;
and to Jack,
my greatest love and biggest fan

—Laura

Contents

Foreword

THE HUMAN RESOURCES function is changing and evolving. When I came into HR over 30 years ago, there were few college offerings in this field of study beyond Labor Relations; now that's changed. The problem is that many of these programs still lack business context.

Working for a business and crafting a strategy is really about telling a compelling story, getting people engaged, and getting people to execute that story to achieve the desired goal. HR professionals have a very definitive role to play in that process. They need to operate as an integral part of achieving business objectives. The problem is that a lot of these HR functions today tend to be satisfied by checking the boxes of an administrative checklist and containing cost. But that's not success—and that's not what the function should be about.

The best HR professionals I have known are some of the best business people I have met who happen to focus on human resources. They are active participants in business discussions and strategy development. They don't speak in HR; they speak in business terms. They understand the financial implications and ROI for every human capital investment and intervention. They are systems thinkers and look for fact-based root causes and holistic solutions.

In *HR's Seat at the Table,* Jack Cage and Laura Larson describe in highly engaging prose *how* an HR executive can do exactly these things in order to set themselves apart from their more typical peers. Having personally worked with Jack over many years and in various industries, there are few that I would consider more qualified to provide the perspective and insight you will find in this book. I encourage you to read it and apply Jack and Laura's suggestions if you are interested in not only having a seat at the table, but also knowing what exactly to say and do once you're there.

Andy Goodman
Executive Vice President/Chief Human Resources Officer

Preface

SEARCH AMAZON.COM with the keywords "HR" or "human resources," and more than 14,000 results pop up. So we had to ask, Does the world really need another book on this topic? Obviously we answered yes—and here's why.

In the last 16 years, working in and with organizations of all types—Fortune 500, midsize, family owned, for-profit, and nonprofit—we've consistently observed the same challenges facing HR professionals just about everywhere. We can put these issues in two general categories that reside on either side of the table:

Where the senior leadership sits, *HR has a credibility problem*. CEOs and other senior leaders complain that HR doesn't understand how business really operates, day-to-day; it's too process-laden and thus slow; and as a result, these executives typically don't turn to HR for help. It certainly wouldn't occur to most of them to talk strategy with their HR colleagues.

Where HR sits, *HR has a talent selection problem*. We've attended far too many meetings in which an HR executive can't comprehensively describe a slate of candidates for a critical role. This lack of clarity is usually the end product of a recruiting process that includes a vague position description and loosely managed (if managed at all) interviews. If the word *fit* is mentioned in a debrief, it usually gets flipped like a switch: good fit or bad fit—with no objective, deep explanation for either.

This book is our attempt to address these two categorical situations in a direct and practical way. We spell out what most business executives want to talk about and then how HR professionals can do so to gain credibility as both a strong talent expert *and* a strategic partner. It's one thing to be asked to sit at the table; it's quite another to know what to actually say once you're there. Equally important, however, is what to do when you step away from the table—which is why we dedicate half the book to talent selection. People are the means through which any organization's strategy gets implemented, and thus knowing how to vet and select great people is perhaps the single most critical function of HR. We believe that HR professionals will have a regular seat at the table *after* they have shown they do understand business and how strategy plays out in their organization, and then consistently deliver strong talent to execute that strategy.

We'd like to underscore an important point: When we discuss HR "becoming a strategic partner" or "taking a seat at the table," this is not as much a judgment call as it is a description of skills that can, indeed, be learned or honed. No matter where you are in your HR career or where you feel you fall on the "strategic business partner" spectrum—from already highly respected and included in high-level discussion, to considered strictly as more of an administrative player on a support team—we offer recommendations that are easy to apply right away and that will make your own work more effective, not to mention valuable to your business colleagues.

Everything we discuss in this book involves ideas and practices we had to learn ourselves over the years and have since put into practice. More than one reviewer told us, "I sure wish I had a book like this when I was starting out!" Jack himself couldn't help but say the same thing. When he retired from the U.S. Army in 1997, he moved from an Army base in Fort Rucker, Alabama, to an executive search firm on Wall Street. Can you say "culture shock"? He'd had some exposure to business while studying at Columbia University in the 1980s, but not directly. For example, he conducted survey-design research for a firm working exclusively with IBM and got a second-hand view of how business functions are finely differentiated to increase sales, profit, and market dominance. However, that minimal exposure wasn't going to cut it in the dog-eat-dog culture and boom days of Manhattan's Financial District.

As a civilian who'd swapped battle dress uniform for pinstripes, Jack had to learn not only how business really operated, but also how to speak the language of business. For Jack, "strategic planning" meant whiteboarding with a couple generals and the national security advisor in the outer tier of the Pentagon; "talent selection" meant vetting officers for combat assaults. In some ways, Jack then was where some of you may be now—also needing to switch gears and learn new ways of operating at work and describing that work to colleagues.

We know you can do it, because we've done it, and you can, too.

INSIDE THIS BOOK

We enjoy a good read as much as anyone, but, frankly, if a book doesn't offer realistic, practical advice we can actually do something with, we're left only with a blur of impressions rather than a slate of actionable ideas. For that reason, much of what we describe here comes straight from our work as executive search and management consultants with HR and business executives around the world.

We combine survey results, research data, and expert opinions from the field with the opinions of executives we know and work with. We use contemporary business news stories to illustrate theories and principles, so it's easy to connect the dots and start viewing business activities through more of a strategy lens.

We know the first step to definitively solving a problem—like the two we described earlier regarding HR's credibility and talent selection challenges—is admitting the problem exists. Thus, we share sometimes unpleasant feedback from colleagues and research findings that point out the gap between what most C-suite executives want from human resource professionals and what many HR teams actually deliver. Our aim is certainly not to offend any readers but, rather, to provide the context for what quickly ensues after those points in the book: explicit recommendations on how to respond—immediately—to such less-than-flattering stereotypical views of HR.

Those stereotypes open the book in the introduction, "Will HR Even Be Invited to the Table?" We discuss how many of these persistent views of HR, combined with the allure of cost and time efficiencies, have led to the rise of human resources outsourcing (HRO) and professional employer organizations (PEOs)—which in turn has meant thousands of unemployed HR folks. Drawing comparisons to the information technology (IT) sector of about 10 years ago, we suggest that HR take a cue from IT colleagues and reposition itself as a future-focused, business-oriented engine that can fuel strategic growth.

The three chapters in Part 1, "Leading Conversations," take the first steps toward helping you heed the oft-repeated advice from CEOs and senior leaders to HR professionals: "Get to know my business." There's no better place to get to know business than to understand strategy. To that end, Chapter 1 sketches out different ways to begin to conceive of strategy generally and also specifically, as it's playing out right now in your organization. *Strategy*, we find, is a term used so much nowadays that much of its meaning has been diluted to apply to nearly any activity that involves more than two people chatting around a conference table. We bring clarity to the term by not simply defining it but also illustrating it through stories of well-known brands like Starbucks, as well as with approachable models and easy-to-use tools that have been invaluable in our own work, including SWOT and PEST analyses and scenario planning. The chapter closes by discussing examples of publicly traded firms' actual strategy documents. We'll show you where to find yours and then how to read it and discuss it in a talent-centric manner so that strategy becomes real for you, infusing your conversations in highly pertinent and business-savvy ways.

Chapter 2's theme is about starting to speak like a knowledgeable business person by acting like a confident salesperson. Many an HR professional refers to business colleagues as "my customers"; this chapter asks you to start walking that talk. We offer ideas for developing what consultative salespeople call situational fluency, showing you how HR professionals are already embodying much of that competency. Tackling the HR stereotype once more, this chapter also explores ways to nurture the self-confidence necessary to lead business conversations. We explain why stereotypes exist in the first place and how to overcome them, by tapping our personal story as an educational example as well as fascinating "power pose" research from Harvard that we've validated in our workplace training programs.

Picking up the thread of the sales metaphor, Chapter 3 describes how you can adapt tools from the Solution Selling® toolbox to prepare and guide your conversations with your CEO and other business leaders. This is the approach that helped Jack finally "break the code" when it came to learning to speak and act like a business person—and thereby earn his own seat at the table as a trusted strategic advisor.

We'll show you how to adapt this approach in HR-relevant ways; for example, what HR theorists and authors like Mark Huselid and Dave Ulrich refer to as an organization's "value chain" is the "pain chain" in sales lingo. Your credibility skyrockets if you can understand the linkages between high-level pain points (e.g., the pain of the CEO) and the lower-level specific causes (e.g., missing new-account revenue targets from the VP, Sales). With this degree of understanding, you can then lead conversations about pertinent challenges and offer your ideas for solving them. Taking this tack will ensure that the topics you discuss with key players in your organization are not HR metrics and data analytics but what truly matters to *them*: solutions to operational problems that will help them execute strategy in their respective businesses. We share lots of examples so that you can start conducting business like this right away.

Treating your business colleagues as your most valuable customers means also that you understand how the different parts of your organization interact and influence each other. This quality of interdependence surfaces most critically when it comes to an organization's talent. If the team in Sales is underperforming, then lower sales numbers will mean Finance must uncover ways to cut costs and expenses (e.g., using an HRO firm to handle some of *your* tasks). Lower revenue, in turn, means your CEO must devise new ways to increase profits or risk losing his job (we've seen this happen, and we'll tell you how it occurred).

Part 2, "Delivering Talent," helps ensure that you are engaged in the best pre-hire practices available to select the high-performing talent any organization needs to survive and thrive. Chapter 4 focuses on the crucial starting block of position descriptions (PDs). We spell out the components of a comprehensive PD, from necessary qualifications and competencies, to the motivation for someone to take the job. Reviewing an actual position description from one of our executive searches, you'll learn how to create a powerful PD that will not only attract well-qualified, highly motivated candidates but also guide you later during focused interviews.

With a nod to the estimated 80 percent of organizations that already use assessment instruments, Chapter 5 makes a powerful argument for the valuable role that these tools play pre-hire—and well after the hire, too. Using the examples of four instruments we use every week, we explain how you can use their results to craft targeted (and legal) interview questions, identify potential derailing behaviors, and evaluate fit—to the position, the team, and the organization—in precise and useful terms.

Chapter 6 applies the learnings from the prior two chapters in discussing what makes for a well-managed interview process. You'll learn how to determine who should conduct interviews and then how to manage that team to best effect. We share ideas for discovering how a candidate's experience ties directly to the position's required outcomes, sidestepping a candidate's "dating behavior," getting to truthful stories instead of canned responses, and seizing control of reference checks so that you can capitalize on the wealth of information from these sources.

We tie many of our opinions and recommendations together in the conclusion, "From Words to Action." There you'll read our interview with Andy Goodman, an accomplished executive vice president of Human Resources and chief human resources officer at E*TRADE Financial and CA Technologies. In his characteristic direct and good-humored way, Andy offers his best advice to HR professionals at all levels. The conclusion also includes a quick self-assessment to help you determine what areas of leading conversations and delivering talent are your strong and weak spots.

A selection of "Additional Resources" appears next; here we list some of the professional associations, educational resources, training programs, and business partners that can help you further hone your business knowledge and talent selection skill set. The book closes with an extensive reference list and index.

HOW TO USE THIS BOOK

Whether you take the conclusion's self-assessment or not, you may already know where your professional focus should be at this stage of your career. As a result, you may opt to not start reading this book at the beginning, with the introduction. That's fine with us. If you've been wondering about how to lower the risk of a bad hire by folding assessment instruments into your recruiting process, then start with Chapter 5. If your curiosity is piqued by how in the world a sales methodology can assist HR, jump into Chapters 2 and 3. Perhaps your boss has suggested you go back to the drawing board when it comes to position descriptions; then Chapter 4 is a great place to start. Maybe you're in the spot we were in several years ago and need to learn the fundamental topics of business conversations. Then starting with Chapter 1 on strategy makes sense.

Throughout the book are boxed features called "Pull Up a Chair!" These sidebars sometimes illustrate a point we're discussing in the chapter, such as how Apple's latest iPhone 5C exemplifies a corporation addressing its stakeholders, business context, and strategy. Sometimes they're a collection of tips on HR topics such as workforce planning analytics and EEOC compliance with assessment instruments. And sometimes they're examples of what *not* to do, such as a weak position description that crossed our path or consumer products that famously flopped partly due to, we suspect, a lack of thorough strategic planning. Reviewers found the Pull Up a Chair features informative and entertaining, and we hope you do, too.

One last point: We are huge proponents of experiential learning, believing that there is no better way to learn new material than by doing it. We often use the metaphor of sports: you can talk about the game of basketball all you like, but until you're actually on the court, dribbling the ball and shooting hoops, you're never really going to get it, let alone perfect the skills it requires. So, as best we can on the pages of a book, we will walk you through the processes of how to

- uncover your organization's business imperatives,
- know the right questions to ask of your stakeholders,
- do your own market research and competitive analysis,
- compose precisely targeted position descriptions,
- evaluate and interview candidates, and even
- hone your professional confidence and presence for stronger influence.

In other words, we've set the table. Are you ready to take your seat? Then, pull up a chair!

Acknowledgments

WE'D LIKE to thank the following people who shared their advice for HR professionals and reviewed the manuscript:

Mike Abbaei
Dorian Anderson
Andus Baker
Mark Barrenechea
Jerry Brennan
Gary Bridge
Monica Burton
Keith Eades
Jack Flanagan
Andy Goodman
David Greenberg
Lena Haas
Janet Jones-Parker
Conrad Lee
John McKinley

Christine McMahon
Sean Moriarty
Victor Nichols
Phil Parisi
Mark Parrish
John Rao
John Roy
Tom Shull
Steve Smith
James Touchstone
Steve Townes
Don Van Eynde
Byron Vielehr
Chuck Wardell
Bill Wray

Thanks to all of you for your professional judgment, which has enhanced every chapter of this book. A very special thank-you to Andy Goodman, a good friend and the best example of an HR executive we've ever met, for his expertise and ongoing support; and to the team at Sales Performance International— Keith Eades, Jimmy Touchstone, Steve Smith, and John Roy—for sharing their insights on Solution Selling® and the figures that appear in Chapter 3.

We owe an immense debt of gratitude to our fabulous production team. Our ever-jolly, always professional book designer and compositor, Andrea Reider, took our ideas for the tone and look of the book and made them a beautiful reality. We could not be happier with the end product, and that's largely due to Andrea's creativity, workmanship, and patience. Kathleen Florio wielded her editorial wisdom, expertise, and kindness to make the text flow and help us not embarrass ourselves—especially when it came to nightmarish variations on the word *assess*. Kathleen did double duty by also proofreading; a special thank-you to her for good-naturedly keeping pace with our harried schedule. Finally, Jim Osborne (www.pd90design.com) delivered a fantastic cover that captured exactly the sense of professionalism and playfulness we were looking for.

Thank you to Catherine Cage for transcribing our interview notes and for cheerfully keeping us company in the wee hours of the night while writing this manuscript. Let's hear it for eight hours of sleep—in a row. And thanks also to Michael Bass of Michael Bass Associates for offering very helpful tips on printing and for role-modeling the Zen approach to book production.

From Laura: I'd like to express special thanks (which hardly seems a big enough word) to Jack, for teaching me everything I know about talent selection, executive search, and love—not necessarily in that order. Because of your undying confidence and faith in me, I've been able to accomplish things I've always dreamed of and do things I never would've imagined. It's a great honor and an all-round blast to share this incredible life with a man like you.

From Jack: How does someone thank the one person who completely changed her life to be with me all the while being my greatest fan? A lifetime of gratitude and love goes to Laurie, my incredible wife and partner. I love you more than words can ever express. You are my real-life hero. I'm honored to be your husband, partner, and love.

Introduction

Will HR Even Be Invited to the Table?

L ET'S FACE IT: HR has a bad rep.
Who can forget the audaciously titled article "Why We Hate HR"—as much as we might like to (Hammonds, 2005). The author, a deputy editor of *Fast Company* at the time, stacked one sharp barb on top of another. For example:

- "HR pursues efficiency in lieu of value . . . because it's easier—and easier to measure."
- "Most human-resources managers aren't particularly interested in, or equipped for, doing business."
- "HR people . . . pursue standardization and uniformity in the face of a workforce that is heterogeneous and complex."
- "Human resources . . . forfeits long-term value for short-term cost efficiency."
- "HR people aren't the sharpest tacks in the box."

Ouch.

To be fair, *Fast Company* offered something of a pain reliever in a blog post for the *Harvard Business Review* called "Why We (Shouldn't) Hate HR." Yes, it came five years later; and yes, it wasn't written by the same fellow who wrote the original hackle-raising article. But at least this author offered more of a middle position:

> [T]oo many organizations aren't as demanding, as rigorous, as creative about the human element in business as they are about finance, marketing, and R&D. If companies and their CEOs aren't serious about the people side of their organizations, how can we expect HR people in those organizations to play as serious a role as we (and they) want them to play? (Taylor, 2010, para. 2)

On the one hand, we agree whole-heartedly with this balanced view. It always takes two people to tango, after all, and HR's colleagues—in Finance, Operations, Sales, IT, and so on, and even the CEO—also have their role to play in developing a more respectful, productive work relationship that benefits not only the individual players but the whole enterprise.

On the other hand, we have to admit that in the course of our own day-to-day work, we still hear comments like this recent one from a senior vice president in Sales at a large health care company: "Sometimes we give HR a special project to do just to have them chase their tails and keep them out of our way." What led to the conversation in the first place, to be honest, was this executive's interest in our firm conducting a talent audit—an HR kind of job if ever there was one. Tapping his own HR team to do this work never even struck him as a viable option. "They're worthless," he said.

This SVP is not unusual. The fact persists that too many people, even those working within your own organization, still generally regard HR professionals as paper pushers with a college degree. HR is sometimes seen as the rule-bound team of data-entry clerks who take in the information required to pay people every two weeks and process health care claims.

At the same time, however, even these kinds of traditional HR functions are increasingly being automated and outsourced in order to save money, especially in an economy that still hasn't regained its balance. The few hundred employees at one company we worked with, for example, managed just fine after its vice president of Human Resources was let go last year, followed soon thereafter by the rest of the small HR team. The CEO saw full-fledged HR as an unnecessary expense—a disposable commodity. If he needed advice or specific assistance, he'd buy it when he needed it.

As part of the human resources outsourcing (HRO) sector, a vast number of firms (e.g., Accenture, ADP, Allegis) have created the ability to take on businesses' payroll and accounting needs, along with retirement plans, benefit packages, training, recruiting, risk management, safety compliance, EEOC discrimination suits and workers' comp claims, and nuances around the Family Medical Leave Act and employment practices liability insurance (EPLI).

All of these areas—from the oversight of comp and benefits to the compliance with zillions of state and federal labor laws—were once firmly under the purview of your friendly neighborhood Department of Human Resources. Now your boss can move them out of your organization altogether by hiring an HRO firm. Take a look at how just one such firm of the hundreds operating in the United States describes its services:

> [We] will help relieve your staff from the cumbersome, day-to-day management of human resources tasks [and] will enable your key personnel to shift its focus from an administrative role to a proactive one that will help contribute to your company's success. . . . Our team of HR professionals and robust on-line payroll system will provide your staff the time to focus on internal operations, employee retention and corporate growth. (www.cpehr.com)

This firm even promotes its "à la carte" menu of options (as do many other HROs). We can hear that CEO client of ours now: "I'll take one 401(k) plan and 50 employee manuals to go, please!"

HR now ranks second behind IT as some of the most commonly outsourced functions in U.S. organizations. Several years ago, 94 percent of large employers surveyed by Hewitt Associates were already outsourcing at least one HR function (Hammonds, 2005). The fact is, the HRO industry has ballooned in size and will only get bigger: Global Industry Analysts, Inc., a business research and forecasting firm, estimates that HRO will be a $162 billion global industry by 2015 and jump to $199.6 billion by 2017.

We're all sadly familiar with downsizing and its resultant cost savings, but when organizations let HR employees go and engage an HRO, they're saving more than just the expense of salaries, insurance, and overhead. By tapping very focused expertise only when required, they're also accruing real savings in things like workers' comp payments and employee benefits—20 percent savings for each, according to some estimates (e.g., HROPlus, 2009). The bottom line is, if an organization has at least 20 employees, it's probably cheaper to engage an HRO or form thereof, such as a professional employer organization (PEO):

> The more successful a business becomes, the more overwhelmed they are with the responsibilities of having employees and the more they need a professional employer organization. . . . A PEO company lets clients grow their bottom line by removing the areas that do not generate revenue, take up valuable space and require several full-time employees to manage. (Employee Leasing Options, 2013, para. 1)

CEOs and other corporate leaders are clearly getting the HROs' marketing message. Shifts in the ways organizations fill their human resources needs have undeniably hit HR professionals hard, by the loss of their full-time jobs. In late 2011, the Society for Human Resource Management (SHRM) estimated that about 43,000 HR professionals in the United States were out of work (Leonard, 2011b). Obviously a sluggish economy has a major role to play in any sector's unemployment rates, but at the same time, you have to admit: outsourcing has come knocking—hard—on HR's door. As bluntly stated in the highly negative article quoted at the start of this introduction, "Most HR organizations have ghettoized themselves literally to the brink of obsolescence" (Hammonds, 2005, para. 10).

You know what? That remark reminds us of what people were saying about IT several years ago. When information technology was the big new thing, in the early 1990s, organizations large and small rushed to establish in-house IT teams charged with writing code and setting up intranet networks, data storage and retrieval capabilities, and other customized information systems.

At first, automating access to organizational data was hugely helpful—just as automating payroll, benefits enrollment, and applicant-tracking data within the HR department is helpful. Eventually, however, a tipping point emerged so that IT professionals' proficiency at mastering the processes that kept their company humming was precisely what also nudged thousands of them right out of a job. Remember, in the world of outsourcing, IT is number one on the hit list. Entire national economies, like those in India, Ireland, and Romania (to name just a few), have been dramatically lifted by the success of their IT outsourcing firms doing business with U.S. corporations that are always seeking ways to lower costs.

Facing "the brink of obsolescence," what did those in-house IT departments do? Pick up their toys and go home? Not exactly. They repositioned themselves to play a more *externally* focused role—gathering competitive intelligence, for example, and measuring local, national, and global trends in the marketplace. They fine-tuned all the more the nature of *key metrics* that parlayed perfectly into supporting their internal business colleagues' core activities and helping solve their business problems. They became more *future oriented* than present-day focused, turning their sights more toward what challenges would be coming up 5, 10, even 15 years down the road and less toward making sure the phones work and the computers don't crash (even—gasp!—in the face of that challenge of once nearly mythical proportions: Y2K). And they learned the *language of business,* translating their data-heavy findings into terms that the executives in the C suite could understand and offering practical ideas for new practices that those colleagues could then share with their own teams. All of these new behaviors and approaches positioned IT professionals differently in the eyes of leadership and served the greater good of the entire organization's ongoing viability and success.

We propose that HR folks follow the IT example. To be true strategic partners to business leaders, you must shift your skill set to become more internal-customer oriented and future focused. For your colleagues to regard you with due respect as a real partner, you must create and deploy key metrics that tie in seamlessly to advance their business activities. To be invited to take your seat at the table—and then have something to contribute—you must speak the language of business fluently, with both internal and external stakeholders, and strive every day to support your customers' operational activities while addressing their challenges. The authors of *The HR Scorecard* summarize this view by noting that HR professionals must "move from a 'bottom-up' perspective (emphasizing compliance and traditional HR) to a 'top-down' perspective (emphasizing the implementation of strategy)" (Becker, Huselid, & Ulrich, 2001, pp. 2–3).

The parallel with IT only goes so far, however. HR professionals deviate in one marked way from their peers in information technology: as their name suggests, they, more than anyone else, work with *human* resources. Over and over, survey data and research clearly state that the top challenge for organizations of all types and sizes is people—finding them, assessing them, hiring them, engaging them, and retaining them.

In 2011, Cornell Advanced HR Studies surveyed 172 chief HR officers, who told researchers that their most critical challenge was, in a word, talent (Wright, Stewart, & Ozias, 2011). Boston Consulting Group found similar results in 2011: recruiting, developing, and retaining talent was a top concern for both "current capability" and "future importance." In a November 2012 survey, SHRM found that HR executives expect their top three challenges over the next 10 years to be all centered on people:

> New economic realities are putting pressure on HR to widen its focus from the administrative role it has traditionally played to a broader, strategic role.
>
> BRIAN BECKER ET AL.

- Retaining and rewarding the best employees
- Developing the next generation of corporate leaders
- Creating a corporate culture that attracts the best employees (Schramm, 2013)

In PwC's *15th Annual Global CEO Survey,* released in 2012, one in four CEOs said they have not been able to pursue a market opportunity or implement a strategic initiative because of talent challenges. One in three admitted they worry that skills shortages will reduce their company's ability to innovate effectively.

Authors of the most recent PwC global CEO survey, of February 2013, sum up the results by noting that business leaders remain interested in "cutting costs, but not cutting people." Alison Cooper, CEO of the Imperial Tobacco

Group in the United Kingdom, exemplifies this view: "The key in this environment is the people agenda. It's one of the easier things to cut in terms of investment when you're in a tough environment, but I think it's essential that companies continue to invest in their people" (PwC, 2013, p. 6).

Another advantage for many HR professionals is derived, ironically, from their employer's increasing use of outsourcing. Yes, many organizations employ HRO or PEO firms to reduce costs, gain access to outside expertise, and improve service quality; in fact, Aon Hewitt (2009) notes that 82 percent of firms that outsource some HR functions achieved exactly those sorts of benefits. But at the same time, many firms that use HROs are doing so to help "remove the day-to-day administrivia of managing HR programs so HR can focus on supporting their most important business challenges" (Aon Hewitt, 2009, para. 8). "The HR function as a whole is under scrutiny and in some cases being reduced, with management's expectation being 'We want our HR department to be strategic, not administrative'" (Miller, 2004, para. 2). This is great news for those HR professionals who want to leverage their role in powerful, strategy-executing ways.

The bottom line is, everything cannot be outsourced. The deep, unique perspective on an organization's talent—both the current workforce and future needs—that a top-notch human resources team can share is a highly valuable skill. Just like spell-check will never replace a human editor reading a manuscript, no HRO in the world will ever completely replace an HR department. Only an HR executive who takes the time to understand the various activities that key players carry out to execute strategy—and, more important, who acts first and foremost like a business person, not an HR staffer—can fully grasp what senior executives want and need out of their departmental teams. When you can talk their talk *and* deliver the solutions (including great talent) they want with a sense of due urgency, you become irreplaceable. In other words, you have earned your seat at the table.

PART 1

Leading Conversations

THE HUMAN RESOURCES role in strategy, and especially its execution, is critical not only for an organization's achievement of core financial goals but also for the survival of many people currently working as HR professionals. Without being able to link—in *business* terms, not HR terms—how human resources directly supports implementing strategy and dramatically reduces the risk in its execution, many HR functions are susceptible to the ever-growing trend of outsourcing, as we've discussed in the introduction. Now we tackle this challenge head-on in the first three chapters:

- Chapter 1: A User's Guide to Strategy: What It Is, Why It's Important, and Where to Find It
- Chapter 2: Look Who's Talking: Getting Yourself Ready for Strategic Conversations
- Chapter 3: The New Rules of Engagement: HR Driving the Business Conversation

When we asked what they believe characterizes the best HR professionals in their experience, executives in both human resources and business roles across the board told us that a genuine and deep understanding of the wider business context—not just HR best practices—was critical. "The best HR professionals take the time to fully understand the business today and where it is going in the future," said John Rao, the managing director and head of U.S. operations for the global Financial Services practice at Navigant. Mike Abbaei, the president of DST Brokerage Solutions and former CIO of Legg-Mason, echoed this view by stating simply, "They have taken the time to learn my business and understand my needs." This core competency applies equally to HR professionals employed in the nonprofit sector, too. Jack Flanagan, the founder of the Center for Effective Nonprofit Governance and Management and a former senior operations executive at the USO (and, earlier, Giant Eagle), remarked, "HR did their best work with me (and my team, and I with them) when they made the effort to truly understand how we added value to the enterprise. We need HR to think and act more like business people with a particular expertise in HR rather than HR über-experts."

> The best HR professionals take the time to learn my business and understand my needs.
>
> MIKE ABBAEI

The question at this point is, How, exactly, do HR professionals take the steps to understand and speak in the terms and to the concerns of executives in other functional areas? How can they apply key HR competencies, such as talent acquisition (the topic of Part 2), to enhance operational effectiveness and, ultimately, the successful execution of strategy, all while keeping their organization's mission and objectives firmly in mind?

Part 1 opens by offering clarity on what, precisely, is even meant by the term *strategy*. You'll learn that strategy is both a preconceived, written document, easily accessible to the public, and also an ever-evolving dynamic entity. It's this latter manifestation of "strategy" that is at the center of conversations with your business colleagues in Finance, Sales, and other units—not to mention with your CEO and president. We also offer simple yet crucial steps you can take to expand your business-oriented knowledge base of the internal and external dynamics that continuously affect strategy as it gets played out in real time. "If you [as an HR professional] want to be a strategic player, you'll have to understand budgets, strategic planning, economic forecasts, and change management" (Sunoo, 2013, para. 11).

The next chapters in Part 1 discuss *how* to apply what you learn about strategy in highly focused, informative discussion with your business partners. The best HR professionals have "an intellectual curiosity that means [they] take the time to convene with their business colleagues," according to Janet Jones-Parker, president of a specialty executive search firm. "They find out what those colleagues are thinking, along with the issues affecting the identification, development, and recruitment of the best talent."

To this end of learning what's really weighing on your colleagues' minds—and how you can explicitly support their efforts and help solve their problems—we cast our recommendations in terms of regarding these business people as your most important internal customers. Many HR professionals already regularly toss around the statement that their business partners are their "customers"; we catch that ball and run with it. We adapt the popular Solution Selling® approach for use by a non-salesperson to help guide your high-level business-centric conversations. Jack offers himself as an example of someone whose core career experience lay outside the business functions that he had to quickly become well versed in when he first entered executive search. This was the game-changing approach that gave him situational fluency, as it's called—the credibility accrued from understanding interconnected functions (the "value chain," in *HR Scorecard* parlance; Becker et al., 2001) and speaking in business terms.

Executives become especially valuable to senior leadership when they can not only work in their functional silo—like human resources—but also communicate and solve problems across the business units in their organization. For HR executives specifically, the most effective ones "partner closely with the business . . . and are engrained in the company above and beyond formal talent review processes," said Lena Haas, a senior vice president at E*TRADE. "They make an extra effort to understand the business and be well versed in strategy and execution priorities." Part 1 will show you how to be just that sort of "true business partner" Lena described to us.

A User's Guide to Strategy
What It Is, Why It's Important, and Where to Find It

LIKE YOU, we review thousands of résumés every year. If we had to guess what single word shows up in most of them—no matter what the industry, sector, or position of the job applicant—it would be some form of *strategy.* "Our sales strategy," "A strategic leader," "Strategic initiatives"—*strategy* pops up everywhere.

The problem is, *strategy* and *strategic* are bandied about so much these days that much of their meaning has become diluted. When someone describes him- or herself to us as a "strategic thinker," we have to ask: "What does that mean? What have you as a strategic thinker *done to help achieve an organization's objectives?*"

This chapter offers ways to start wrapping your head around the sometimes "squishy" topic of strategy. We envision our approach as going from the wide-angle view down to the close-up. The wide angle considers what strategy means in the general sense as it applies to any organization. Then we'll start zooming in by looking at the written strategy of real companies. Nearly every firm has such a document, and we'll show you where to find it and what parts of it are especially pertinent to you as a business executive. The next chapter will discuss how to focus on a close-up of strategy, as it's playing out today in the various departments of your organization.

We're fans of reverse engineering: starting with the end in mind and winding back from that point. So, if this book is to help you deliver strategic results, let's start by defining what we mean by "strategic results"—or *strategy*.

STRATEGY DEFINED

In his first career, as an Army officer, Jack helped create and implement *strategy* in its original military sense: a demonstration of generalship, according to the Greek *stratēgia*. In his second career, as an executive search and management consultant, he knows it as most business people do: a carefully thought-out plan to achieve success—usually in the form of market position, revenue and profit, or market share.

> Strategy has been variously described as a way to define an economic entity and what business it is in, a plan of how an economic entity will achieve its goals, and a co-created process of innovation and discovery between the economic entity and external stakeholders. These definitions illustrate wide-ranging views toward strategy—from an internal, deliberate planning process to an explanation of an unplanned emergent behavior. (Swanson & Holton, 2009, pp. 406–407, reference citations omitted)

We mentioned at the start of this chapter that many organizations have prepared, in writing, a strategy, and we'll show you how to find that document later. Such documents fall into the category of what Swanson and Holton (2009) describe here as a preplanned, "co-created" definition of what an organization is and does.

> Strategy can *form* as well as be *formulated.*
>
> HENRY MINTZBERG

But it's important to highlight the other type of strategy also mentioned in Swanson and Holton's quote: an "explanation" of events that are unfolding in real time. In other words, a strategy can be *proactive,* and another strategy, even for the same organization, *reactive.* Strategy can be defined before, during, and after events taking place in the business marketplace. It's "a dynamic phenomenon that necessarily unfolds over a period of time in a business environment that is inherently unstable" (Swanson & Holton, 2009, p. 369). In other words, to paraphrase another favorite theorist of ours—John Lennon—strategy is what happens while you're busy making other plans.

To explore the meaning of strategy in a bit more detail, we take our cue from *Forbes* magazine, which noted recently that "there are two people, and only two, whose ideas must be taught to every MBA in the world: Michael Porter and Henry Mintzberg" (Moore, 2011, para. 1). Scores of business scholars have committed their careers to defining the nuances of strategy and elaborating on its meaning in various contexts around the world, but we're huge fans of both Mintzberg and Porter and have employed their ideas in our own work. (Laura has also come to know Henry by working on three of his best-selling books.) We further simplify our discussion by choosing just one piece of work from each of these scholars: a classic strategy model from Mintzberg, and a classic strategy article from Porter. More comprehensive treatment is well beyond the scope of this book, but we encourage you to read a broader range of both men's works, among others', to appreciate their relevance to modern business. See the Pull Up a Chair feature for a few recommendations.

PULL UP A CHAIR!
Recommended Reading

We're both voracious readers, of print books, digital books, magazines, newspapers, online newsletters, cereal boxes—you name it. So we clearly agree with our friend and colleague Jack Flanagan, who has had a successful career as a senior-level operator in both the for-profit (Giant Eagle, Costco) and nonprofit (Center for Effective Nonprofit Governance and Management, USO) sectors, when he responded this way to our survey asking business colleagues for their advice to HR professionals:

(continued on next page)

One tip I'd offer is that HR folks [should] read a lot more about business—some theoretical, some corporate history about both successful and unsuccessful organizations, some general business—so as to better understand the theory and reality of enterprise value creation. If I, as an operator, can find the time over the years to become a student of Peter Senge, Noel Tichy, and Dave Ulrich (to name three of my HR/OD [organizational development] heroes), I don't think it's too much to ask any salaried HR person to understand "how we make money" or "how we increase market share."

To that point, and in addition to the references listed at the end of this book, here's just a handful of titles we recommend for being both content-rich and highly engaging:

- *Good to Great: Why Some Companies Make the Leap . . . and Others Don't* by Jim Collins (HarperBusiness, 2001) and, with Jerry Porras, *Built to Last: Successful Habits of Visionary Companies* (Harper Business Essentials, 1990). These two books combined have sold over four million copies and have been perpetual best-sellers for decades now—for good reason. Tapping his ongoing research, at his private firm as well as at Stanford University's Graduate School of Business, Jim Collins drills down on what makes or breaks a company. He's famous for using the metaphor of "getting the right people on the bus" when he describes the importance of targeted and timely talent management. All of Collins's work is superb, but start with these two books (and if you work in a nonprofit, you may also enjoy Collins's 2005 title, *Good to Great and the Social Sectors*).
- *The Essential Drucker: The Best of Sixty Years of Peter Drucker's Essential Writings on Management* by Peter Drucker (HarperBusiness, 2008). The "father of modern management" passed away in 2005, but he spent the great portion of his 95 years thinking and writing about management philosophy and practice. He coined the term *knowledge worker*, predicting the decline of a blue-collar workforce. He also was the person who first described what we know now as outsourcing,

distinguishing between front-room functions, which are integral to supporting a business, and back-room activities (or the "back office," as we hear modern executives say all the time), which are not—they don't generate revenue and so should be passed along to other companies for which they *are* the front-room activities. If you want to appreciate the background thinking that undoubtedly inspires many of your colleagues' views on business today, dive into Drucker.

• *SuperCorp: How Vanguard Companies Create Innovation, Profits, Growth, and Social Good* (Crown Business, 2009) and *World Class: Thriving Locally in the Global Economy* (Free Press, 1997), among more than a dozen others, by Rosabeth Moss Kanter. Kanter is the former editor of the *Harvard Business Review* and currently a professor at Harvard Business School and chair and director of the university's Advanced Leadership Initiative. She writes eloquently on how organizations can thrive amid the global churn of innovation and technology, as well as the factors accounting for an individual's career success (e.g., her book *Confidence*). Like her Harvard colleague Michael Porter (discussed later in the main text), Kanter describes how strategy and management will need to adapt in the face of ongoing global economic and cultural change in order to maintain a competitive advantage—precisely the sort of future- and outward-focused orientation often required of HR professionals today.

MINTZBERG: STRATEGY IN FIVE EASY PIECES

McGill University professor Henry Mintzberg, a Distinguished Scholar of the Academy of Management and winner of two McKinsey Awards for his articles in the *Harvard Business Review,* has studied strategy formation and other areas of managerial work for decades. To help clarify the multifaceted and dynamic nature of strategy, he proposed the now-classic Five *P*s model (Mintzberg, 1987; see Figure 1.1). Each part of this model looks at a different component of strategy:

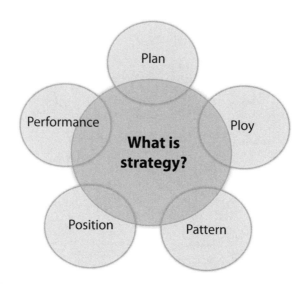

FIGURE 1.1 Five *Ps* Model

- *Plan:* A strategy is developed with purpose and in advance.
- *Ploy:* A strategy tries to outsmart an organization's competitors.
- *Pattern:* A strategy identifies what approach was successful in the past that may also be successful in the future.
- *Position:* A strategy describes where the organization is situated in the marketplace and how it can distinguish its products or services.
- *Perspective:* A strategy recognizes how the firm's organizational culture—ways of getting things done—and collective thinking affect its strategic decision making.

Let's take a closer look at each *P* in turn.

Perhaps the most common way one thinks of a strategy is as a *plan*. Most executives are comfortable with planning: put simply, gathering and reviewing information, seeking ideas from their team, and brainstorming ways to put those ideas into action is how they already spend a good portion of their time. A strategy needs to be more than a plan, however, and that's where the other *Ps* come in.

Strategy, more specifically, needs to act as a *ploy* by spelling out what the organization will do to outperform its competition. Perhaps it will promise its supply chain high-volume contracts in exchange for rock-bottom costs so that it can transfer those savings to consumers in the form of low-priced merchandise (e.g., Walmart), gaining massive market share and revenues. Perhaps, taking a cue from Admiral Nelson, it will purchase property for expansion where rivals have already carved out a dedicated customer base for the same goods (e.g., a Burger King opening up near a McDonald's, Barnes & Noble operating in a neighborhood with inde-

> No captain can do very wrong if he places his ship alongside that of the enemy.
>
> ADM. HORATIO NELSON

pendent bookstores). Perhaps it will cut out the middleman and sell made-to-order wares directly to consumers, rather than in retail stores (e.g., Dell Inc.). Anything an organization can do to get the upper hand on its competition is a ploy, in Mintzberg's parlance, that should appear embedded in a strategy.

The two *P*s discussed so far, plan and ploy, are purpose-driven exercises looking to the future. But sometimes a strategy can also derive from the past. Think of the *pattern* aspect of strategy as an example of the adage "If it ain't broke, don't fix it." Or, put more gracefully, in the words of Confucius: "Study the past if you would define the future." Pattern-based strategy considers practices that have already proven successful and then maintains or elaborates on them. The next Pull Up a Chair feature describes Starbucks' renaissance over the last five years as an example of a pattern strategy successfully implemented.

 PULL UP A CHAIR!

"A Grande Double-*P* Latte, Please":
Pattern and Ploy at Starbucks

Many an MBA classroom has studied Starbucks' rise and fall and rise again over the last few decades. The company is a great example of two of the Five *P*s of Mintzberg's (1987) model of strategy: pattern and ploy.

(continued on next page)

Consider the company's "comeback" in the late 2000s. The company had seen the departure of its passionate CEO, Howard Schultz, in 2000. By then, it had grown from 6 stores in 1982, when he first joined the company, to just over 3,500 (Miller, 2011). Starbucks had become a ubiquitous brand that was entrenched in American culture much as McDonald's had 30 years earlier.

During Schultz's eight years away, however, Starbucks' star started to lose its shine. It had grown too much, too fast. In New York, where we live, we were alarmed to see a Starbucks on one Manhattan street corner and another Starbucks on the very next corner, just one short block away. This was market saturation writ large. Consumers abroad also yelled, "Enough!" When a Starbucks was going to open in his posh London neighborhood, charmingly peppered with small, independent shops, actor Rupert Everett of *My Best Friend's Wedding* told an English newspaper, "Starbucks is spreading like a cancer. Nobody in the neighbourhood wants it, including me" (*Daily Mail*, 2006, paras. 4–5).

At the same time, customers began to complain about the quality of the coffee, calling it "Charbucks." The grand Italian espresso machines, once a unique ploy in Starbuck's strategy, had been replaced with machines that could brew coffee faster. Store design had also been tweaked so that the walls around the prep area were now a bit higher, which meant customers no longer could watch the engaging "theater" of baristas brewing lattes (Simon, 2009). All told, same-store sales started to slip.

Schultz returned as CEO about then, in January 2008. The last straw came when the recession hit hard later that year. Many Starbucks customers—coauthor Jack included—had reached their tipping point when it came to the price of a Starbucks coffee (Jack could not bring himself to pay $2.01 for a grande cup of regular roast—$1.98, OK; but not $2-plus). Sales took a nose dive, and much to Schultz's chagrin, the company was forced to close 900 locations around the world and cut $560 million in costs.

Enter a pattern strategy. Taking the "Charbucks" wisecracks to heart, Schultz harkened back to the kind of coffee and the kind of place he had originally envisioned and created for Starbucks: a vibrant community replicating the espresso bars of Italy, where very high quality coffee beans, roasted just right, were the star of the show, served by exuberant experts

The true original site of the first Starbucks was razed in 1974, and so the shop moved to this still thriving location a block away, at Seattle's Pike Place Market. It's a hugely popular tourist destination.

who created coffee beverages before the customers' eyes. This was the element that had made Starbucks distinctive and rise head and shoulders above its competition—a ploy strategy back in the late 1980s to early 1990s, resuscitated as a pattern strategy in 2008.

With great publicity, Schultz crafted a "transformational agenda" (Miller, 2011), as he called it—an actual written document, in fact—that included this example of a pattern strategy. He ordered all Starbucks locations—every store in the United States—to close for three hours one day so that all servers could be retrained on how to brew delicious coffee. Teams were also ordered to throw away any unused brewed coffee after half an hour so that the coffee they served would always be fresh. An ad campaign touted Starbucks as *the* place for distinctive high-quality coffee.

(*continued on next page*)

Slowly Starbucks regained its footing. Same-store sales did a U-turn and started increasing again just 16 months after Schultz's return. More recently, for the third quarter in 2013, they were up 8 percent in the United States and 9 percent in China. Profits jumped 25 percent—a third-quarter record for the company. It's understandable, then, that in reponse to Dunkin' Brands' announcement that it will open 45 new Dunkin' Donuts stores in California, where Starbucks operates 3,000 locations, CEO Schultz told CNBC, "I'm not losing sleep over Dunkin' Donuts" (Toscano, 2013, para. 5).

Looks like Schultz will be catching some zzz's now that he's figured out his *P*'s.

> # Strategy and culture should have breakfast together.
> MAX McKEOWN

Position is the fourth way Mintzberg (1987) suggests we look at strategy. Very similar to the plan and ploy components, position specifies where your organization is compared to competitors in the marketplace. It looks at the big picture by considering issues external to your organization. For example, if you're Dunkin' Donuts moving into an area like Southern California, where arch-rival Starbucks has several hundred more locations, you might develop a product to distinguish yourself—say, a wide variety of donuts and other baked products prepared right on the premises.

The final *P* of the Five *P*s model is *perspective*. "Just as patterns of behavior can emerge as strategy, patterns of thinking will shape an organization's perspective and the things that it is able to do well" (MindTools, 2013, para. 24). This is where organizational culture can influence strategy, as patterns of thinking and getting things done is simply another term for *culture*. Many companies tout innovative cultures, for example, after enough years have passed during which they've actually *done* innovative things so that those activities have become well entrenched into their cultures. Such firms now can fold into their strategies these patterns of thinking and acting—their culture—by stating strategic goals in terms of "developing innovative consumer products" or "designing creative and cutting-edge technology" (see the feature in Chapter 2 for one of the most recent examples from Apple Inc.).

Remember, Mintzberg's Five Ps do *not* describe chronological steps in a strategy-writing process. Think of them more as reminders during the planning stage of some key elements an organization will want its preconceived or "formulated" strategy to encompass. Use them to reality-check initial ideas, to make sure they're practical, and also to help craft a strategy that's comprehensive, consistent, and actionable in the real world.

SWOT AND PEST: DEBUGGING YOUR FIRM'S STRATEGY

Two fundamental but very helpful tools to start thinking about an organization from more of a business person's point of view (i.e., the way your CEO and other non-HR colleagues do) than a strictly HR point of view are SWOT (strengths, weaknesses, opportunities, threats) and PEST (political, economic, sociocultural, technical) analyses. They're very similar, but SWOT takes a slightly more *micro*-analytic and internal-looking view, zooming in on your organization to determine what it does especially well and where it has some room to improve vis-à-vis the competition. PEST takes a more *macro*-analytic view, looking not so much at your organization but rather all of the current forces in greater society that affect your organization. SWOT focuses both internally and externally, whereas PEST is really only externally oriented.

If you master nothing but these two tools—in fact, even if you only perform one (SWOT)—you've taken a big step toward understanding and discussing strategy as it pertains specifically to your organization and its business. It's not enough to be well versed and highly competent in HR practices such as recruiting, comp and benefits, and training and development. "These efforts are important, but they are not *the business*. They are in support of the business" (Ulrich, Younger, Brockbank, & Ulrich, 2012, p. 7). As we state throughout this book, speaking in the same business terms as your CEO and

> By leading a SWOT analysis, you increase your value to the organization.
>
> HARVARD BUSINESS SCHOOL & SHRM

other non-HR colleagues is how you as an HR professional put to rest once and for all the less-than-flattering stereotypes that we've shared in the introduction (and address specifically in the next chapter). It's how you start to be viewed as a fellow business person—a *strategic business partner*—and not simply as "the HR person." In short, it's how you perform so that you not only get invited to take a seat at the table but also have something smart to contribute once you're there.

Let's take a big step toward the table now by looking at SWOT and PEST analyses.

SWOT: A PIP for Business

Whether for individuals (to structure personal or career development plans), business units or departments (including Human Resources), or entire organizations, a SWOT analysis is an extremely useful and flexible tool to help build your strategy focus. Think of it, in simple terms, as a rough draft of a "performance improvement plan" (PIP) for your organization. Just as you do with an employee, consider what your organization does really well and not as well, and what it must do to address both those areas. Specifically, you're evaluating the following factors:

Strengths: your organization's forte—those capabilities that it enacts to implement its strategy and objectives

Weaknesses: factors that are preventing your organization from performing at its best

Opportunities: events, trends, and other forces inside or outside your organization that it can fold into its strategy to capitalize on and, ultimately, increase revenues/profits

Threats: any possible forces or events that could adversely affect your organization's performance or standing in the marketplace

Reading this brief list, you probably see now what we meant when we mentioned earlier that SWOT is focused both internally and externally. Alone or with your HR team, brainstorm how your organization fares in these various ways, using a single sheet of paper, a flipchart, or a whiteboard.

S *How can we build on our strengths?*	W *How can we address our weaknesses?*
Internal • • • External • • •	Internal • • • External • • •
O *How can we seize new opportunities?*	T *How can we avoid or minimize threats?*
Internal • • • External • • •	Internal • • • External • • •

FIGURE 1.2   Internal/External SWOT Template

Note: See the text for sample questions that are externally and internally focused to help you complete this chart.

The next sections offer some sample questions to help you identify your organization's strengths, weaknesses, opportunities, and threats; and the template in Figure 1.2 includes additional follow-up questions after you've filled in your SWOT chart.

INTERNAL

Many internally oriented SWOT factors play to an HR professional's sweet spot. Here you can really leverage your highly developed knowledge base about your organization. Thinking about its senior leadership and workforce (skills, background, experience, performance, etc.) as well as its culture (values, mission, branding, image, etc.), consider questions like these:

Strengths

- What sets our brand apart? Who or what do we have going for us that our competitors do not?
- Why do talented people like working here?
- What's special about the current composition and/or location of our workforce that gives us an advantage?

Weaknesses

- What gaps on our org chart do we currently have? What key positions are open?
- What skills do our employees need to develop or learn right now? In the next one to two years?
- What areas do we need to work on according to the results of our latest all-employee survey?

Opportunities

- How can we incent our employees to refer new customers to us, thus increasing our revenues?
- How are we mentoring and developing—and keeping—our high-potential employees?
- What creative products are in our R&D pipeline?
- Do we have the right talent to create new products or offer new services?

Threats

- Why do A-player employees leave our organization for the competition?
- Do we have cash flow or accounts receivable problems that must be resolved? Do we have the right people to resolve them?
- How is our benefits package composed to provide what our workforce wants and needs so that we retain top talent?

EXTERNAL

Factors outside your organization that can powerfully affect its business—and therefore the ever-evolving quality of its strategy (the "forming" nature of strategy, as Mintzberg conceives it)—are front-page news every day. These are the big-picture topics, many beyond your control, that weigh on your senior leadership's mind—things like, first and foremost, the state of the economy; the actions of the Federal Reserve Board (the Fed) and their influence on interest rates; health care (e.g., Obamacare) policy; federal laws and regulations; population and social trends; and more. These factors come into play again for PEST analyses, too (discussed in the next section), so start thinking about your responses to questions like these:

Strengths

- What do our external customers say that they like most about us? Why do they buy from or hire us as opposed to our competitors?
- What advantages do we accrue from our business partners in joint ventures?
- How do our vendor contracts strengthen our competitive position?

Weaknesses

- What do dissatisfied customers tell us we could do better? What do they tell potential customers?
- Who's our biggest competition, and what do they do better than us?
- What challenges do our suppliers and distributors have that can potentially affect our business performance?
- Do we have the talent we need in critical roles? If not, what can we do?

Opportunities

- How can we change our talent, insource/outsource ratios, operations, logistics, and marketing to generate new clients and revenue?
- What cultural trends play to our strengths?
- What new governmental policies might work in our favor, for market expansion at home and abroad?

Threats

- How does health care reform legislation affect us?
- What new economic policies or compliance requirements are obstacles to our growth?
- What technological advances are already out there that could make our products/services obsolete one day?
- What's the political landscape like in the new markets we want to enter?

PEST: What Keeps Business Leaders Up at Night

As we've stated, performing a SWOT analysis—of not only your business but also your HR team—goes a long way to enhancing your strategy-formulating and strategy-supporting role in an organization. Considering the immense influence that external forces exert in the market, however, you may want to give particular attention to them by also conducting a PEST analysis (Figure 1.3), which describes those external factors as follows:

Political: the effects of governmental involvement at various local, state, and national levels, such as tax laws and Obamacare

Economic: the ramifications to your organization's business of inflation, interest rates, tariffs, and so on

Sociocultural: society-wide trends such as buying criteria and consumer preferences, demographics, safety concerns, cultural fads, and more

Technological: cutting-edge ways of doing business, and novel products and services that are powered by evolving technology

As part of the strategy-crafting endeavor, PEST gives you and your business colleagues an overview of the different macro or big-picture factors to consider. These issues combine to flesh out everyone's understanding of (1) market growth or decline (including financial performance) and (2) the position and direction of the industry your business is in (i.e., not so much the organization itself, which is more the purview of SWOT). In sum, these are the nitty-gritty operational and strategic topics your colleagues discuss

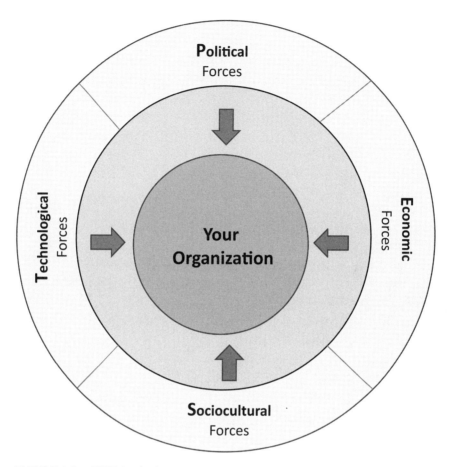

FIGURE 1.3 PEST Analysis

around the conference table. They infuse the conversations you'll be having with these executives, as we describe those discussions in the chapters to come. Like a mosquito buzzing in one's ear at bedtime, PEST is the persistent and attention-seeking stuff that keeps your CEO up at night.

A good starting point for performing a PEST analysis is the content you created for the T quadrant of your SWOT exercise with your ideas about, specifically, *external* threats (revisit Figure 1.2). Some analysts expound on these by taking the anagram play to major league level by adding *L* for *legal* (changing PEST to SLEPT), one or two *E*s for environmental and/or ecological (PESTLE), and even *D* for *demographics* (STEEPLED). We prefer to keep things simple, so let's stick with the model's original four-letter name, PEST—though we do recommend you include these other forms of external threats (legal, demographic, etc.) in your analysis, just within, say, the socio-cultural category.

Often describing a more glass-half-empty perspective, PEST analysis is particularly useful for alerting executives to possible "red flags" about conducting their business—that is, executing their strategy within a larger context. We describe potential derailers in job candidates in Chapter 5 on pre-hire assessments, but it's important to realize that entire lines of business can have "potential derailers," too. Remember the flop that was New Coke? Or Chevrolet's embarrassment over marketing a car in Latin and South America whose name translated into "no go" (Nova)? As another example, Kodak just emerged from Chap-

> A company's ability to respond to an unplanned event, good or bad, is a prime indicator of its ability to compete.
>
> BILL GATES

ter 11 bankruptcy, as that once massive corporation was upended by the technical capabilities of digital photography. The Pull Up a Chair feature lists five of our other favorites among products that dramatically flopped.

PULL UP A CHAIR!
Build It and They Will Come—Then Again, Maybe Not

Where's a good PEST when you need one? Besides the business blunders we mention in the main text, many other consumer products have famously flopped—to the extent we'd love to ask their companies, "What part of PEST don't you understand?" Imagine how a different (read "better") strategic analysis might have helped businesses avoid bringing these consumer products to the market:

1. **The Segway.** This "personal transporter" rolled off into the sunset of the mass consumer marketplace soon after its debut in 2000 because many people found it too expensive (and a bit odd, in the decidedly not-cool way) and municipal governments outlawed its use on roadways and sidewalks. Other than security guards trolling the mall, law enforcement officials patrolling public spaces, and travel groups choosing fresh air over a tour bus, few people have opted for the "future of walking" over, well, walking.

2. **Green ketchup.** Consumers (including us) went wild for *Shrek,* the inspiration to Heinz to make this product, but they weren't so fond of goop the color of "blastin' green" on their food. Ditto for "funky purple," a sister flop in the ketchup category.

3. **Cocaine Energy Drink.** This beverage didn't actually contain the drug, but with a name like this, and riding the wave of energy-drink popularity, what possibly could go wrong? Parents pitched a fit (imagine!), city governments (including New York's) immediately outlawed the drink, and the Food and Drug Administration banned it.

4. **Thirsty Dog! and Thirsty Cat! bottled water.** Unless they know how to read or have sophisticated palates, animals don't much care if their water has vitamins or tastes like "Crispy Beef" or "Tangy Fish."

5. **Gerber Singles.** Tasty food like "Beef Burgundy" and "Mediterranean Vegetables," in convenient one-serving jars from a trusted brand—what's the problem? Gerber was targeting these products to single adults and college students, who found it strange, if not depressing, to eat baby mush for dinner.

As you've done for SWOT, now consider the following questions to begin addressing the big-picture themes for PEST:

Political

- How could the outcome of the next elections, at home and abroad, influence business? What do candidates' platforms reveal about their views on business?

- What legislation (e.g., on regulations, discrimination, safety) will have an impact on your business? Are there changes to tax laws affecting you?
- Is there corruption in the governments of countries where you want to enter new markets?

Economic

- What's the current state of the economy at home and abroad—stagnant, growing, slipping?
- What's the level of talent in places you need it? How, in any way, does it affect your ability to find the specific individuals your organization needs to remain competitive?
- How do income levels where you operate (or want to) affect consumer spending?
- How do current interest rates influence your organization's capacity to expand operations and increase R&D?

Sociocultural

- What impact do demographic trends such as an aging population and the rise of the Millennial (or Y) generation have on your business?
- What cultural trends are driving or shrinking demand for your products or services? How long will these trends endure?
- What impact do the health and education of the population have on your ability to find talent and customers?
- Does organized crime affect your organization's doing business in new locations, whether at home or abroad?
- What religious and cultural factors must you consider before entering new markets in foreign countries? What's taboo in these places?

Technological

- What new technology is being developed that could affect the demand for your business and thus your revenues?
- Do competitors have a technological edge that threatens your market share?

- Is automation influencing how your business performs key activities? What operations may be offshored, outsourced, or eliminated?
- How is technology affecting employees' preferred way to work (e.g., telecommuting, job sharing)?

Questions like these serve to "create fear, uncertainty, and doubt" so that the senior executives in an organization are compelled to take action (Mirza, 2012, para. 13). Human beings are more strongly motivated to avoid a negative outcome than to achieve a positive one. This is why many people quit smoking or lose weight only when their doctor looks them in the eye and tells them they won't live to see their children grow up: death is as negative a consequence to avoid as we can think of. Your business colleagues are fearful of and want to avoid the potential negative consequences of increasing costs, mismanaging cash flow, missing sales targets, having inadequate talent, and all the other possible worst-case scenarios within their realm. You are ideally placed to help them via a well-done PEST (and SWOT) analysis.

A few more points on PEST before we exterminate this section. First, depending on the industry, the four PEST forces and the questions they inspire will be of varying importance to the strategy your organization adopts. A manufacturing company that generates most of its profits from defense contracts, such as Boeing or Northrop Grumman, is going to be especially sensitive to political/governmental forces such as the congressional sequester in 2013. Consumer electronics companies such as Samsung and Sony pay special attention to technological trends. Fashion retailers are plugged into fickle and rapidly evolving cultural fads.

Second, one or more of the four categories of PEST considerations may be highly pertinent in foreign markets for your organization and its broader business sector, but less so in your domestic market—or vice versa. Some strategists thus perform separate PEST analyses for domestic and foreign considerations.

Finally, PEST analysis bears a strong resemblance to and lays a solid foundation for the strategy-crafting tool known as scenario planning. Scenario planning, like the PEST approach, is externally focused but very strongly emphasizes a future orientation. For the professional engaging in HR "from the outside in" (Ulrich et al., 2012), the external and future focus of scenario planning is ideal. We briefly describe this tool in the next Pull Up a Chair feature.

PULL UP A CHAIR!

Scenario Planning: A Vision Quest for Your Business

Coping with change and uncertainty is a mainstay among executive competencies today. You can assist your business colleagues in navigating a turbulent global marketplace by engaging in scenario planning. A *scenario* in the strategy-planning context is "a story or plot line that allows the organization members to explore fully a rich story of possible future events. These scenarios are stories describing the current and future states of the business environment, and they become stories about alternative possible futures" (Chermack, in Swanson & Holton, 2009, p. 371).

As noted in the main text, scenario planning builds upon the trends you've identified in PEST analysis. In effect, it answers the question "We've identified these political, economic, sociocultural, and technological forces affecting our business—now what do we do about them?" Entire books have been written on scenario planning (see, e.g., Chermack, 2011; Swanson & Chermack, 2013), so we're greatly simplifying with this "shortcut" approach. This exercise can be done as a group around the conference table or in one-on-one interviews you conduct with your colleagues. Either way, it creates an ideal context for engaging in a business-savvy conversation.

Step 1: Rank the issues that surfaced in your PEST analysis. Ask your business colleagues which threats are of particular concern to your organization—which ones could have the greatest impact? This ordering helps you and your team know where to focus your attention and, ultimately, what to detail in your strategy.

Step 2: Brainstorm storylines. Take notes during this step. Ask what are called "the seven questions" in scenario planning. Shell Oil originally created these questions for its own use, but now strategists everywhere use them "to comprehend the strategic agenda" (Swanson & Holton, 2009, pp. 372–373):

a. If you could speak to someone five years from now, what would you like to know about the organization?

b. If the organization collapsed in five years, what would have caused the failure?
c. If the organization has grown and is moving in a positive direction in five years, what would it have done between now and then?
d. What's surprised you—pleasantly and unpleasantly—in the past five years?
e. What do you believe are the major challenges ahead, and the obstacles to overcome?
f. What forces would prevent us from moving past those obstacles?
g. If your business or product line had to be cut, what would your argument be for keeping it?

Step 3: Create scenarios. Write the stories and plotlines that incorporate the statements and opinions that surfaced (which you jotted down or otherwise recorded) in step 2. You're not writing the Great American Novel here—just compose the headline and a couple paragraphs that flesh out the scenario. If this event were to actually occur, what would the newspaper article or TV news account be?

Step 4: Use your scenarios to "wind-tunnel" the strategic plan in discussion with business colleagues. "Wind tunneling" here simply means to check the strategy for any weaknesses and to uncover additional opportunities and risks that may not be included in the plan at this point. You're using the scenarios in the same way you might use Mintzberg's Five *P*s (described earlier) to make sure a strategic plan is as robust and comprehensive as it needs to be. Moreover, as an HR professional specifically, you're wind-tunneling to align HR capabilities with business objectives spelled out in the strategy. Vis-à-vis each scenario, what will *you* need to do to minimize that risk, avoid that obstacle, or otherwise partner with your colleagues to execute that component of the strategy?

The benefit of wind tunneling and, more generally, scenario planning is that people often realize they need to "adjust their thinking based on evidence of flawed assumptions" (van der Merwe, 2008, p. 233). You and your colleagues can course-correct to capitalize on heretofore unseen opportunities and to avoid New Coke–like missteps.

DISCOVERING REAL-DEAL STRATEGY

So far we've spent considerable time defining *strategy* and offering ways to evaluate it as well as the factors that influence it. Now let's discuss how, exactly, you figure out what your organization's strategy actually is.

Some of you may be thinking, "Of course I know what my organization's strategy is! I'm one of the firm's senior executives, and that's the world I operate in." That reaction makes sense if you do know clearly every nuance of your board's and CEO's opinions about the strategy as well as the key activities to execute it; but if you did—no offense—wouldn't you already have a regular seat at the table?

Our experience suggests that what HR executives believe and what business executives believe about the value that HR delivers and the average HR professional's business know-how are often two very different things. Many C-level executives are not entirely confident about HR executives' level of business expertise. The consulting firm KPMG (2012) goes so far as to say, "It is practically a business truism that HR is not well respected in many organizations" (p. 14). In support of this statement, KPMG shares data accrued from its 2012 global survey of both business and HR executives, 37 percent of whom identified themselves as C-suite executives:

> Whether deserved or not, this stigma is clearly evident in our survey results.
>
> - Only 15 percent of our survey respondents see HR as able to provide insightful and predictive workforce analytics.
> - Only 17 percent view it as able to demonstrate measurably its value to the business. (KPMG, 2012, p. 14)
>
> There clearly remains a vast gulf between the perceived importance and the perceived effectiveness of HR today. At the very least, HR has a perception problem. (p. 15)

We address the persistent stereotype and offer suggestions to address it in chapters to come (see, especially, Chapter 2). In fact, it's a primary reason we wrote this book. But for now, let's return to strategy as a key element to enhance the contributions that you make in your organization.

Porter: Defining Strategy for Everyone

If it's any comfort, we've also found over the years that even among senior leadership not working in HR, there's often a lack of consistency and clarity about an organization's strategy, especially in one with a top-down or command-and-control management style. We sat in on a senior team's meeting once when everyone around the table was totally blindsided as their boss, the CEO, announced a multimillion-dollar capital campaign that veered 180 degrees from the organization's long-held mission and strategy. The CFO looked like he needed something stronger than coffee in his mug to absorb that news.

As we stated at the opening of this chapter, executives—in and outside HR—often talk about strategy in broad terms. Enter one of the world's most preeminent management scholars, who has literally written *the book* on strategy: Michael Porter. He's actually written many books dedicated to strategy; *Competitive Strategy* (1998b), for example, was voted the ninth-most influential management book of the 20th century by the Academy of Management. A professor at Harvard Business School, Porter also leads the school's program designed expressly for new CEOs, to help *them* get clear on what strategy is. For this chapter, we're going to rely on one of his classic articles from the *Harvard Business Review,* titled, aptly enough for our discussion, "What Is Strategy?" (Porter, 1996).

"GOOD" ≠ "STRATEGIC"

Porter (1996) starts off by saying what strategy is *not*: it is not operational effectiveness (doing business to high quality standards while also managing costs carefully), which is necessary but not enough to transform a company in a competitive market.

Many of us recognize the value of best practices in execution. To name just a few examples, total quality management, benchmarking of talent, and even outsourcing have been embraced to maximize performance while, ideally, reducing costs. Several firms apply these approaches—and so do their competitors. As these best practices and outsourcing efforts take hold, they're no longer the "next big thing." This is how competitive companies become more and more alike over time. For example, we bet many of you today regularly employ HR practices that at one time were highly distinctive, even unique, to GE's famed Human Resources team—they're not so unique anymore. In business terms, the name of the game in competition is differentiation. Organizations that rely only on best practices (which can be easily copied) and strong operational effectiveness are not doing enough to become—and stay—successful.

WALKING THE STRATEGY TALK

To this key point of differentiation within the marketplace, Porter (1996) notes that "competitive strategy means deliberately choosing a different set of activities [versus competitors] to deliver a unique mix of value" (p. 64).

Recall this chapter's earlier Pull Up a Chair feature on Starbucks. Back in the 1980s, when Howard Schultz bought the company and became CEO, he very deliberately chose to have customer-facing employees perform a set of activities that were distinctive at the time: overseeing the careful roasting of coffee beans, making theater out of preparing espresso drinks one at a time, and engaging in a well-trained yet friendly way with customers to

> The essence of strategy is choosing to perform activities differently than rivals do.
>
> MICHAEL PORTER

nurture a sense of vibrant community. This mix of activities delivered unique value to consumers and powerfully brought the company's underlying strategy to life: simply put, to make money selling coffee.

For another example of a corporation successfully executing its strategy, Porter discusses one in an industry very different from Starbucks': financial services. A stalwart then and now, the Vanguard Group is an investment management company that currently manages about $2 trillion in assets while offering mutual funds, exchange-traded funds (ETFs), and other products and services.

Vanguard's competitive differentiation derives from its "variety-based" strategic position, as Porter calls it: it offers an array of investment products, but those products share a critical quality in common: they are low-risk/low-cost. For example, Vanguard is especially famous for its solidly performing index funds, which spread risk out among dozens of different companies' stocks rather than "betting the farm" on just a handful.

In addition, Porter notes that Vanguard "aligns all activities with its low-cost strategy" (p. 71). These activities still serve as the firm's "unique mix"—the differentiator, as mentioned, Porter believes gives an organization a true competitive advantage. These activities (illustrated in Figure 1.4) include

- an emphasis on no-load index funds, which means there are no sales fees attached to the purchase of these lower-risk investment products;
- infrequently buying/selling stocks and bonds, and holding them longer, which means not only minimal expenses but lower-paid fund managers (compared with their peers in other brokerage firms) because a highly sophisticated, analysis-heavy investing skill set is not as critical for this sort of low-volume trading;
- using direct distribution, meaning there's no stockbroker as a middleman—you can buy these investment products and services directly from Vanguard online—and no commissions;
- favoring word-of-mouth recommendations over large amounts of expensive advertising and marketing; and
- structuring compensation packages so that employees' bonuses are tied to cost savings.

Senior executives at Vanguard undoubtedly commit the bulk of their time and energy laser-focused on performing activities like these, and on managing the performance of such activities, that implement the firm's low-cost strategy. In turn, HR professionals at the firm are best served by describing how, explicitly, they're supporting these business executives in that work. For example, you might lead a conversation with the chief information officer (CIO) by asking him how well he thinks two key players on his team, the heads of IT infrastructure and IT applications, are doing—specifically, "How are they reducing overall costs?" This open-ended question tells the CIO that you not only understand the firm's core strategy but are really plugged in to perform the activities supporting it, such as tying bonuses to cost savings.

FIGURE 1.4 Sample Activities Supporting Vanguard's Low-Cost Strategy

As Porter states, nearly all firms work toward operational efficiency, but the truly successful ones—like Vanguard—orient their efforts clearly and directly to their strategy and its related activities. Without a differentiating strategy and a unique set of activities to support it, Vanguard would scarcely differ from rival firms such as Fidelity Investments, T. Rowe Price, Charles Schwab, and scores of others.

WHY HR METRICS DON'T PLAY IN THE STRATEGY SANDBOX

At this point, some of you may be thinking that focusing on strategy alone is not realistic. Specifically, you can rightfully say that much of human resources centers on *measurable* HR variables that ensure that people perform at a high level to achieve important, and also measurable, outcomes. The HR metrics that most of you are deeply familiar with play a key role in your organization, guiding what you do and how you do it. Clearly, you're right: a major part of HR professionals' job is to maximize measurable performance *while reducing cost.* That's why many of you have a series of widely recognized metrics that benchmark your performance against world-class standards. You either work toward these standards or get an outsourcing firm to do it for you. (We briefly discuss data analytics in HR in Chapter 3.)

Yet here's the rub:

> *Your metrics may not mean very much*
> *to the other executives in your organization.*

More troublesome, if you're continually talking about these HR metrics when speaking with other business unit or departmental executives, you may inadvertently be "reducing what should be a dynamic dialogue to a form or template to be filled out" (Mirza, 2012, para. 7). That is, you may be describing HR efficiency, whereas your business colleagues want to talk about their business outcomes—those strategy-supporting activities that Michael Porter describes. This divergence is at the core of remarks like "HR just doesn't get my business." Major General Dorian Anderson, the former commander of the U.S. Army's Human Resources Command (i.e., its enormous, global "HR department"), told us when HR professionals speak too much about HR metrics and not enough about a role's critical requirements and, especially, the people to carry them out, "I feel like the process is more important than the prospect."

> To be effective, HR must have a sincere curiosity and a sincere desire to understand business.
>
> ANDY GOODMAN

So what do your business colleagues want to talk about, and what *do* they talk about when you're not (for now) at the table? The next section will tell you, and the Pull Up a Chair feature makes sure you're defining some key business terms the same way they do.

PULL UP A CHAIR!

Getting in Your Business: No Cause for Embarrassment

It's happened to all of us: we find ourselves in a conversation in which we quickly realize that other people are far better informed on the subject at hand than we are. Sometimes we all need a quick review to get up to speed. The *Washington Post* openly recognizes this fact via its WorldViews blogs called "9 Questions about ___ You Were Too Embarrassed to Ask." Fill in the blank: Syria, Egypt, Chechnya. Example: "1. What is Syria?" Just as any good teacher will tell you, there are no dumb questions.

So before we barrel along, let's clarify how we're using some terms in this book and define a few others, to be on the safe side.

In this book, the term *business unit* (or simply *business*) or *function* means specifically a particular division or department within an organization. These units may be organized by geography, type of product or service, or internal function in your organization; and each has, as its head, a person we often refer to as a "key player." Heads of these "businesses" may have titles such as Managing Partner, San Francisco (geography); Senior Vice President, Retail Brokerage (business line). Other examples would be the executive who manages the women's clothing *business* at a corporation like TJMaxx, or the executive who runs the Specialty Care and Oncology *business* in a pharmaceutical firm like Pfizer. Key players also manage the Finance, Sales, and Operations functions or teams in your firm. If you lead the HR team, you're a key player, too.

You'll likely hear several hard-core business terms in conversations with your colleagues or read them in documents like annual reports, sales reports, and 10-K forms (discussed in the next section). We list some of those here. Note how they all have to do with the core purpose of any organization, whether for-profit or nonprofit: bringing in money (and for corporations more specifically, generating both revenue and profits).

- *Revenue*: the amount of money brought into a company by its business activities

- *Revenue per share*: the amount of revenue divided by the number of common shares of the company's stock that are in the market
- *Profit* or *loss*: the money a business makes or doesn't make after accounting for all expenses. The two terms frequently appear together and abbreviated. For example, a "P&L statement" is simply the organization's income report. Key players or job candidates may say they "manage a P&L of $100 million," meaning that they manage the elements that affect both revenue/profit and also costs (or losses) in their business (as defined earlier).
- *Gross profit*: company revenue minus cost of goods sold; that is, the money left over after selling a product or service and deducting the cost associated with its production and sale
- *Profit margin*: a ratio of profitability calculated as net income divided by revenues, or net profits divided by sales. It measures how much out of every dollar of sales a company actually keeps in earnings.
- *Market cap*: the total dollar market value of all of a company's outstanding shares
- *Market share*: the proportion of an industry's total sales earned by a specific company over a certain period of time. It's calculated by dividing a firm's sales during that time by the total sales of that firm and all of its competitors, so it's a way investors see how well a particular firm is doing and how well it's adapting its strategy in the face of the dynamic forces we discussed earlier in this chapter.
- *Top line*: a reference to a company's gross sales or revenues. "Top" relates to the fact that on a company's income or P&L statement, the first line at the top of the page is generally reserved for gross sales or revenue. A company that increases its revenues is thus said to be "growing its top line" or "generating top-line growth."
- *Bottom line*: as with *top line*, a reference to where the amount—in this case, the organization's net income—appears on the income or P&L statement: almost always the last line at the bottom of the page. This number is what remains after all expenses have been taken out of revenues, and there's nothing left to subtract. Most companies

(continued on next page)

aim to improve their bottom lines through two simultaneous methods: growing revenues (i.e., generating top-line growth) and increasing efficiency (or cutting costs—e.g., Vanguard's activities shown in Figure 1.4).

Unless you enroll in a financial certification course or an MBA program (see the Additional Resources), you might consider inviting one of your Finance colleagues to present a one- or two-hour seminar to the HR team on the basics of finance for nonfinance professionals. Consider the invitation another reason to engage with a key player and to signal you're starting to speak the language of business.

FROM THEORY TO PRACTICE: WHERE TO FIND YOUR STRATEGY AND WHAT TO DO WITH IT

You and others in your organization can talk about strategy all you like, but sometimes you want the actual document that goes by the name "our strategy." Happily, finding it is easier than you might think, especially if you work in a publicly traded company in the United States. (And if you don't, it may be as simple as walking down the hall to ask for the actual written document your organization calls its strategy.) All you have to do is go online to dig up your firm's "Form 10-K," an annual report required by the U.S. Securities and Exchange Commission (SEC), whose purpose is to provide a thorough summary of a company's performance. Usually, but not always, this form is *not* the same as the document that a company sends to its shareholders called "the annual report."

The 10-K is extremely useful for getting at the heart of a company. It typically covers topics such as the firm's structure, objectives, competition, financial information, and management discussion of the firm—exactly the information you need to build your business knowledge base and to talk shop with your CEO and other non-HR colleagues. A publicly traded company must make its 10-K readily available to everyone who might have an interest; most firms post it on an investor relations page on their company website, among the other required SEC filings.

The 10-K is also a *pro forma* document, meaning it's a template that every public company uses to cover the same basic sections required by law. Some firms do more than what's required and compose additional sections. But the foundational standardization of all 10-Ks means that the tips we share later in digesting one will apply to just about every publicly traded firm in the United States.

This document provides regulators and investors with the most valid information about what's going on in a company. Therefore, as you might imagine, a company's leadership and staff spend considerable time getting the 10-K just right. The rest of this chapter will explore two firms' 10-Ks and then offer ideas for follow-up strategic questions with key players in each organization.

E*TRADE: Strategy Example 1

The investing-savvy baby in E*TRADE commercials has yet to tell TV viewers where to locate the company's strategy document, but we can do that for you: simply go to www.etrade.com and find it in the guise of the 10-K form on the Investor Relations page.

The best place to start exploring a 10-K is right at the beginning. The first page is a pro forma cover sheet for the document. The next few pages are the document's table of contents—a very useful page, especially if you're looking at the 10-K in HTML: a single click on a link will take you directly to the page you want. A few pages in, you'll usually find "Item 1. Business"; below this line is typically an "Overview" section describing the nature of and metrics about the company.

E*TRADE has placed a section overtly labeled "Strategy" below the Overview. Here's an extract of the firm's description of its strategy:

> Building on the strengths of this franchise, our strategy is focused on:
>
> - *Strengthening our overall financial and franchise position.* We are focused on achieving a more efficient distribution of capital between our regulated entities, improving capital ratios by reducing risk, deleveraging the balance sheet and reducing costs, and enhancing our enterprise-wide risk management culture and capabilities.

- *Improving our market position in our retail brokerage business.*
  We plan to accelerate the growth in our customer franchise and to
  continue enhancing the customer experience.
- *Capitalizing on the value of our complementary brokerage businesses.* Our corporate services and market making businesses enhance
  our strategy by allowing us to realize additional economic benefit
  from our retail brokerage business.
- *Enhancing our position in retirement and investing.* We believe
  growing our retirement and investing products and services is key to
  our long term success. Our primary focus is to expand the reach of
  our brand along with the awareness of our products to this key customer segment.

In short order and in plain English, you've learned the overriding approach
the board of directors and the senior executives will take as the firm moves
forward.

Further into the 10-K is the section "Item 1A. Risk Factors." This section
describes in detail what seems like the outcome of SWOT and PEST analyses, maybe even scenario planning: things that can go wrong. What you need
to consider is how these elements can detract from the implementation of the
strategy and cause the firm to derail in the market, and what HR can do to
help prevent that occurrence.

The other key section you should study is "Item 7. Management's Discussion and Analysis of Financial Condition and Results of Operations." It's
a mouthful, we know, but this section serves as the "fly on the wall" for
those people who weren't in the room when executives and board members
discussed at length issues that they regard as truly important in achieving the
firm's economic objectives—which collectively represent its strategy. Review
this section to get a rich and fairly current view of your organization's most
significant matters. It delivers to you on a silver platter precisely what your
business colleagues want to talk about.

HR'S ROLE

Let's take a deeper look at E*TRADE's strategy and those elements that can
align the strategy and activities—just as management theorist Michael Porter

has suggested—with HR's role in the firm. Consider again this component in the 10-K:

> **Enhancing our position in retirement and investing.** We believe growing our retirement and investing products and services is key to our long term success. Our primary focus is to expand the reach of our brand along with the awareness of our products to this key customer segment.

At the heart of any senior executive's expectation for Human Resources is whether or not the HR professional can talk about and act on key business activities. In this specific case, the issue centers on what HR staff can do to "enhance the organization's position in retirement and investing."

Let's imagine E*TRADE employs a senior executive in charge of the firm's efforts in long-term investing (e.g., retirement accounts, college funds), as opposed to stock trading. You, as an HR professional at this firm, should shy away from explicit discussion of any HR metrics; that's not the topic that your colleague is interested in based on her charter. She doesn't want to know how you "make the sausage." Instead, you might focus the chat on your colleague's *strategic outcome* (two equally important words) that entails enhancing the firm's position in retirement and investing—that is, long-term investing, *her* domain:

- How do you think things are going as you work to enhance long-term investment?
- As you consider your team in place, do you have the capabilities you need to further our goal of "enhancing our position in retirement and investing"?
- Let's say we brought in someone with the right skills to help you manage our retirement products. What would that person's responsibilities entail?
- If we did bring this person onboard and a year from now you're thrilled with his or her performance, what exactly would that person have accomplished or done? What does success look like in this role?

The next example, Limited Brands, is probably another familiar company, as the corporation owns the well-known businesses of Victoria's Secret and Bath & Body Works.

Limited Brands: Strategy Example 2

As another publicly traded U.S. corporation, Limited Brands also must make its strategy-containing 10-K form readily available. Indeed, like E*TRADE, the company has posted it on the Investors page of its website, where it is part of the firm's annual report and proxy statement. You can also search for it online using the keywords "Limited Brands 10-K." The results show this webpage: www.limitedbrands.com/investors/company_info/sec_filings.aspx.

Opening the document, you find the same pro forma formatted page that you did for E*TRADE, with a brief description of the corporation and its businesses. This time, though, there's not a clear "Strategy" section like what we found in E*TRADE's 10-K, so jump ahead to the same "Item 7" section as we did before: "Management's Discussion and Analysis of Financial Condition and Results of Operations." In the "Executive Overview," you strike strategy gold:

STRATEGY

Our strategy supports our mission to build a family of the world's best fashion retail brands offering captivating customer experiences that drive long-term loyalty.

Now look at the detail around the following "unique mix of activities," as Michael Porter would put it, that comes next—paying special attention to the parts we've underlined and to the superscripted numbers (they tie later to suggested follow-up questions):

To execute our strategy, we are focused on these key strategic imperatives:

Grow and maximize profitability of our core brands in current channels and geographies[1];
- Extend our core brands into new channels and geographies[2];
- Build enabling infrastructure and capabilities[3];
- Become the top destination for talent[4]; and
- Return value to our shareholders.

The following is a discussion of certain of our key strategic imperatives:

Grow and maximize profitability of our core brands in current channels and geographies

Our overriding focus is on the substantial growth opportunity in North America.

The core of Victoria's Secret is bras and panties. We see clear opportunities for substantial growth in these categories by focusing on <u>product newness and innovation</u>[4]and expanding into <u>under-penetrated market and price segments.</u>[5] In 2013, we plan to increase our square footage at Victoria's Secret by about 3.5% through expansions of existing stores and the <u>opening of approximately 50 new stores</u>. In our direct channel, we have the infrastructure in place to support growth well into the future. We believe our direct channel is an important form of brand advertising given the ubiquitous nature of the internet and our large customer file.

Extend our core brands into new channels and geographies

We began our international expansion with the acquisition of La Senza at the beginning of 2007. Since 2008, we have opened 71 Bath & Body Works stores, 16 Victoria's Secret full assortment stores and 10 Victoria's Secret Pink stores in Canada. <u>Based on the success we have experienced in Canada,</u>[6] we plan to open an additional 8 Bath & Body Works stores and 8 Victoria's Secret stores in Canada in 2013.

Build enabling infrastructure and capabilities

Over the past five years, we have opened a new Direct to Consumer <u>distribution center</u>, launched <u>new merchandise planning systems, new supply chain management systems, new financial and other support systems and a new point-of-sale system</u>[7] in our stores. We are using these capabilities to be able to productively and quickly react to current market conditions, improve inventory accuracy, turnover and in-stock levels and deliver more targeted assortments at the store level. In 2013, we plan to continue to roll out new point-of-sale systems to our stores, continue to build new cross-channel functionality at Victoria's Secret and invest in international support systems.

HR'S ROLE

Based on this summary of the Limited Brands strategy and the follow-up description of supporting actions, here's a sampling of the many talent-centric questions that you, as an HR professional in the firm, might ask your business colleagues (the numbers here align with the superscripted numbers in the excerpt):

1. How many store managers and regional managers on your team can expand profit in their current locations?
2. Have you thought about internal candidates we might consider moving into new channels and geographies? Who do you consider the true star players on your teams in the United States and Canada?
3. What talent do you need to build out our infrastructure capabilities, such as the IT systems that support our distribution centers?
4. Do you have the right talent with retail (women's clothing) expertise who can create innovative products? Can you think of things we could do to attract and retain top talent?
5. Do you have key people who have worked in retail clothing and have penetrated new markets at different price points?
5/6. Are you comfortable with the number and talent of your staff in opening retail stores in both the United States and Canada?
7. As the CIO [or CTO], do you have the right talent to make the most of your new merchandise planning systems? What about the new supply chain management systems? The new financial systems?

In two industries, financial services and retail, we've gone to the companies' easy-to-access documents (by visiting their websites or by searching online for their SEC Form 10-K) to find their preconceived or "formulated" strategy, as theorist Henry Mintzberg would call it. For E*TRADE and Limited Brands, we've identified the activities that support and distinguish that strategy as it plays out, and we created some sample HR-related questions that can inspire your own discussions with business colleagues about how you can best assist them.

These are examples of the close-up shots, at the business unit level, that you can take of strategy, after regarding the wide-angle view we took at the start of this chapter. Now that you know *what* kinds of business-oriented topics to discuss, we'll start describing *how* to talk about them in Chapter 2.

Look Who's Talking
Getting Yourself Ready for Strategic Conversations

Imagine you're sitting in the conference room with the president of your firm. This meeting is the first closed-door executive meeting to which you've been invited. You quickly learn your company may merge with a 20,000-employee firm overseas. But just as you're biting into a sugar-glazed doughnut, the president turns to you and asks, "What do you think are the key HR and talent management issues at stake?" Instead of responding, you shake your head to signal that speaking with food in your mouth is impolite. The truth? You have no idea what to say. (Sunoo, 2013, para. 1)

HAVEN'T WE all experienced a situation like the one described here? We're caught off-guard by a comment or question, and because we're afraid we may sound "stupid" by responding with whatever pops into our head, we opt to say nothing instead. Unfortunately, saying nothing actually makes a worse impression. Later we replay (and re-replay) the scene and have the "V8 moment" where we smack our forehead and think, "Oh! I should've said ___!"

This is not the effect we're going for.

Remember a key point in Chapter 1 about strategy that management theorist Henry Mintzberg has made: strategy is *formulated* ahead of time, but it also *forms* as day-to-day business takes place. That is, it is both *preconceived,* like the written documents whose excerpts we explored in Chapter 1; and *dynamic,* ever-evolving through day-to-day activities in the face of market realities. Your role as a business-savvy HR executive comes into play during discussion about those sorts of mission-critical activities. This chapter gets you ready to engage in the "strategic implementation" conversation— even initiate the conversation—so that, as Jack likes to say, you always have something smart to say. Never will you respond by taking another bite of a doughnut.

CLEARING THE AIR FIRST: THE HR STEREOTYPE

We suspect we don't need to tell you what the stereotype is about human resources professionals. You know it already. And so do a lot of other people.

A consulting partner at KPMG, Robert Bolton, is typical of many observers of the HR field. "HR functions have tried for the past 15 years to transform themselves into strategic players and earn a place at the leadership table," he says. Bolton envisions HR professionals as being stuck in a vicious circle he calls a "doom loop": frequently offering generic responses and universal best practices instead of "customized solutions that support the value drivers of the business" (Maurer, 2012, p. 3). If we follow Bolton's train of thought, this practice knocks HR's standing down a notch (and inspires those negative comments we've reported), which in turn lessens its role in strategy creation and execution, which means most HR professionals (still) aren't at the table. Even accomplished HR executives with Harvard MBAs admit:

> We, too, have become a bit cynical hearing companies grandly proclaim, "People are our greatest asset!" only to watch most of them show true little commitment to developing and leveraging those people's abilities. We are also aware of the less-than-flattering stereotypes of HR professionals—you know, "administriviators"—and of the reality that many traditional HR activities, such as benefits management, are increasingly being outsourced. (Breitfelder & Dowling, 2008, para. 3)

We understand this perspective, too; as we mention throughout this book, we've observed and experienced HR practices that do nothing but support this unflattering view. But we also believe HR professionals can do something to sidestep the "doom loop" and begin deflating stereotypes about their field. The first step is admitting this challenge exists.

In the spirit of transparency, we coauthors have had to take this step ourselves, as we've been on the receiving end of stereotypes. For example, Laura vividly remembers French students in Avignon throwing stones at her and another college classmate as they walked home from class because they were stereotyped as "typical Americans." And we (Jack and Laura) were subjected to stereotypes—from each other—in the early days of our relationship.

When we met, at a Spanish language school in Antigua, Guatemala, Jack was a freshly minted colonel and Laura was a freelance writer-editor. Laura accepted Jack's invitation to brunch—what turned into our first, eight-hour date—solely because she had never interacted in any way with an active-duty military person and thought this would be an interesting bit of "research" in case she ever wrote a story about "gun-toting Army lugs." Her dad and uncles had served in World War II and were deeply patriotic; but Laura's father hated pretty much every second of

> There is no truth. There is only perception.
>
> GUSTAVE FLAUBERT

the "three years, three months, and zero days," as he always put it, that he served—too much "being told what to do" for an independent thinker like him. The apple didn't fall far from that tree, so, in 1995, Laura's socializing with a straight-laced, "arch-conservative" colonel would've been akin to her schmoozing with the head of the KGB—in Siberia. She figured if nothing else, she'd pass an hour listening to acronym-laden gobbledygook and maybe finally figure out what the difference is between a battalion and a brigade. That'd be better than doing her homework conjugating irregular Spanish verbs. Plus, a gal has to eat, right?

Jack, meanwhile, perceived Laura as a carefree gadabout who was traveling around the world, dabbling in foreign languages, and generally living the romantic life of a "struggling writer." Sporting Birkenstocks, hand-woven Mayan shorts from the local market, and zero makeup (and—let's

Coauthor Jack Cage busting stereotypes in Guatemala, 1995.

be honest—some leg stubble), she was an exotic "hippie chick," in his view. When she told him she wanted to learn Spanish to better serve the inner-city Latino women she did volunteer work with, he didn't roll his eyeballs, but labels like "bleeding-heart liberal" did float through his head.

And then came brunch. Happily, it took about 20 minutes into a spread of Guatemalan coffee, fresh pineapple, and granola for us to figure out that we each blew the other's stereotypes into smithereens. Neither Jack nor Laura was on the political extreme, as they had originally assumed, but actually more centrist. Yes, Jack was indeed a decorated officer, but he also was passionately interested in music, travel, and psychology; and he was an animal nut, evidenced by his buying a stray dog we named Pancho a chicken sandwich. Yes, Laura was indeed a freelancer who loved to travel, but she spent most of her time home in Chicago—and had even turned down a job in Berlin—so that she could help care for her mom, who had Alzheimer's. Moreover, she wasn't struggling financially but actually earning more than most in-house editors.

We share this bit of personal history to underscore the point that we all have been on the giving and receiving end of stereotypes. The fact is, stereotypes exist for a reason: there *is* some truth to them, to some small degree. Jack *was* toting guns—he was an infantry officer, after all; Laura *was* a carefree traveler in Guatemala—her freelance career enabled her to be one. So those parts of our respective stereotypical views were accurate, but obviously there was, and is, more to us than that.

We've worked with HR professionals on both ends of their own stereotype spectrum: those who speak in what a senior operations executive once described to us as "HR happy-talk" and those who are revered organization-wide for how well they discuss and understand business—and by that we mean how an organization drives revenue and profit, pure and simple.

Maybe you're confident that you already have great relationships with your non-HR peers and are thinking, "*My* CEO and president love me!" If that's the case, awesome—and congratulations, because we have to say: you're probably in the minority. This view is supported by published research findings as well as much of our own "boots on the ground" experience. For example:

- The authors of *The HR Scorecard: Linking People, Strategy, and Performance* cite a "review of HR professionals in 300 firms [in which] the rating of *technical proficiency* of HR professionals was 35% higher than the mean level of performance in *strategic* HRM proficiency" (Becker et al., 2001, p. 12). This conclusion reflects that persistent view of HR being dramatically better at performing more administrative and technical functions (as mentioned in our introduction) than those bigger-picture activities related to a business and its strategy (described in Chapter 1).
- Reviewing its global survey of C-suite and other senior-level executives, consulting firm KPMG (2012) reports that "the HR function is often dismissed as non-essential or ineffective," and "just 17 percent [of survey respondents] maintain that HR does a good job of demonstrating its value to the business" (p. 2). Commenting on this survey, Tim Payne of KPMG's HR Transformation Center of Excellence remarks, "[T]here is often a gap between the ambition and rhetoric of talent management and the practice on the ground. Many talent processes have unfortunately become annual form-filling exercises" (KPMG, 2012, p. 9). A KPMG colleague in the UK, Mark Spears, notes in the

report's foreword, "The HR function must push beyond the basics to enhance its reputation" (p. E).

- Even SHRM, HR's trade association, has stated that 4 out of 10 of its surveyed members "agree or strongly agree that HR professionals are held in high esteem today" (Claus & Collison, 2005, p. x). That means 60 percent—no small number, in our minds—admit they're *not* held in high regard.

- Another SHRM (2008) survey found that HR professionals believed that 53 to 65 percent of their colleagues, from manager to C-suite level, regard them as "equally strategic and transactional" (Figure 2.1). A more recent survey of HR professionals shares a similar number—66 percent—who agree with the statement "My organiza-

> # Many business leaders don't feel that HR is delivering for them.
>
> TIM PAYNE

tion views HR as a strategic function" (Fallaw & Kantrowitz, 2013, p. 10). These opinions make sense, given the day-to-day realities of most HR professionals and the fact it was HR, not other executives, responding to this survey. Nevertheless, we think the "strategic" side of this view can and should be enhanced to raise these numbers, especially when 26 to 45 percent of non-HR colleagues in the SHRM survey are perceived as thinking of HR as "primarily transactional."

As we mentioned, data points like these are verified today among the opinions we commonly hear in the real-world workplace:

- "The best HR professionals don't get an issue bogged down in process and policy," Bill Wray, COO of a major Blue Cross Blue Shield organization, told us. "The process and policy need to exist but should not be painful to deal with. That's like having to sit on a couch without enough cushioning: you know it needs a support framework, but you wish it didn't hurt so much while it was doing its job."
- Jack Flanagan, a senior operations executive in both the retail and nonprofit sectors, said what never has served his and his team's purposes

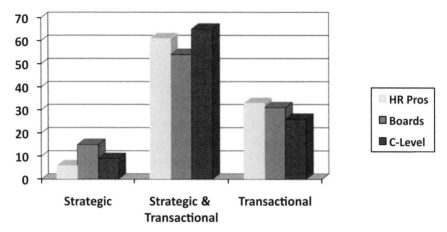

FIGURE 2.1   HR Professionals' Perceptions of How Groups View HR

toward "enterprise value creation," yet is a regular occurrence, is the "worst-case, legalistic, after-the-fact 'root canal' from the HR admin side of the house."

• Major General Dorian Anderson, who led the U.S. Army's Human Resources Command, chimed in: "HR is a very demanding field that many people dread dealing with due to filling out forms, meeting deadlines, providing detailed information, and sometimes even being obstacles to success. A typical HR professional does nothing to overcome this label."

We give the last word to a person who has scrutinized the HR field for over 25 years: University of Michigan business school professor Dave Ulrich (see, e.g., *HR from the Outside In,* 2012, among many other of his stellar works). SHRM's *HR Magazine* voted Ulrich "the #1 most influential international thought leader in HR" in 2011. What does he have to say?

"HR must give value or give notice."

As Jack the Army lug would say, "Roger that." But the logical next question, in our opinion, is "How, exactly, does HR give value?" That's what the following sections in this chapter—indeed, in the rest of the book—will address.

REACTION FORMATION:
START THINKING LIKE A SALESPERSON

In psychology, a *reaction formation* is a defense mechanism in which an offended person reduces his or her anxiety by behaving ardently in the opposite way from the real belief. Think of the last time someone gave you a present that was truly awful. You, as polite gift recipient, probably didn't react by saying, "What in the world were you thinking? This stinks!" but, rather, "How very thoughtful of you—I *love* it!" We know a man who once gave his wife an IOU for an iron for her birthday—not even an actual iron, which would be bad enough, but an IOU for one. We don't know what her "reaction formation" was, but we're grateful we weren't there to witness it!

In this chapter, and in the introduction, we've shared some unflattering opinions and data from researchers and executives about human resources. No matter what the vibe is around the role of human resources in your organization—whether HR is respected as a critical player at the strategy table or dissed as a time- and cost-inefficient exercise in frustration—we suggest you accept that unpleasant stereotypes do exist and probably, in general, aren't going away anytime soon. That said, you can't control what other people think, but you *can* control what you think and what you do. That's where your own reaction formation might come into play. We recommend you react like a salesperson.

Who Is Your Customer, Really?

Many HR professionals already refer to the employees in their organization as "my customers." In our opinion, that's a good news/bad news situation. It's good news because by getting to know the firm's "customers" so well, a great HR team learns the "strengths/weaknesses of the 'people' assets of the organization," as the USO's CFO, Phil Parisi, told us. "This speaks to [creating] an authentic environment, trusting relationships, and true teaming." According to John Rao, head of U.S. operations at Navigant, a global professional services firm:

> The best HR professionals have a deep understanding of what characteristics will lead to success and the type of cultural things needed to be

effective in our organization. They work with us [i.e., business heads] to make our organizations the most effective they can be, covering important aspects such as leadership, communications, empowerment, employee engagement, employee development, performance management, compensation, and succession planning.

All such things are vital to establish and nurture a thriving organizational culture—a topic that will surface very importantly in Part 2 when we discuss talent acquisition.

But here's the bad news. Our sense is that HR professionals sometimes miss the forest for the trees by regarding the majority of the workforce—from top executives to the most junior employees—as their customers. We disagree with this way of thinking. We believe that HR has one group of customers that matters the most: the CEO and the heads of businesses or functional units—the so-called key players. We believe these are the most critical customers because, no matter what the industry or sector, they're most directly responsible for generating revenue/profits and controlling costs. If they don't succeed in their roles in executing the strategy and its associated activities, the whole organization suffers and even possibly shuts down.

> HR isn't about being a do-gooder.
>
> ARNOLD KANARICK

We understand this point is hard to swallow for those HR professionals who entered the field "to help people." But as Arnold Kanarick, an EVP at the Telsey Advisory Group and former EVP and chief human resources officer at The Limited (which is highly regarded for its talent management), said, "When people have come to me and said, 'I want to work with people,' I say, 'Good, go be a social worker'" (Hammonds, 2005, para. 14).

We're not suggesting that you not help people or that you stop helping or developing people. We're suggesting that you consider specific business factors, requirements, and critical needs as much as, if not more than, those "people" considerations. Especially if you're the head of the HR team, we believe that you should be spending the great majority of your time on business issues rather than people issues. Delegate the latter to your capable staff or, dare we say, outsource those functions. That being said, we agree with Ulrich and his coauthors (2012): "Balancing the trade-off between people and business is not always easy." As they put it, "Overemphasis on people turns business enterprises into social agencies that may lose the credibility to meet market requirements. Overemphasis on business drives results without attention to how they are generated" (p. 22).

Of course, you should continue to ensure that your workforce is engaged and performing at its best—that's critical for making sure you develop and retain top talent, after all, which is also important for your organization to remain a strong contender in the years ahead (we touch on retention in Chapter 4). But if you want to enhance your standing among your non-HR business colleagues, treat *them* as your primary and most important internal customers.

> [E]very business person must speak in the language of their customers. HR is no different. For HR [professionals] hoping to stand out, be competitive and make an impact, speaking the language of bottom-line results is a must. (Grensing-Pophal, 2012, para. 21)

How Well Do You Know Your Customers?

If your organization employs sales teams, you may already know that the best salespeople take the time to drill down on both their prospects and their current customers, including studying every factor inside and outside those customer organizations that affect their business performance. Many organizations dedicate entire departments to scrutinizing leads and customers, in the form of business development teams that identify buying criteria, scour the marketplace for leads, and deliver the most viable leads to the sales force. This point applies to nonprofits, too: their development teams are continuously seeking new sources of donor dollars—a nonprofit's revenues—or in-kind donations; and they target their requests very carefully depending on the prospect: individual, corporation, high-net-worth family, and so on. Whether in a for-profit or nonprofit, so-called rainmakers are always doing their homework and striving to go deeper and deeper in their appreciation for and understanding of their current and prospective customers' needs.

Following this line of thought about salespeople, what should you, an HR professional, understand about your internal customers? Again, by "internal customers," we mean the heads of business units and functional areas (e.g., Sales, Finance, Information Technology, etc.) and the firm's president and CEO. Dave Ulrich, the HR researcher mentioned earlier, and his coauthors state that knowing what key internal customers and their groups do daily is not enough. You must also understand fully what those activities mean in terms of furthering the organization's objectives (Ulrich et al., 2012). This point reminds us of Michael Porter's (1996) emphasis on the specific *strategy-supporting* activities across a firm that we discussed in the last chapter (remember the Vanguard example?). To genuinely comprehend how a business operates, Ulrich and his coauthors believe that HR executives must understand the environment in which the firm operates. Some ways to define that set of conditions include the

- *context* (e.g., the global economic state, societal trends, market conditions);
- *stakeholders* (which include the actual external customers who buy your organization's products or services, as well as investors, regulators, and your colleagues in the workforce); and
- *strategies* (how your firm will achieve its objectives).

Reminiscent of our discussion in Chapter 1, these three areas are what you must know—comprehensively and profoundly—in order not just to support your internal customers but to help them execute the mission-critical strategies and activities on which the entire organization depends. If you perform a SWOT or PEST analysis, as described in Chapter 1, you'll go a long way toward understanding the contexts and stakeholders—especially key internal and external customers—that affect your organization's strategy and its implementation (see the Pull Up a Chair box for an example featuring Apple's iPhone). Also helpful are the various lenses through which you can view business strategy, such as Mintzberg's Five *P* model, which we also described in the previous chapter.

PULL UP A CHAIR!

Apple's iPhone: Forbidden Fruit for Some People— for Now

Any time Apple announces a new iPhone model, the buzz in the business media rivals that of tabloids' announcing every detail of, say, Prince William and Kate Middleton's "new model": their son, born on July 22, 2013. Only one of these deliveries pertains to our discussion, alas.

With less expensive plastic materials instead of aluminum for its casing, Apple's iPhone 5C is a new option for smartphone users around the world. The introduction of this model is a perfect example of how a company interacts deftly with all three aforementioned business factors that Dave Ulrich et al. (2012) believe any top-notch HR professional must comprehend: business context, business stakeholders (especially, in this case, external customers), and business strategy. What led to this offering?

CONTEXT

For the last few years, Apple had enjoyed "spectacular expansion," increasing shipments of its iPhone by more than 50 percent each quarter throughout 2010 and in all but one quarter in 2011 and 2012 (Luk & Sherr, 2013, para. 11). Then, in 2013, those shipments rose by only 7 percent in the first quarter, which led analysts to wonder if "the smartphone market may be slowing, particularly in Western markets" (para. 12).

So if its markets in the West are starting to dry up, where might Apple turn its focus? East, of course, to the huge markets in Asia and especially China, which has the world's largest mobile carrier, with 700 million or so subscribers. The catch: it's also the only Chinese mobile carrier that doesn't offer the iPhone. Indeed, Apple reported in mid-August 2013 that its sales in greater China, including Taiwan and Hong Kong, had slipped 4 percent from the previous quarter (Lee, 2013).

STAKEHOLDERS

Apple's *prospective* customers represent one set of stakeholders. These are either folks who don't own a smartphone or those who do own one but not an Apple, because they find the $649 USD price tag for the iPhone 5 too high. (This is the current price in the United States of an unlocked device purchased at an Apple store, not at a U.S. mobile carrier, which discounts the price of a phone with a two-year contract.) "The iPhone in China [has been] submerged under the waves of cheap Android smartphones," such as rival Samsung's Galaxy, Google phones, and "sub-$200 homegrown Android devices" (Sutherland, 2013, para. 1). When Jack was in Beijing in January 2013, he noticed that the iPhone was clearly a status symbol for wealthy business people, who usually put theirs right in the middle of a table for all to see, but it wasn't in the hands or pockets of most Chinese.

Apple's investors are another set of stakeholders. When sales increase, market share expands, and the value of Apple's stock rises. Recently these stakeholders have been observing the opposite trend. "A perception that Apple's pace of innovation has slowed, along with some uncharacteristic missteps by the company, helped push its shares down [in value] by more than 40 percent in the span of six months" (Luk & Sherr, 2013, para. 9). The stock price went from a high of just over $702 on September 19, 2012, to a low of just $390 seven months later, on April 19, 2013. As of this writing, it's back up to $521.

Apple must also contend with the powerful stakeholder that is the Chinese government, which is heavily involved in an array of business matters in China. On September 11, 2013, for example, the government said iPhones could run on the new network of that gigantic carrier (and another stakeholder), China Mobile (Chen & Pfanner, 2013). In exchange, China Mobile is hoping Apple will lower the cost of iPhones (which are priced higher in China).

STRATEGY

Enter Apple's strategy, manifest in the form of the iPhone 5C. The hope is that it will attract the Chinese consumers who don't own a smartphone

(continued on next page)

yet but said they would choose an iPhone if and when they do: 23 percent of respondents report these results in a recent Morgan Stanley survey. The number rises to 29 percent if the iPhone were compatible with China Mobile. Those same consumers said they would pay up to $486 for an iPhone (Elmer-DeWitt, 2013)—well below the 5C's price tag in China of $733 (Chen & Pfanner, 2013).

Meanwhile, Apple CEO Tim Cook has been doing what he can to hammer out a deal with China Mobile, meeting with the firm's chairman at the end of July 2013. Analysts project that if Apple can swing such a deal, it "could easily turn things around for Apple in the country. The demand is certainly there—[China Mobile] tracks more than 10 million unlocked iPhones on its network" (Lee, 2013, para. 9). The same survey mentioned earlier also says that the repurchase rate for iPhones is higher than that for other smartphones—that is, more people who own an iPhone will buy another iPhone in the future, compared with owners of other smartphone brands (Elmer-DeWitt, 2013).

This iPhone strategy well played, then, would attract more brand-new Apple customers as well as current customers who buy the new 5C model—several million people in China alone but elsewhere around the world, too. Investors would be thrilled if Apple's market share increases as predicted (while competitor Samsung's is predicted to decline) due in part to the iPhone 5C. As *Fortune* magazine said, "Apple could find itself, once again, the No. 1 vendor in the world's largest smartphone market" (Elmer-DeWitt, 2013, para. 9).

Thus far, we've "set the table" by expanding a bit on the notion of starting to think and act like a salesperson when it comes to drilling down on what matters most to your business colleagues (who are, in fact, your most valuable customers): *their* challenges, described in business terms (not HR metrics). The next chapter elaborates on an approach that actual salespeople use to engage deeply with their critical customers, because we believe it is similarly suitable for HR professionals who also want to have these sorts of business- and strategy-focused conversations. Why do we believe that? Because we're not salespeople, yet we've used this approach to speak more effectively with business people who work in industry sectors and functional areas outside our own. We think HR professionals can do so, too.

If you still find this hard to believe, read on and see how much of what you probably already know and do has in common with customer-centric salespeople.

HOW SALESPEOPLE LEARN TO SPEAK BUSINESS— AND HR CAN, TOO

As mentioned, we suspect you already regard your CEO and president, as well as the key players who head business units, as customers. So now replace the words *buyers* and *salespeople* with *business leaders* and *HR professionals* in the following quote, and see how precisely the same ideas pertain to human resources:

> Buyers want to do business with salespeople who understand them— their jobs and their problems. They want to do business with someone who has situational fluency—in other words, a person who has a good understanding of their situation as well as a good working knowledge of the capabilities necessary to help them solve their problems. (Eades, 2004, p. 10)

Or compare the earlier-cited quote from HR guru Dave Ulrich—

> "HR must give value or give notice"

—with this one:

> "Salespeople must add value to the situation or they won't survive."

See what we mean? The second quote is from *The New Solution Selling* by Keith Eades (2004, p. 10). We'll be hearing more from Eades in the next chapter, but for now let's explore his idea of situational fluency, mentioned above, as it pertains to facilitating your strategic conversations—and helping eradicate any negative HR stereotypes. The good news is that we suspect most of our readers already have some of the skills, or are well on the way to developing them, that comprise situational fluency:

- People skills
- Selling (influence) skills
- Situational knowledge
- Capability knowledge

The *H* in HR: People and Selling (Influence) Skills

These "human-oriented" components of situational fluency are what define many HR professionals. They have the ability to engage and connect effectively with a variety of people; they can pivot their interpersonal skills to build relationships across the organization (see Table 2.1). If you're familiar with the behavioral DISC model, discussed at length in Chapter 5, you may regard yourself and many of your HR colleagues as very high on the Influence scale: optimistic, enthusiastic, motivational. These qualities define the people and selling skills that are critical for situational fluency.

It's natural qualities like these, in fact, that often attract people to the human resources profession. "The top two reasons HR professionals give for selecting HR as a career were that they found HR appealing and wanted to work with people. Taken together, these two reasons account for one-third of all responses to this question" in a global survey by SHRM—especially for those working in North America (Claus & Collison, 2005, p. 10).

> The best HR professionals do not speak HR; they talk in business terms.
>
> ANDY GOODMAN

These data are dramatically confirmed by another global survey, the more recent *2013 State of Talent Managers Report,* published by the New Talent Management Network (NTMN; see www.newtmn.com). It found that 77 percent of HR professionals cite "I want to help people grow and develop" as the "primary reason" they're in the HR field (Effron, 2013, p. 3). This top reason stands true around the world: 76 percent of HR professionals in North America, 77 percent in Asia Pacific, and 69 percent in Western Europe—as well as by HR function: HR business partner, 72 percent; talent management, 76 percent; and learning and development, 92 percent (see Table 2.2).

Table 2.1 Interpersonal Style Cheat Sheet

When speaking with this *personality type**	Adapt your *body language*	Use this *tone of voice*	Adjust your *pace*	Inject these *key words*
Rules Follower Common examples: • Accountants • Auditors • Technologists • Programmers • Data entry staff	• Arm's-length (at least) distance • No touching (except for a quick, firm hand-shake) • Direct eye contact • Straight posture • No or minimal gestures	• Direct • Thoughtful • Steady • Little inflection	• Methodical • Deliberate • Slow	• "According to the data. . . ." • "The facts are . . ." • *analysis* • *proven* • *research* • *statistics* • *compliance* • *risk management* • *established procedures* • *protocol* • *field-tested*
Solid Joe/Jane Common examples: • Middle managers • Line staff	• Comfortable distance • Friendly eye contact • Relaxed stance • Leaning back • Small gestures	• Warm, soft • Steady • Low volume • Calm	• Steady • A beat slower than normal	• "Help me to . . ." • "Think about it" • "We're counting on you to . . ." • *step-by-step* • *team* • *loyal* • *trusted* • *dependable, reliable* • *logical* • *stability*

(continued on next page)

Table 2.1 Interpersonal Style Cheat Sheet (*continued*)

When speaking with this *personality type**	Adapt your *body language*	Use this *tone of voice*	Adjust your *pace*	Inject these *key words*
Dominant Force Common examples: • CEO, president • C-suite executive • Department head • Project/program manager	• Arm's-length (at least) distance • No touching (except for a strong handshake) • Direct eye contact • Lean forward • Controlled gestures	• Strong • Clear, loud • Confident • Direct	• To-the-point • Fast	• "We lead the field in . . ." • "Results show . . ." • "Top performers . . ." • *modern* • *new, novel* • *cutting-edge* • *challenge* • *results* • *dominant* • *best practices* • *leading*

When speaking with this *personality type**	Adapt your *body language*	Use this *tone of voice*	Adjust your *pace*	Inject these *key words*
Energetic Enthusiast Common examples: • Top salespeople • Customer service reps • Executive coach • Corporate trainers	• Conversational distance, at times leaning in • Firm handshake, plus quick, light touch on arm (*only* in appropriate context between two people who already know each other very well) • Friendly eye contact • Relaxed and open posture • Animated gestures	• Expressive • High and low modulation • Friendly • Dynamic	• Skipping around • Fast	• "I feel . . ." • "This will be great!" • *social* • *looking good* • *fun* • *exciting* • *adventure* • *funny*

*The personality types and their common examples are generalizations based on our experience and the research of assessment developers. These tips are suggestions only; exceptions obviously can occur.

Table 2.2 Reasons HR Professionals Chose the Profession, by Function

Reason	Function within HR		
	HR Business Partner	Talent Management	Learning & Development
I want to help people grow and develop.	72%	76%	92%
I want to help my company maximize its profitability.	68%	58%	35%
I want to help balance the needs of an organization and its employees.	56%	53%	55%
I want to represent the needs of employees in my organization.	30%	26%	35%
I enjoy being part of a for-profit organization.	28%	15%	18%
It's one of many different business functions I want to learn about.	13%	7%	10%

Source: Effron (2013), *2013 State of Talent Managers Report*, p. 4. Published by the New Talent Management Network; publicly available at and downloaded from www.newtmn.com.

We believe their typically strong people skills are a real asset for the great majority of human resources professionals. We've met a few exceptions, for sure, but by and large we would say this point holds true. We also believe, however, that the great majority of HR folks have room to expand their skill set in situational fluency's other two factors that are more business oriented: situational knowledge and capability knowledge (remember what we noted earlier about there being some small kernel of truth to all stereotypes). These are not only a main focus of this book but also the absolute requirements to gain further respect from your internal customers. According to HR consultant Brenda VanderMeulen:

> HR folks enhance their credibility immensely by having a good understanding of the financial aspects of an organization. Having these skills and knowing how to use them in conversations with managers adds credibility because it demonstrates that you understand the business

and are proposing solutions to organizations' problems—not "fluff" that "just makes people feel good." (in Grensing-Pophal, 2012, para. 13)

Business Savvy: Situational and Capability Knowledge

The other components of situational fluency, situational knowledge and capability knowledge, are collectively what we'd regard as business knowledge, in the context of this book. "The real key to getting good management-level meetings and having meaningful conversations is to have good situational knowledge, which is knowledge developed through personal experience, training, reading, research, and planning" (Eades, 2004, p. 47).

In the sales realm, this is called "pre-call planning." In the HR context and what we're discussing in this book, it's many of the activities, for example, described in the previous chapter. You're on the path to developing these competencies of situational fluency when you dig up your firm's Form 10-K or start using strategy models and business practices like scenario planning and SWOT or PEST analysis. When business people suggest that HR professionals should be "business leaders first and managers of people and process second"—as Sean Moriarty, the former CEO of Ticketmaster, told us—it's these components of situational fluency they have in mind. Polishing this side of the situational fluency coin is what will help business executives—your most important internal customers—regard you as more of a strategic player in your organization.

As noted, this half of the situational fluency skill set is also where we think many HR professionals have an opportunity to improve. Some research indicates that this orientation doesn't come as naturally to many HR professionals as the people and influence skills described earlier. The NTMN survey cited in the prior section reveals that "way down the scale was business growth and development as a career choice driver" for HR professionals, coming in at 58 percent (Zappe, 2013, p. 1). We don't agree that 58 percent warrants being described as "way down the scale" or "a distant second," as the author of the survey views it (Effron, 2013, p. 2). But we do agree with the bottom-line impressions and recommendations that emerge from data like these.

Effron, the founder of NTMN, is himself a highly experienced Fortune 500 HR executive, with an MBA from Yale. With this distinctive HR-business background, he comments on his group's survey results by underscoring the critical difference between a "humanistic" and a "capitalistic" motivation among HR professionals:

> The dominant humanistic reasons for being in HR suggests [*sic*] that our love for people meaningfully outweighs our love for business. Whether this is proper or troubling depends on your point of view. When a chair at the table is occupied by someone whose fundamental motivation differs from their teammates, it's likely they will have less influence on the business agenda and outcomes. (Effron, 2013, p. 6)

Effron succinctly sums up his recommendation by stating, "Humanism dominates; capitalism differentiates" (p. 3).

Even SHRM's response to the infamous "Why We Hate HR" article, excerpts of which open the introduction to this book, admits, "There are many truths in this article: HR professionals need business acumen and skills, performance metrics are imperative for HR practices, and *there has to be a balance with concern for people and concern for the organizational bottom line,* not one extreme or the other" (Berkley, 2006, p. 7, emphasis added). To take steps toward healing the "adversarial relationship" that often exists between business executives and HR professionals, the author of this paper offers this advice:

> You shouldn't ask for a "seat at the table" if you have no interest in what's being served there.
>
> MARC EFFRON

> Top management speaks the language of profit and loss. If HR is to get their attention, it is important to know how to speak that language. Therefore, it is important for HR to understand finance, accounting and economics. Further, HR professionals need to understand how HR practices are linked to company strategy. (p. 7)

Let's look at an example of how speaking this business language like a salesperson with situational fluency can affect an HR professional's effectiveness. We'll use a recruiting scenario probably familiar to many readers: hiring salespeople.

PULL UP A CHAIR!
Fact Sometimes *Is* Stranger Than Fiction

In doing our "pre-call planning" by researching a prospective client firm, we came across this position description posted online for—coincidentally—a "Solution Sales Executive":

As part of a regional Sales Team reporting to the VP of Sales, the Solution Sales Executive will support regional objectives to achieve quota. The Solution Sales Executive should have experience in health information exchange (HIE), meaningful use, EMR interoperability and analytics.

Duties and Responsibilities
- Meet regional revenue targets by developing qualified prospects into contracts.
- Present [firm's] value proposition.
- Work in team environment.
- Translate complex technologies and business models into winning business plans for customers.
- Write clean and concise RFP.
- Present deep dive technical and business cases.

Knowledge, Skills and Abilities
- Excellent mix of HIE experience and sales success required.
- Optimal candidate will be able to hit ground running having previously sold HIE.
- Ability to adapt the [firm's] story to the level of expertise desired by prospects (high-level vs. technical) through outstanding presentation skills.
- Experience delivering compelling product demos for different kinds of audiences (administrative, clinical, technical, business, executives).

(continued on next page)

Our concern with this PD was that the only thing that really aligns with Solution Selling is the name of the role. For example, nowhere is there a clear definition of what this sales approach means in this particular firm. Where's mention of diagnosing a customer's challenges, establishing value, creating solutions, demonstrating value, negotiating a win-win, and so on? Chapter 4 describes in detail how to craft position descriptions that align with your business colleagues' requirements to execute on their strategic objectives.

Using Situational Fluency to Recruit Salespeople

The so-called skills shortage has gotten a lot of press (e.g., Cappelli, 2011; Friedman, 2013; Wright, 2013). In a May 2013 survey, 35 percent of about 40,000 employers in 42 countries reported difficulty finding workers with required skills; 39 percent of about 1,000 employers in the United States echoed that view. ManpowerGroup, which conducted this survey, specified that one of the consistently toughest roles to fill around the world is top-notch salespeople. Among the top 10 most difficult roles to fill, sales reps ranked second in the United States and Mexico, fourth in Canada, and third globally (Staffing Industry Analysts, 2013).

Imagine you're in charge of talent management at a pharmaceutical company that was one of the employer respondents to the skills shortage survey. You've had plenty of conversations with your firm's SVP, Sales—some during staff meetings, and some, like one that took place recently, when the SVP has asked to meet with you when jobs in her business open up. These one-on-one conversations typically have been driven by the SVP, who cites her requirements as you jot down notes for the content of a position description. This most recent meeting was no different.

You thought all was progressing well in the search for salespeople: you generated 15 résumés of individuals who currently work in other pharmaceutical companies and seem like a great match. But then the SVP, Sales reviews them and barks, "These candidates are way off!" Now you have to not only start from square one with your search, but also paddle through some choppy waters with this SVP—a customer you very much want to keep happy.

We suspect the trouble identifying the "right" salespeople is an unfortunate by-product of the imbalanced conversation that occurred before you even wrote your position description. In fact, we'd go so far as to say that the well-publicized global skills shortage can be partially attributed to thousands of "imbalanced conversations," like the one just outlined, that take place every day. It takes two people to tango, however, and two people to communicate clearly with each other so that both parties walk away knowing what to do next. Therefore, the SVP in our fictional scenario here had a role to play, too, in things going awry. We note in Part 2 that we've observed scores of senior business executives really stumble when it comes to things like specifying requirements for a key role or interviewing the candidates who show up. We're on the receiving end of those unhelpful conversations all the time in our own work. Trust us when we say we're doing our best to help these people so that they can make the job of their HR teams a bit easier! But right now, we're hoping to do that for you as it pertains to your interactions with an "unhappy customer." Back to our story . . . .

Let's rewind the tape a bit further to better understand the situational knowledge (or lack thereof) that affected the recruiting scenario. The fictional pharmaceutical organization may have a history of selling individual products—let's say, prescription medications—to physicians in medical practices. But several months ago, the CEO announced a shift in strategy so that the company could ride a major trend within the health care industry: selling not just products (prescription drugs, in this case) but services, too, and not just to physician practices but to large organizations, such as hospitals and HMOs. Specifically, your firm will now be offering the option—selling the service—of managing the distribution and delivery of prescription drugs, at the best prices, to these large businesses; these businesses are in effect outsourcing much of their in-house pharmacies to companies like yours. The bottom line is, your CEO wants to raise the firm's bottom line by increasing revenues via new customers and new offerings. This new strategy was communicated in an all-staff meeting and the online employee newsletter delivered every month. This is how you, the fictitious HR professional in the story, learned about the strategy—or should have. You may not have been invited to the meeting where the SVP, Sales heard about it in detail from the CEO, but you still would've known about it.

What we've just described regarding prescription drug delivery and distribution is actually playing out today. HR executives with situational fluency not only will be aware of this trend in the broader pharmaceutical industry (*situational knowledge*) but also will be able to talk about it in the language of business with a range of colleagues (*people* and *influence skills*). They will understand how this trend trickles down to affect

- their organization's strategy;
- problems for key players, like the SVP, Sales; and
- the capacity to offer solutions (*capability knowledge*).

In the recruiting context of our story, those once-appealing candidates for the sales role turned out to be inappropriate because they've spent their entire careers selling medications (products) to doctors (individuals). The SVP, Sales now must build a team of sales stars who know how to sell pharmaceutical *services* to health care *corporations,* to include hospitals and HMOs. This is the business problem weighing on her mind: to implement the strategy—increase revenue in new ways to new customers—she must have the right sales talent. If you as the HR professional in this story don't understand the distinction between these two types of salespeople, you're not solving this executive's core problem. It's an unhappy ending to a story like this one that leads many actual business executives to lament, "HR doesn't understand my business!"

How can you avoid your own unhappy ending and not disappoint your internal customers? Two tools in a true solution sales executive's toolkit will further help you develop the situational fluency you need to have powerful, high-level conversations. The next chapter describes them in HR-relevant detail.

The New Rules of Engagement
HR Driving the Business Conversation

NOW THAT we've pinpointed who an HR professional's most important customers are and have begun to cue you as to how to start thinking like a salesperson, let's discuss further the approach that we introduced in the last chapter as apt for HR professionals' business conversations: Solution Selling.*

We imagine some readers grumbling, "OK, you're losing me. I got how situational fluency is a lot like what we already do to adapt our style when we're talking to different types of people, but aren't you taking this sales metaphor too far? Do you actually expect to teach me, an HR executive, how to sell—like, for real?" Yes, we do—to an extent. Bear with us.

Remember we mentioned in the prior chapter that we, who also are very much *not* professional salespeople, use this approach in our own work. For instance, when coauthor Jack showed up to work at a Wall Street executive search firm—his first job as a civilian after 22 years in the Army—he was thrown into a role for which he had very little preparation. To be blunt, he didn't have a clue. He knew he had to both find prospective clients and

---

Solution Selling is a registered trademarked term of Sales Performance International (www.spisales.com).

nurture ever-deeper relationships with current clients, but he spoke "Army" and they spoke "business." He knew what to do, in theory ("Find search work. Do search work. Repeat."), but not *how* to do it. He also had to figure out how to connect with these business people and figure out what mattered to them. He had to talk shop with people who did things beyond his experience, at a level and in a domain different from what he was used to. And, to really get these business people's respect and trust, so that he could uncover what their real needs were, he had to do all of this not just well but fast. He didn't have a formal business background, but he did have a strong desire to be regarded seriously and invited to take a seat at the table.

Does this remind you of anyone you know?

Jack set out to learn as much as he could about the executive search business as well as the businesses his clients were in, primarily financial services technology. He

> Job titles don't matter. Everyone is in sales.
>
> HARVEY MACKAY

read books, subscribed to the *Wall Street Journal* and *Investor's Business Daily,* listened to CD programs, scoured the Internet, and asked his colleagues a lot of questions. But the real game-changer came with *The New Solution Selling,* the best-seller we cited in Chapter 2 (Eades, 2004).

We're not asking you to switch teams and play for Sales. But when it comes to honing your ability to engage deeply on the business problems and issues your colleagues are struggling with, we think you should take at least a few practice swings with the Solution Selling bat. Play ball!

SOLUTION SELLING: IT'S NOT JUST FOR SALESPEOPLE ANYMORE

Eades (2004) notes that Solution Selling is a sales process that includes a philosophy, a map, a methodology, and a sales management system. For our purposes, we're interested mainly in the philosophy and map components, so let's delve into those two areas a bit more—including how they can translate into the HR arena.

PULL UP A CHAIR!

A Lexicon from Solution Selling

To help begin thinking about your CEO's and other business colleagues' challenges and objectives differently—dare we say strategically—familiarize yourself with some of the terms and specific definitions that come from Solution Selling. In this context, your "customers" or "clients" are your CEO and the heads of business units and functions; and what you're "selling" is HR's capabilities to help solve *their* problems and drive *their* business agendas.

- **Solution**: a mutually agreed-upon answer to a recognized problem that offers measurable improvement
- **Pain**: a critical business issue that compels a person to make a change
- **Situational fluency**: a set of four integrated competencies—people skills, selling/influence skills, situational knowledge, and capability knowledge—that establish credibility by developing deep understanding of both a customer's pain and ways to resolve it (see Chapter 2)
- **Key Players List**: a list of the senior executives in an organization that identifies and connects their specific problems and challenges in their part of the business—their pain points
- **Pain Chain**®: a flowchart of the key players and their pains, the reasons for those problems, and the effect those problems have on other key players in the organization

This chapter will look at how these terms and tools will come up in your strategic conversations with business colleagues.

Philosophy: Focus on Your Customer

As a philosophy, Solution Selling believes that "the customer is the focal point. Helping customers solve their business problems and achieve positive, measurable results is the basis of all actions" (Eades, 2004, p. 5). The parallels here to your context in HR are very clear. HR professionals desire the opportunity to help tackle the big, hairy problems in their firms—the "strategic issues." That's what being "invited to the table" is all about. Solution Selling is a way to speak your customers' language so that you can discover their problems and then determine how HR can help address those issues. When you do that, you're clearing the path for your business colleagues to achieve their goals and objectives. This is the business-savvy HR professional's way to really "help people."

Be mindful, however, of what you offer as a so-called solution. Later in this chapter we discuss how a real business problem and solution can emerge from the conversations with your colleagues; but for now let's say you have "for sale" to your internal customers—the key players—the following:

- Recruiting
- Talent management
- Training and development
- Coaching and mentoring
- Onboarding

This list of capabilities is a great starting point from an HR perspective; these functions, after all, represent what human resources is all about and how it can address key business problems in your organization. Yet *none* of these activities alone is a real *solution* to your internal customers' problems. In fact, each of them is better defined as a service.

Remember how Solution Selling defines a solution: an answer to a recognized and somewhat significant problem, and it's framed to include measurable improvement. Ideally, you and your customer should be in full accord around exactly what the challenge is—the "before" picture; what the solution you will provide entails; and how you can measure the resultant change—the "after" picture. (Measuring just a few critical HR functions is discussed in the Pull Up a Chair feature.)

PULL UP A CHAIR!

Measure Twice ... No, Make That Three Times (at Least)

We'd like to underscore something just mentioned in the text when it comes to delivering impactful solutions to your internal customers. Being able to *measure* your work is immensely important, because it enables you to do at least three things:

1. **Continually demonstrate HR's value**, measured in dollars, because HR is a function that does not generate revenue. In blunt terms, HR departments spend money rather than make money; they're cost centers. This is why many organizations are outsourcing much of the HR function, as we noted in the introduction, "Will HR Even Be Invited to the Table?" These organizations know they need to provide HR-type services to their employees—payroll, health insurance, and so forth—but they can do so today at lower costs via HRO or PEO firms rather than an in-house department. Measuring the business change that derives from HR efforts proves the value—and justifies the existence—of a dynamic in-house HR team.

2. **Master data analytics**—what has been called "the next technological quantum leap for HR" (KPMG, 2012, p. 2). KPMG's global survey of human resources found that 57 percent of respondents—who represented both business (42 percent) and HR (58 percent) executives—acknowledge that the use of data analytics is much more common today than in 2009, especially for gathering business intelligence and identifying risk (i.e., the ingredients of good SWOT and PEST analyses and scenario planning; see Chapter 1). "Data analytics gives HR departments the long-overdue chance to become more empirical, to provide hard evidence for their opinions, thereby gaining much-needed credibility at the highest levels

(continued on next page)

of the business" (KPMG, 2012, p. 11). One of the writers of the KPMG survey, managing director Paulette Welsing, goes so far as to say that "the ultimate killer metric" is the demonstrated return on human performance. A step in that direction, if you're not already doing so, is benchmarking talent (see Chapter 5).

3. **Deliver strategic workforce planning**. This area taps data analytics, too, and it parlays into the findings of survey after survey that state that talent management—recruiting, developing, and retaining high-performing employees—is, if not the number-one priority for CEOs, at least among the top three (see, e.g., Boston Consulting Group, 2011; SHRM, 2008; Wright et al., 2011). As Victor Nichols, the CEO of Experian North America and Experian Consumer Services, told us, "Strategic planning long has been financially oriented. We now make it equally talent oriented—defining what talent will be needed over a three-year strategic time frame in terms of skills, knowledge, quantities [of employees], location—and then we hire and cross-train accordingly." The key to strategic workforce planning is to ask *open-ended questions* of your business colleagues about the challenges they foresee and the outcomes they'd like to achieve. Then direct the conversation about possible ways to address those needs, in a balanced, mutually informative give-and-take.

No matter what context your measurement takes—HR's functional value, data analytics, or strategic workforce planning—follow these three tips:

1. *Describe the executive summary of your research.* No need to share every exciting data point. Remember our advice in the section in Chapter 1 about HR metrics not playing well in the strategy sandbox. "Only data that is relevant, meaningful, and accurate is of any real value in designing and implementing initiatives and evaluating their success" (Fallaw & Kantrowitz, 2013, p. 28).

2. *Wait for answers and suggestions in your discussions.* "Some HR leaders shortchange the conversation . . . by leaping to conclusions and providing the solutions they think are needed instead of probing to find out what their peers and senior leaders consider the problems to be" (Mirza, 2012, para. 8). We'll talk more about this recommendation later in the chapter.

3. *Engage in a true conversation, not a compliance exercise.* Asking your colleagues to complete a template is about as dynamic and instructional as watching paint dry. You want your interactions to come off with a more strategic than transactional bent.

Map: Determining the Destination

As a map, Solution Selling shows you "how to get from where you are to where you want to be. [It] provides an end-to-end series of next steps to follow," including preparing for the conversation with your customer, "diagnosing the problem, vision processing, . . . and [giving you] the ability to predict . . . success or failure" (Eades, 2004, p. 6).

Most organizations, whether for-profit or nonprofit, have—at a minimum— as their destination "greater revenue." Companies are judged as strong and viable forces in the market when they can demonstrate quarter-over-quarter or, even better, year-over-year sustained growth (think of the Starbucks example we described in Chapter 1). This is how they grow the following all-critical metrics for the business stakeholders who are investors (among others, including employees who want to keep their jobs): revenue, profit, earnings per share, stock price, and market share.

If a business partner tells you, loud and clear, that higher revenues is his or her strategic destination, here are some ideas for how HR can map its way to some solutions. And even if your colleagues don't say that out loud, it's OK, even smart, for you to assume they *always* have this financial outcome as a goal; therefore, these are activities you should be *continually* engaged in.

- Work with your business colleagues to assess the talent on their current teams. For example, who are the A-, B-, and C-level salespeople in the firm? Assist the head of Sales in retaining the As, enhancing the capabilities of the Bs, and redeploying or removing the Cs.
- Start identifying the requirements for critical roles and create lists of possible candidates. These people may currently work in your firm, or they may be talented people outside your organization.
- Tap your workforce analytics skills to predict staffing requirements across the firm. Perform PEST analysis and scenario planning to anticipate challenges to meeting these needs (see Chapter 1). How can you course-correct now to avoid some of those obstacles?
- Determine the best sources for that talent—in-house as well as external to your firm, especially if you plan to operate outside the United States.
- If there are higher-level roles to be filled in the foreseeable future, start sourcing and screening possible candidates now. This approach is often called building bench strength; you connect and vet but keep them on the string *outside* the organization. Then leverage your people and influence skills—key elements of situational fluency (discussed in the previous chapter)—to keep them "warm." For example, send a quick e-mail or call them periodically, until your business colleagues are ready to begin face-to-face interviews.

> Successful executives don't allow recruiting to become a one-time event. They are always on the lookout for new talent, before a new hire is really needed.
>
> GEOFF SMART & RANDY STREET

- Orient the entire HR team, not just yourself, to support the business units and functional groups in the firm that are experiencing fast growth or rising demand.

- Begin identifying ways HR can find and support the right talent as the firm enters brand-new markets. Think of the story in Chapter 2 about Apple angling itself to enter the low-cost smartphone market in China. To best support the company's various business units in this endeavor (product development, retail sales, etc.), what talent, in what locations, does Apple's HR team need to identify and potentially hire? In other words, how are they serving their internal customers?
- Craft a well-thought-out integration plan to manage mergers and acquisitions, if that's a way your organization plans to grow its top line and increase revenues. A couple years ago, a company that had acquired a competitor hired us for the express purpose of helping them integrate the two highly distinct (and still competitive) cultures.
- Similarly, anticipate how talent management needs may change if your company is being purchased by a private equity firm. If new owners are likely to ask you to help cut costs through a reduction in force, determine *now* where your organization might let some employees go. Then sketch out how those functions can still be handled with fewer but more highly skilled people. For example, will you need training programs, designation of part-time roles, or temporary workers?
- Standardize major HR functions (e.g., the recruiting process—see Part 2). Run a cost/benefit analysis to see if outsourcing makes sense and saves the company money (i.e., reduces costs). Some commonly outsourced HR functions, according to a SHRM survey, include employee assistance counseling, flexible spending account administration, and background checks (SHRM, 2008, p. 16). The decision around what gets outsourced is most often tied to the organization's business strategy (according to 50 percent of respondents), competencies of the HR team (45 percent), and the organization's workforce management needs (40 percent) (p. 18). Commenting

> Part of HR's value proposition has to be our intimate knowledge of our internal customers' business and industry.
>
> TRELLIS USHER-MAYS

on these findings, Trellis Usher-Mays, a member of SHRM's Organizational Development panel, noted, "The more closely aligned HR is to the organization's strategic objectives, . . . the less we have to worry about being outsourced or eliminated" (p. 19).

Table 3.1 shares some other "destinations," or strategic business goals, and ways that HR can link itself to them. Also included are possible metrics—so you can *measure* the impact HR has on these strategic endeavors.

When you think and act like a salesperson, you'll learn how to determine priorities like these and map out a strategy-supporting set of activities for your colleagues. Let's see now how a couple of the specific components of Solution Selling we've defined at the start of this chapter—namely, the Key Players List and the Pain Chain—can help you do this.

KEY PLAYERS LIST

Sheryl Sandberg (2013) has shined a bright spotlight on the importance of women, and men, "leaning in" to have direct conversations around business topics. Women still represent about three-fourths of the human resources profession (HRxAnalysts, 2011; Ramirez, 2012), but the Key Players List applies to any HR professional, male or female, or even any professional who needs to engage with executives outside his or her own field. The Key Players List was a huge help to coauthor Jack, for example, when he was learning how to conduct executive search and, specifically, unravel the complicated talent-centric problems he needed to discuss, as an outsider, with prospects and clients in various sectors.

As Eades (2004) defines it in *The New Solution Selling,* "A Key Players List is a starting point for developing situational knowledge [one of the core business-related competencies for situational fluency]. This list identifies, connects, and leverages the pains [challenges] of key players" (p. 54). Table 3.2 is an example of a Key Players List for a manufacturing organization. As you see, it's simply a list of the key players in your organization—your most important internal customers—and a corresponding list of the pains or challenges that you know or suspect each of those executives is experiencing. Let's start drafting your Key Players List for your own organization.

Table 3.1 Measurable Links to HR That Drive Business Goals

Business Goal	HR Links	Metric
Lower costs	• Uncover ways HR can lower its own operating costs (e.g., using an HRO firm to handle those HR functions mentioned in the main text that are commonly outsourced). • Determine whether other functions might be outsourced or offshored; conduct a cost/benefit analysis. • Manage outsourcing implementation. • Review compensation and especially bonus structures. • Oversee any change process to keep productivity and morale up.	Decrease costs for the business unit by 7% by end of quarter 2.
Increase customer satisfaction	• Analyze the retention–customer satisfaction connection: are departing employees taking customers with them? • Nurture the organization's brand and image in the marketplace, starting with its internal culture and workforce. • Cite a customer-centric focus as an explicit required competency in all position descriptions. • Assess and interview for a strong customer orientation and collaborative problem-solving skills.	Raise customer satisfaction scores by 10% by year end.
Decrease turnover	• Ensure that compensation is appropriate for your geographic area. • Train all managers in active listening, emotional intelligence, providing balanced feedback, and other coaching skills that support their teams. • Recognize and reward star performance, including in nonmonetary forms (certificates, plaques, lunch with the CEO, etc.; see Kaye & Jordan-Evans, 2014). • Communicate openly and regularly, organization-wide; tap multiple forms of media to share news and views with the workforce.	Reduce turnover by 10% this year.

Table 3.2 Key Players List

Key Players (Job Title)	Potential Pains
Chief Executive Officer (CEO)	• Not meeting investors' expectations • Declining stock price • Decreasing EPS/shareholder value
Chief Operating Officer (COO)	• Rising operational costs • Declining margins • Inability to consistently reach productivity goals
Chief Financial Officer (CFO)/VP Finance	• Declining cash flow • Declining ROI and ROA • Eroding profits
Chief Information Officer (CIO)/VP Information Technology	• Inability to meet users' technology demands • Trouble keeping up with technology change • Difficulty implementing new technologies • Lack of resources
VP Sales	• Missing revenue goals/new account sales targets • Inability to accurately predict sales revenue • Declining customer satisfaction
VP Manufacturing	• Not meeting manufacturing and shipment schedules • Excessive inventory levels • Lack of capital for equipment
VP Engineering	• Inability to get new products to market on timely basis • Escalating design costs • Inability to develop a new product plan

Source: Reprinted with permission from Keith Eades, *The New Solution Selling* (New York: McGraw-Hill, 2004), p. 55.

Who Are the Key Players?

In the last chapter, we asked you, "Who are your customers, really?" Now we want you to drill down into more detail. Who are the executives in your firm whom you most need to assist? We use the word *need* very specifically here. Step back for a moment and ponder these questions:

- Which people make the most essential decisions about strategy, key activities that support the strategy, target markets, and revenue/profits?

- Who has the team that brings in the most revenue?
- Who has the largest team?
- Who are the people who manage the most risk?
- Which executives have the biggest effect on the firm's reputation?
- Which executives have the biggest direct effect on the market and on customers/clients (or end users, in nonprofits)?

A postscript to this section's head might very well be ". . . and Do You Want to Talk to Them?" When you identify the key players based on these questions, you may realize that you've actually had less than an ideal level of substantive interaction with them. It may be that these folks—like you—are extremely engaged in their work, and neither of you has had a lot of time to talk shop in a deep way (again, from the perspective of your customer). We once worked with a brilliant SVP, HR who had an international MBA and endless ideas— great, viable ones—for strategic action, but whenever she'd share one with us, she was quick to add, "But when am I going to find the time to do *that,* when I have everything else to do?"

> I don't like that man. I must get to know him better.
>
> ABRAHAM LINCOLN

Maybe you've had plenty of contact with your organization's key players, but now you realize that, really, most of your "conversations" have consisted of your being on the receiving end of their requirements (much like the experience of the fictional recruiter in our story at the end of Chapter 2). Maybe you simply don't like them and therefore avoid them—in which case we're compelled to quote from, first, *The Godfather:* "It's not personal—it's business"; and then *Moonstruck:* "Snap out of it!"

But maybe there's yet another reason: Truth be told, you might be slightly intimidated by one or two of these people because you don't fully understand their business and its problems, and therefore you don't know precisely what to say. Perhaps you can relate a bit too much to the scenario that opens Chapter 2 in which it's easier to take another bite of the doughnut than risk saying something your colleagues might regard as what one HR blogger calls "Fuzzy Wuzzy HR (you know, all of the team building, cry on my shoulder, let's hold hands and sing kum-ba-ya HR philosophies)"

(Haun, 2009, para. 3). Sandberg (2013) may have had women in mind when she made the following statement, but we've been firsthand observers of men feeling the same way and doing (or not doing, as it turns out) the same things: "We hold ourselves back in ways both big and small, by lacking self-confidence, by not raising our hands, and by pulling back when we should be leaning in" (p. 8). Whether women or men, in HR or not, all professionals are subject at some point to the same human qualities of insecurity, anxiety, and fear. The Pull Up a Chair feature describes an outstanding tip that we've seen work before our eyes in helping men and women become more confident when they're called on to speak at a meeting or to present more formally.

We're suggesting that no matter what the nature of your current relationship with the CEO, president, and other key players in your firm, we bet there's room to improve the nature of your conversations so that they're more about your colleague-customers' business problems than your HR services.

PULL UP A CHAIR!

Wonder Woman, Hormones, and You: Tips for Speaking Up with Confidence

In creating a two-day course for the City of New York called "Powerful Project Presentations," we stumbled upon an outstanding TED Talk by Amy Cuddy, a social psychologist and associate professor at the Harvard Business School. If you're unfamiliar with TED.com, it's a forum of people from all walks of life and all parts of the world, speaking briefly on any topic you can think of. We recommend it to the participants in our class for not only great content but also role models of public speaking done well (or poorly). Cuddy's presentation is a consistently popular highlight in our class; indeed, it's had well over seven million views since it was posted on TED.com in October 2012.

Cuddy reminds us of the critical role body language plays in communication, relating experiment results in which hiring and promoting decisions were influenced by the experiment subjects' body language. In addition, her colleagues have found that a mere *1-second* view of a political candidate's face leads to a 70 percent accuracy rate in predicting the outcome of senatorial and gubernatorial elections, and, similarly, a 30-second video clip—with no sound—of doctor-patient interaction strongly predicted whether the patient would file a medical malpractice suit.

Anyone who has had to deliver an unpleasant performance review or fire someone is acutely aware of the power of nonverbal communication. But, as Cuddy notes, "We forget about the other audience influenced by our nonverbals: ourselves." People who project power—think of pairs of victorious presidential and vice presidential candidates, hands clasped and both arms raised over their heads—not only are perceived by others as self-confident, optimistic, and assertive, but actually have biochemical differences compared to their more timid counterparts: their levels of testosterone, the assertiveness hormone, are higher; and their levels of cortisol, the stress hormone, are lower. This got Cuddy to wonder, "Do our bodies change our minds"—literally?

She found her answer by putting research volunteers into two groups: one that was asked to assume slouching "low-power" poses, with arms folded and face cast downward; and one that was asked to assume upright "high-power" poses, with hands on hips and chin tilted upward (this one's colloquially called the "Wonder Woman" pose). Members of each experimental group held their respective pose for two minutes; then they spit in cups, and Cuddy measured the hormone levels in the saliva samples. *Spoiler alert:* The results were pretty striking (especially in the context of the teeny units of hormonal measurement):

	HIGH-POWER POSE	LOW-POWER POSE
Testosterone:	↑20%	↓10%
Cortisol:	↓25%	↑15%

What this simply means is that *after only two minutes* striking a confident, even exaggerated, high-power pose, people's biochemistry had automatically reacted to that nonverbal signal so that, whether they wanted to

(continued on next page)

or not, they actually *did* feel more self-confident and assertive (the spike in testosterone) as well as relaxed and comfortable (the drop in cortisol).

Hey, we love a cool social psychology experiment as much as the next guy, but we also like to see for ourselves whether and how things like this play out in the real world. What better bunch of research volunteers for us to find out, we thought, than the folks in our own presentation classes. The people typically in these classes are extremely intelligent and accomplished professionals who work for New York City—the man who oversaw the entire rebuilding of the 9/11 memorial site, for example, and an architect who counted a "genius award" from the MacArthur Fellows Program among her many accomplishments. What about 90 percent of them have in common is a fear of public speaking, even in the context of a small staff meeting around the conference table. Thus we added into our workshop a segment on day 1 in which we ask every person to show us what their own personal power pose is going to be. We tell them that we'll be asking them to do this pose, even for a few seconds, before they stand up in front of the class on day 2 of the workshop to present an actual speech (always at least an uncomfortable, if not terrifying, prospect for these people; some even skip day 2 to avoid it!).

One fellow, a civil engineer named Trevor, told the class he'd opt for the power pose of fist-pumping both arms over his head. He also told us that on a public-speaking comfort scale from 1 to 10, where 1 is very low and 10 is very high self-confidence, he was a 2. Day 2 comes, and Trevor, seated in a corner in the back of the large classroom, gets up to present his speech while his classmates clap and cheer him on. To everyone's delight, this shy middle-aged man of small stature strides to the podium, fist-pumping the whole way. He gives his speech—flawlessly—and returns to his seat with a big smile on his face. When we ask him where he is on the scale now, he replies, "I'm a 9!"

"Fist Pump" Trevor, Wonder Woman—pick your public-speaking role model, and check out Amy Cuddy's talk at www.ted.com/talks/amy_cuddy_your_body_language_shapes_who_you_are.html.

Where's Their Pain?

The Solution Selling model describes three levels of need that include latent pain and admitted pain (see Figure 3.1). We imagine that you, as an HR professional, are privy to a lot of *admitted pain* in your organization, in which a person

> is willing to discuss problems, difficulties, or dissatisfaction with the existing situation. [He or she] admits the problem but doesn't know how to solve it. At this level, [people] tell us their problems but aren't taking action. (Eades, 2004, p. 19)

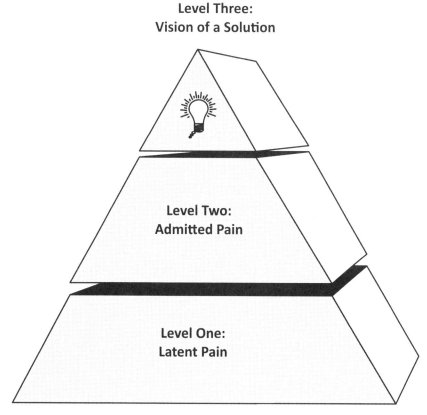

Level Three:
Vision of a Solution

Level Two:
Admitted Pain

Level One:
Latent Pain

FIGURE 3.1 Three Levels of Buyer Need

Source: Reprinted with permission from Keith Eades, *The New Solution Selling* (New York: McGraw-Hill, 2004), p. 18.

Are you vigorously nodding your head and thinking, "This is an average day for me!"? You're probably also well familiar with how Eades suggests that you, acting like a customer-focused salesperson, respond: "confirm the pain that they're having and lead them to a vision of a solution" (p. 20). For instance, in our Chapter 2 example of a pharma company, we looked at the difference between finding product sales talent and service sales talent in the marketplace to assist the head of Sales to significantly grow revenue. Grasping the difference provided a level of clarity that started an HR professional down the path toward full situational fluency. That degree of understanding required the kind of active listening that often involves saying things like "If I'm hearing you accurately, you want . . . ." But when you're responding to the admitted pain of a *business*-related matter, we actually strongly advise *against* using that kind of language, because some (or most) people will dismiss it as precisely the kind of "Fuzzy Wuzzy HR" or "HR happy-talk" you want to avoid. (The section on "Using Pain Chains" later in this chapter will show you a better approach.)

Latent pain gives you the opportunity to rise to the "strategic player" challenge and really be useful in a way that your business colleagues will likely find refreshing. People who

> are not looking and not actively trying to solve a problem are in latent pain. There are two primary reasons for [people] being at this level of need: ignorance or rationalization. Ignorance means they're unaware of the problem, and rationalization means that they know about the problem, but they may not believe a solution exists or they may have failed at previous attempts to solve the problem. (Eades, 2004, p. 19)

Ignorance on the part of your colleagues in this context is by no means a derogatory thing; it's simply not knowing about or anticipating future events or consequences of business decisions and actions. This is where you can tap the research and analysis you've done—reading your organization's strategy statement online, sketching out a SWOT analysis, reading a business-focused book, and the like—to truly serve in a strategic advisory role. As Mary Young, a principal researcher of human capital at the Conference Board, notes, "Engage business leaders so you can prepare [and have] the agility and flexibility to respond quickly to changes in the operating environment" (in Mirza, 2013, para. 4). For example, if your head of Sales is determined to increase revenue by moving into new markets, you can spot his latent pain (finding brand-new customers for the same products or services) and then craft a solution for his pain (addressing any regulations, laws, talent availability, and other barriers that exist in the new markets) before "latent" becomes "admitted" pain. Remove all the obstacles you can to clear this new revenue-generating path for your business partner well *before* he deploys his sales team there.

In other circumstances, to guide key player colleagues from the latent pain point to admitted pain so that you can offer a viable solution (see Figure 3.1), try the approach we described in the earlier feature on measurement in this chapter: open-ended questions within a balanced dialogue. Look at what these senior executives told us they liked about the best HR professionals in their own experience:

> The best HR professionals bring insights and questions to the table that others do not always consider. Do we have the capability to execute? Do we understand the talent pool, both internally and externally to build that capability? What are alternative approaches to consider?—*Andy Goodman, EVP, HR*

> I particularly valued HR when they came to me or a member of my team with talent management insights that were not obvious—at least to us. Some of that proactive approach was to help us better understand where there were opportunities we were missing or not maximizing. Other cases were where they could see—ahead of time—potential or likely outcomes to be avoided.—*Jack Flanagan, senior retail and non-profit executive*

> The best HR professionals become "business partners" with us by adapting our objectives as their own in terms of HR. The very best are proactive in bringing ideas and recommendations to us that will add value to our business.—*John Rao, managing director and Operations head*

What HR professionals can do to best work with me is strategic work-force planning with business segments to plan and execute, in detail, on talent and team member composition, in the short and long term. —*Victor Nichols, CEO*

Latent pain for business executives like these four may also be resolved through the future-oriented and strategic "HR from the outside in" that management professor and HR guru Dave Ulrich describes (see, e.g., Figure 1.4 in Ulrich et al., 2012, p. 25). As "strategic positioners," in the words of Ulrich's HR competency model,

> high-performing HR professionals understand the global business context—the social, political, economic, environment, technological, and demographic trends that bear on their business—and translate these trends into business implications. They understand the structure and logic of their own industries and the underlying competitive dynamics of the markets they serve, including [external] customer, competitor, and supplier trends. They then apply this knowledge to developing a personal vision for the future of their own company. (Ulrich et al., 2012, p. 52)

To develop this "vision for the future" of the company, or what in Solution Selling parlance *is* the solution to business problems, let's turn now to the next tool in that protocol.

PAIN CHAIN: CONNECTING THE DOTS

The Pain Chain picks up where your Key Players List left off. It cites in brief terms not just the key players and their pains or challenges, but also the reasons for the pains and the effects of those pains on other key players (see Figure 3.2). In the situation displayed in Figure 3.2, the CEO is facing a decrease in earnings per share due to "eroding profits," which is the pain for the VP Finance. In turn, one reason for this pain is because new account revenue targets are being missed, which is the pain for the VP Sales. By "connecting

	Pain:	Missing new account revenue targets
	Job Title & Industry:	VP Sales, manufacturing company
	Our Offering:	e-Commerce Applications

Reasons	Impact	Capabilities
Is it because...; Today...?	*Is this (pain) causing?*	*What if...; Would it help if...?*
A. salespeople spend too much time handling repeat business in existing accounts (i.e. "order taking" vs. selling)?	• missed overall revenue targets? • lower profits? *Is the VP Finance concerned?*	A. *when:* wanting to place orders *(who:)* your customers *(what:)* could view inventory levels, place an order and have it allocated and confirmed, all over the Internet?
B. salespeople spend too much time answering frequently asked questions (FAQs) from current customers?	• impact on growth? • declining stock price? *Is the Chief Executive Officer affected?*	B. *when:* customers have questions *(who:)* they *(what:)* could click on a FAQ web menu to get answers or select an "I need help" option to be connected to the appropriate person in the company?
C. prospects are unaware of your promotions?		C. *when:* offering promotions *(who:)* your salespeople *(what:)* could create personalized messages and broadcast them to all of the prospects via e-mail?
D. salespeople fail to ask customers for referrals or leads?		D. *when:* visiting your website *(who:)* your customers *(what:)* could be prompted to submit referrals in exchange for discounts or promotional items?

FIGURE 3.2
Pain Chain

Source:
Reprinted with permission from Keith Eades, *The New Solution Selling* (New York: McGraw-Hill, 2004), p. 57.

the dots" in this way, Pain Chains differentiate you by giving your business colleagues the impression that you truly understand their business activities and challenges on multiple levels, simultaneously. "Your ability to build and confirm a Pain Chain with a customer demonstrates an understanding of his or her business environment. The customer will respect that" (Eades, 2004, p. 58). In a similar vein, the authors of *The HR Scorecard* state:

> Organizations are complex systems that involve interactions with and between many different subsystems. . . . [I]t's the *interactions* between systems [i.e., business units] and among a system's parts [e.g., key players and HR] that generate both problems and potential leverage points for change. Depending on the situation, different system interactions will be more or less important at various times. Skilled managers—including those HR professionals who want to be more than just administrators—know which interactions most require their attention, and when. (Becker et al., 2001, p. 15, emphasis in original)

See? As we mentioned before, we think the parallels between HR professionals leading business conversations and salespeople engaging with their customers are really quite marked.

Eades (2004) makes two critical points about what Pain Chains are *not*:

- They are *not* organizational charts, though they may look like them. Your org chart might be a helpful starting point for names and titles of key players, but you're going to have to do some research—online and face-to-face with your colleagues—to add the reasons for your colleagues' problems and to reflect on how they link to other problems. "Pain Chains trace the flow of pain or problems throughout an organization. Generally the pain at one level becomes the reasons for another pain at a higher level" (p. 58).
- Pain Chains are also *not* static documents created once and then preserved in acetate. Instead, you should continually update and revise this tool so that it accurately reflects the business realities that surface in your research and in your conversations with your internal customers—the key players.

PULL UP A CHAIR!

"If Mama Ain't Happy, Ain't Nobody Happy": Pain Chains and Family Systems Theory

Keith Eades (2004) notes that his view of Pain Chains has been dramatically influenced by the theory of organizational interdependence described by W. Edwards Deming, the pioneer of total quality management (TQM; see Deming, 2000). We also see the connection to systems theory (Senge, 2006) and, specifically, family systems theory—a theory we all live with every day.

Murray Bowen originated family systems theory to describe the incredibly complex emotional connections the members of a family experience with one another. Unlike in the business context, in a family context the Pain Chain really *is* a living entity, as the feelings and behaviors of one person cascade over all the other family members. Dad experiencing the pain of being laid off? Mom feels that pain as a tighter household budget, and the kids feel it as fewer toys at the holidays. Eldest child feeling the pain of maintaining the status of an overachiever? Middle child spins that pain by veering in the opposite (i.e., rebellious) direction.

The connectedness of all members of a family (even those in which the black sheep may claim to be detached) makes the functioning of relatives—just like that of the key players in your workplace—highly interdependent. "When family members get anxious, the anxiety can escalate by spreading infectiously among them. As anxiety goes up, the emotional connectedness of family members becomes more stressful than comforting. Eventually, one or more members feel overwhelmed, isolated, or out of control" (see www.thebowencenter.org).

So the next time you describe your organization as "a big family," beware of the darker implications of that statement. It may not have been a coincidence that the father of family systems theory, Murray Bowen, was a psychiatrist.

Using Pain Chains

The core of a Pain Chain is actually what some theorists call a "strategy map" (Kaplan & Norton, 2000)—remember Eades calls the Solution Selling approach partly a map—or a "value chain." A value chain is "a solid comprehension, throughout the firm, of what kind of value the organization generates and exactly how that value is created" (Becker et al., 2001, p. 19). Based on the "pre-call planning" you've done using some of the tools described in Chapter 1, you should be familiar with these strategy-related topics in your organization as you lead discussions with business colleagues.

The Pain Chains you create can help you exercise the situational fluency you've started to develop, as discussed in the previous chapter. Specifically, these flowcharts will help you

1. identify a key player's pains or *problems,*
2. uncover the *reasons* for those pains,
3. determine their *impact* on their business, and
4. brainstorm ways HR *capabilities* can help resolve those pains.

In an HR-business context, you use Pain Chains at three points: before your conversation with a business colleague, during the solution-creating process, and at the end of your HR-driven solution.

BEFORE YOUR CONVERSATION

As an amped-up Key Players List, the Pain Chain provides you with a checklist or "cheat sheet" as you prepare to speak with a business colleague. You stand to gain huge benefits in terms of both valuable data points and your professional reputation when you can confidently ask about the potential problems (latent pain) or address previously discussed issues (admitted pain). A key player is likely going to

> Understanding how to identify points of intersection in your firm is the key to securing a strategic role for HR.
>
> BRIAN BECKER ET AL.

perk up dramatically if you lead the discussion by asking, "What challenges are you dealing with as a result of the missed revenue targets on new-account sales?" All of a sudden, with this more specific question, you start coming across as a true business partner.

DURING YOUR SOLUTION CREATION PROCESS

Just as it does for a salesperson, the Pain Chain serves to underscore the benefits of your prospective solution in the terms that are most valuable to each senior executive in your organization (and *not* in the terms of HR metrics, as advised in the previous chapter). It's in your subsequent conversations that you're gathering the real-time, boots-on-the-ground information that fleshes out in greater detail your colleagues' problems and their interconnectedness across the organization. "I expect the HR professional to establish and sustain an open two-way line of communications," Major General Dorian Anderson, who headed the U.S. Army's global Human Resources Command, told us. "Having conversations throughout the [talent management] process is very helpful and allows for fine-tuning the requirements." Few people want to be sold, but most of us want to buy from someone who we trust understands our situation, needs, and goals.

AT THE END (FOR NOW) OF AN HR SOLUTION

Because of its ever-evolving nature amid strong forces inside and outside the organization, we don't see HR's work coming to a full stop now or in the future. But a Pain Chain underscores the value of an HR-led undertaking just as it does for a sales proposition. The further along in your strategic conversations, the more data analytics and other research you should have performed that stack one strong benefit of your initiatives on top of another. As you refine your Pain Chain, you should also be verifying and updating the connections to other pain points. Your goal is to offer customized, targeted solutions that your internal customers have told you *they* want and need. As our colleague Dorian Anderson advises HR professionals, "Do not try to fit [your customer] in an already established box." You're not an order taker—you're a business partner.

Solution Selling in the HR Arena

To conclude this chapter, let's revisit our fictional pharmaceutical corporation and pull together those elements we've adapted from Solution Selling to look at a couple of key players' business challenges (Eades, Touchstone, & Sullivan, 2005).

SVP, SALES

Heads of Sales—and the entire sale force, for that matter—always bear the pressure of increasing revenues amid a churning global economy, fickle consumer tastes, scattered supply chains, and dozens of other factors. What are the typical problems that these executives face?

- Inability to get new products to market quickly
- Increased number of stalled sales opportunities
- Poor customer service
- Inability to develop new customers

Because you've created a Pain Chain in your organization, you recognize that these pain points themselves are creating challenges for the CEO in terms of lowered profits.

With these problems identified, here are some questions to ask of the SVP, Sales:

- As you think about it, how is your sales team doing in getting newer products to the market quickly? Are there any specific aspects of this problem that suggest you need enhanced talent, salespeople who truly can accelerate getting new products to the market?
- As I understand it, stalled sales opportunities are ongoing problems with sales executives in various pharmaceutical firms. Is this a challenge for you, and where does it primarily show up? Do you think that some people could use specific training to reduce this problem? Are there some people who just can't solve this problem, and you might need to replace them?

- In the research I've seen, I understand that customer service is sometimes a challenge in pharma companies. How do you think it's working here? Do you think we have the right people following up with customers after the sale?
- I'd imagine that an ongoing problem for your team is the ability to break into a new client company. How is it going for you in this regard? Are there any gaps that you see or areas where you need help?

By now you should see how taking the time to do your research, individually and in regular dialogues with your internal customers, lends you the situational fluency you need to have a meaningful, content-rich conversation with your head of Sales. You may rephrase these questions any way that you want, but the point is that you're orienting your approach based on the language and problem sets of a key executive, in this case, the head of Sales.

> Every person I work with knows something better than I—my job is to listen long enough to find it and use it.
>
> JACK NICKLAUS

Like the president and COO, you must work across all functional areas of the firm. How do you have conversations similar to the one we just outlined with, say, your VP, Finance or chief financial officer?

CFO

As we've mentioned, every organization, no matter the sector or industry, must make money to survive. No wonder, then, that one of the especially "key" key players is the CFO. What are the pain points a typical CFO faces?

- Poor investor relations
- Rising cost of capital
- Poor cash flow
- Increased cost of R&D
- Increased cost of marketing

What's interesting about this list is that many of the people responsible for each issue don't work for the CFO. For example, much of the cause of "poor cash flow" pain resides with the head of Sales: if sales increased or at least stayed steady, cash flow obviously wouldn't be as big an issue. The head of Research and Development also has a major role to play in the status of cash flow, by how well he or she manages the cost of R&D: research can't lean too far in front of the revenues that pay for it.

Again, organizations, like families, are tightly linked and interdependent; so, in turn, the problems of one group (R&D) may be caused by the performance of another group (in this case, Sales), which all combine to be one big headache for the CFO. How can you engage with the CFO to begin addressing his or her problems and formulating solutions as you did with the head of Sales? Consider these possibilities:

- From what I understand, investor relations is a big deal as the market and shareholders view a corporation. What's your perception of how investors view our firm? Is there anything I can do to assist your efforts to engage investors in the best possible way? Do you have the right people on your team to handle investors?
- I've spent some time with ___ [head of Sales]. What's your view of the firm's cash flow? What's your advice to me on ways I could assist Sales in increasing cash flow?
- It's pretty amazing how much firms like ours spend on R&D. In your view, what could we do to reduce that amount or find the appropriate amount to spend? What do you think I could do to assist ___ [head of R&D]? Do you think there are specific skills that he's missing on his team, skills that can be learned, developed, or acquired?
- I've come to realize that many pharma companies spend massive amounts of money on marketing. What's your view of how much we're spending? Is it about right or too much? Do you think I can help ___ [head of Marketing] in reducing that cost? What, or who, does she need to perform even better?

———

Now that you've learned in Part 1 how to view and discuss—in business terms—strategy and the challenging operational issues that inevitably emerge in executing it, you can apply these lessons to the focus of Part 2: delivering talent. We've already used it often in our examples, but undoubtedly in your real-life conversations with business colleagues, an ongoing challenge they'll share is the requirement for exceptional talent they need to successfully execute their key activities and thus the firm's strategy. In fact, a SHRM (2008) survey indicated that the functional area in HR that is "most critical to contributing to the organization's current business strategy" was "staffing/employment/recruitment," at 52 percent (p. 6).

Most CEOs and heads of major business units talk about the need for great talent to create a stark and vivid business advantage in the market. But the concept of talent is fairly broad and relatively imprecise. Critical questions about talent center on *what* talent, *where* in the organization, doing *what*, and *why* or *to what end*—all ingredients of powerful position descriptions, the subject of the next chapter.

PART 2

Delivering Talent

I F THERE'S a single bottom-line function expected of a great human resources executive, it's the ability to attract, identify, hire, develop, and retain outstanding talent for his or her organization. For the rest of this book, we discuss the pre-hire components of this skill:

- Chapter 4: Position Descriptions: Defining the Role and Selling the Job
- Chapter 5: Online Assessment: The Pre-Hire Gift That Keeps on Giving
- Chapter 6: Hiring Interviews: How to Shift from Gut Feel to Real Deal

In sum, these three chapters will help you put into effect many of the topics of the strategic conversations you've had with your colleagues in other business units—what we've discussed in Part 1.

When we asked business executives to share their thoughts on what makes for a great HR partner when it comes specifically to delivering talent, two themes emerged very clearly among their responses: (1) a sharp understanding of the business requirements for the role and (2) a strong understanding of cultural fit. Let's look at each of these points in turn.

It seems nearly impossible to get in too much detail when it comes to determining what an open position's required skills and competencies are. This consideration comes up when you're customizing a position description for a specific role, selecting assessment instruments to help screen for behavioral style and motivation, and then probing for real-life examples of those skills and competencies in interviews. "[The HR executive and I] must have a shared understanding of the requirements and why these requirements are important" Dorian Anderson, a retired major general of the U.S. Army Human Resources Command, told us. Bill Wray, a chief operating officer of Blue Cross Blue Shield, agrees, suggesting that HR professionals "get to know me and my team and my mission in a profound way, so that the talent acquisition is targeted to solve not just the immediate issue but also serve the larger context of succession, team effectiveness, and the like." Another executive who spoke with us, John Rao, a managing director and the head of U.S. operations of the global Financial Services practice at Navigant, elaborated on this idea:

> It is critical that [HR professionals] understand our business, the skills and traits of highly successful professionals in the jobs we are trying to fill, and the culture of our organization. Often the HR professional does not have more than a high-level general understanding and may not fully understand the skills critical to success. When they do have this knowledge, they can more easily find candidates who have all the traits needed to be successful.
>
> The other critical aspect is to be able to find candidates who will fit our organization's culture. The cultural fit is essential and often overlooked. Can the candidate assimilate to our culture and flourish?

John's thoughts here segue into the second theme we mentioned earlier: cultural fit. SmartRecruiters notes that more than half of hiring managers "have decided not to hire anyone *at all* because they couldn't find the right fit" (Li, 2012, p. 4, emphasis added). Phil Parisi, the CFO of the USO and a former executive at AOL, believes that the best HR executives "show genuine care in finding the 'right' person versus just filling the position." Such HR executives know how to strike the proper balance between presenting highly suitable candidates and presenting those candidates in a time-efficient way. Well-done position descriptions cover both these bases by (1) painting a compelling portrait of the role and the organization to attract the best and brightest and (2) screening out, through self-selection, less suitable individuals for the role. Online assessments follow up as they cast a spotlight on those candidates whose natural tendencies align with your culture. If the hiring manager—say, your colleague in IT—tells you he wants candidates who thrive in a creative environment with a lot of unsupervised freedom to innovate, you can choose instruments that will spotlight those qualities (creativity, autonomy, innovation).

> The business value of talent assessments must be understood and embraced by everyone, especially the CEO.
>
> BILL CONATY

Similarly, interviews should not be left to the whims of the interviewers (especially those who personify the decidedly unhelpful "archetypes" we describe in Chapter 6) or candidates who are engaged in their very best "dating behavior" in order to win the hearts of the interviewing team—and the job. Instead, hiring interviews must be managed to explicitly seek out not just the required skill set but also a strong cultural match. According to Sean Moriarty, the chairman at Metacloud and former CEO of Ticketmaster, this search for cultural fit begins as soon as a candidate shows up for an interview. "It starts the moment a candidate walks through the door for the first time, and the signal should get stronger with every subsequent conversation." Sean told us that in his experience, the most effective HR professionals "develop a highly accurate picture with respect to cultural fit when evaluating candidates. . . . They truly evaluate a candidate beyond the résumé—[looking for] work ethic and tempo, worldview, regard for others, source of personal motivation, and authenticity."

The chapters in Part 2 will describe what we believe are best practices in writing position descriptions, using online assessment, and conducting interviews (including with references). We go a step further, however, by also guiding you explicitly in *how* to do these things, using real-life examples that illustrate how you can link interview questions to an assessment report or parts of a position description. We believe when you master these three skills, you are genuinely partnering with your CEO and other colleagues to help deliver not only superb talent but also the strategic results your organization wants and needs.

Position Descriptions
Defining the Role and Selling the Job

THE WORLD is full of position descriptions. And like most things in the world, there are good ones and bad ones. What makes the difference, and what role does the position description play in recruiting talent?

The essential purpose of a position description is to provide a summary of the skills, responsibilities, qualifications, and competencies required of an individual for a specific role. The best position descriptions are clear, specific, and concise. They show that you, and your partners in other business units, share a solid understanding of the type of person who is optimal for the role. As this chapter's subtitle suggests, a strong position description (or PD) also describes in a compelling way *why* a person would want to take on this role. In other words, a great PD tells *and* sells.

Sometimes the hiring manager or someone on his or her team takes the first stab at a position description, focusing especially on job-specific skills. Other times, you as the HR executive are asked to meet with the hiring manager and gather his or her viewpoints of the requirements, and then you are essentially tasked with preparing a document from scratch that becomes the position description. In either case, our experience over the last two decades tells us that, unfortunately, there is a good chance that this document will fall short in both describing the role with necessary precision and in helping you effectively screen—and attract—strong candidates.

In this chapter, you will learn what components should appear in every position description, no matter what level the job is, and what makes those components really strong. To illustrate, we will take you step-by-step through an actual position description we wrote, sharing the thinking behind each part. That way, you can begin to see how our recommendations—as well as the sort of information you gather through the strategic conversations we describe in Part 1—manifest in real life.

WHAT'S WRONG WITH MOST POSITION DESCRIPTIONS?

Creating a great position description is one of those tasks that seems simple enough, or at least pretty straightforward, but is actually quite difficult. Part of the difficulty lies in finding and gathering the kind of specific information you need to power up your PDs. The chapters in Part 1, we hope, have started to alleviate that issue by describing what to ask of your colleagues who serve as hiring managers and interviewing partners.

Another part of the difficulty, however, lies in three problematic issues surrounding most PDs. First, typically no single person is in charge of this effort; consequently, the PD gets stitched together in piecemeal fashion as it passes from one person to another for input. It becomes a patchwork of different people's ideas, opinions, and even writing styles. The resultant verbiage is so muddled that the document is not very helpful to either a candidate or a recruiting executive (in-house or external).

> Organizations need to examine role clarity, priorities, and performance expectations beyond the financials.
>
> RAM CHARAN ET AL.

Second, many position descriptions are basically a laundry list of what an individual in the role does today. That is, they hardly focus at all on what this person will be expected to accomplish *in the future*. In most cases, a person in a key role is hired not just to continue to carry out current responsibilities but

(1) to solve specific problems and (2) to achieve specific goals. Both of these elements will occur in the future.

Finally, the content and tone of position descriptions are often geared more for people already inside the organization rather than for people who know little about the company or corporation and absolutely nothing about the role. This issue generates two subproblems. For one thing, folks contributing to the PD "assume" that people will know what they are talking about, so they either use a vague shorthand—such as "Collaborate with Sales & Marketing"; "Develop a strong team"—or skip discussing important elements altogether due to the mistaken belief that "People will know what this means—I don't have to get into that level of detail." The problem is that people don't know what, precisely, is happening when the person in this role is "collaborating" with Sales & Marketing. And what size is the team to be developed, doing what, where? Does "develop" mean making the most of the staff already there, or hiring and training new people? You see what we mean.

The other problem with PDs that speak primarily in sound bites is that they do not offer enough detail to draw really talented people to the role. That is, they don't *sell* the role or the organization. There is little description of the company, the business situation at hand, or the rationale for someone to consider taking the role, especially if it means leaving a great job he or she may have today, not to mention a home, children's schools, and a spouse's current job.

THE ABCs OF PDs

Mastering the fundamentals of a strong position description will help you avoid potential problems like those just discussed. We suggest including the following elements in your position description:

1. Organizational and functional titles
2. Title of the new hire's boss
3. Location
4. Overview of the role
5. Detailed look at the organization
6. Description of the role
7. Explicit draw for candidates

8. Primary responsibilities (and, ideally, measurable outcomes)
9. Necessary qualifications
10. Critical competencies

Let's look at each of these elements in more detail. As promised, you'll see how they surface in an actual position description we used to recruit a senior executive into a financial services firm. To honor our client's confidentiality, we have changed the company name to "MetroFinancial," but all other parts of the sample PD are authentic.

Who, What, Where

1. **Organizational and functional titles**
2. **Title of the new hire's boss**
3. **Location**

Put these initial elements right at the top of the document so your reader knows immediately the who, what, and where of the role:

METROFINANCIAL

Position: Senior Vice President, Product Management and Long-Term Investments

Reports to: President, MetroFinancial Securities

Location: New York, NY

Let's take a moment to comment briefly on each of these first three elements.

"POSITION": ORGANIZATIONAL AND FUNCTIONAL TITLES

Of course, 99.99 percent of position descriptions do include the name of the organization and job title. Do make sure, however, that the job title is accurate and corresponds clearly to the details that come up later in the position description. It is generally better to use a descriptive functional title rather than a generic title you might assume "everyone uses today." For example, "SVP, Product Management and Long-Term Investments" is far more precise than merely "SVP, Product Management"—especially for candidates outside the organization.

Remember the position description in Chapter 2's feature with the headline "Solution Sales Executive" that did not define solution sales (there's that assumption problem noted in the last section) and did not describe the responsibilities of the role in any way resembling those of someone engaged in Solution Selling. Don't assume "everyone knows" what a "Solutions Sales Executive" or any other role is or does—tell them what it means in *your* organization, today and in the future. It's better to use a clear title as opposed to a generic description that means nothing to an external candidate.

"REPORTS TO": TITLE OF THE NEW HIRE'S BOSS

Many candidates want to know, naturally, who their boss would be. Put your-self in their shoes: wouldn't you want to know? If the role reports to a senior executive in the company, especially the CEO or president, this line is also a magnetic bit of data for applicants who like working with and learning from high-level executives.

The reporting line also suggests important things—again, from a candi-date's point of view—about how things are structured or even valued in the organization. These things may not be deal breakers for a job hunter, but they may highlight questions the person needs answered before deciding whether to discuss, much less pursue, this opportunity.

Consider these two reporting lines, for example, for the open position of Senior Vice President, Human Resources:

Reports to: Chief Executive Officer

versus

Reports to: EVP, Chief Operating Officer

A candidate might believe that HR is more valued if the head of the depart-ment reports directly to the CEO. Another might be drawn to an organiza-tion that has a COO, as in our example, believing there is a well-delineated hierarchy in place and liking such structure. Another may interpret the reporting line more negatively, thinking that having a COO between the SVP and the CEO is just creating more layers in a bureaucratic maze, and that this organization "just doesn't value HR" because the role doesn't report to the CEO. Many HR executives might, in fact, take offense in reporting to a COO; we know one human resources professional who resigned when the reporting structure changed this way with new leadership.

Whether or not these first impressions are valid is not the point. What is more important is that you take the care to start considering the messages your position description might be sending. Is the PD working right off the bat to attract optimal candidates and screen out less desirable ones?

LOCATION

The location detail may fall victim to that earlier-noted problem of assuming "everyone" knows this information already or will look it up on their own. Plus, many firms have multiple locations around the country and around the world. If you work for a household-name company like Microsoft, readers of your PD likely know that your headquarters is just outside Seattle, in Redmond, Washington. But perhaps this role operates in a Microsoft office in a city located in one of the corporation's other nine geographic districts besides the Northwest sector—like Edina, Minnesota. Many job hunters will be drawn to one location but not another.

Don't set someone up for a surprise by doing a sort of bait-and-switch in promoting one location on your PD and then specifying later in the interview that the job actually operates somewhere else. Great cities both, but Redmond and Edina are apples and oranges.

Selling the Job, Part 1

4. Overview of the role

The next necessary element in a position description is the overview. This is where you begin to sell someone on both the job and the organization. Like the lead paragraph of a front-page news story that draws readers in, this single powerful paragraph should quickly compel an appropriately talented executive to read on, learn more, and express interest in this position.

Overview: The SVP will lead the Advice and Long-Term Investing Product Management team at MetroFinancial. This executive will help set the direction of the firm's product strategy and address the expanding advice and long-term investing needs of retail and institutional clients. Working across the organization, this person will develop new products, tools, and services that will differentiate and point individuals toward a partner that will service them across their lifetime.

As this sample shows, the overview quickly tells someone what this job entails—what the real-life definition is of "SVP, Product Management and Long-Term Investing" in this particular organization.

The next required element of a position description also helps sell the position:

5. Detailed look at the organization

The Company

MetroFinancial (www.fakeurl.com) is an innovative financial services company offering a full suite of easy-to-use online brokerage, investing, and related banking solutions, delivered at a competitive price. It empowers individuals to take control of their financial futures by providing the products, tools, and services needed to meet their near- and long-term investing goals. The corporation has approximately 6,000 employees (as of September 30, 2012) and over 2 million customers, and annual revenues are just over $6 billion.

MetroFinancial is primarily focused on profitably growing the online brokerage business, which includes active trader and long-term investing customers. Its competitive strategy is to attract and retain customers by emphasizing low cost, ease of use, and innovation, with delivery of its products and services primarily through online and technology-intensive channels.

MetroFinancial operates directly and through numerous subsidiaries, many of which are overseen by governmental and self-regulatory organizations. It provides services to customers in the U.S.

through its website. In addition to the website, the firm also provides services through a network of customer service representatives, relationship managers, and investment advisors.

MetroFinancial helps clients trade stock but also offers mutual funds, options, fixed-income products, exchange-traded funds, and portfolio management services. For corporate clients, the company performs market making, trade clearing, and employee stock option plan administration services.

This entire section came directly from the company's website. Don't reinvent the wheel. As we mentioned when discussing 10-K forms in Chapter 1, most organizations invest a great deal of brainpower in describing very carefully who they are and what they do, especially how they differentiate themselves from other firms in the same sector. Take advantage of the expertise of your marketing and communications colleagues by using their verbiage from your website. The "About Us" page usually provides you with an overview ready to copy-and-paste into your position descriptions.

Using the same text to describe your organization also lends a sense of cohesiveness between the marketing vehicles of the website and the PD. A strong, consistent message is always desirable. And yes, the PD is a marketing tool—remember, one of its purposes is to sell attractive candidates on the role and the organization. That's exactly what a good overview helps you to do.

Selling the Job, Part 2

6. Description of the role

7. Explicit draw for candidates

Now it's time for the position description to flesh out the details of what the role entails and the reasons that someone would be motivated to take this job. You want to lay out the context for your readers so it becomes easy for them to start imagining what it would be like to disengage from their current job and move into your organization. Take a look at the sample:

The Role

Today, MetroFinancial has built a powerful retail brokerage capability but wants to do so much more. The senior leadership of the corporation has decided to find an executive who can work across the entire firm and help shape the products, investor tools, and multi-channeled services that will provide a long-term or life-cycle set of capabilities for their clients. This executive, due to his or her background, will bring those advice-centered capabilities that will attract and maintain clients all of their lives.

This section makes the point that the key players in the firm have very consciously thought about this role, that they haven't just decided to "fill an open slot." This paragraph suggests to a discerning reader that the company's leaders really want a top executive in this role, someone they will partner with across the organization and rely on to help them raise the entire firm to a new level. Most candidates want to feel like their job has direct pertinence to strategic goals like those cited in this description.

With this initial depiction of the role, the PD is now putting the open job in a bigger, exciting context that will attract strong talent. But don't stop there: underscore explicitly why a person would want this job—even quit a perfectly viable current job to do so:

What's the draw? That is, why would a qualified candidate be interested in moving to MetroFinancial and this role?

- Executives are viewed as being "just a bit better" when they work for a company with a great brand. MetroFinancial has that type of brand, and so this role will look good in the overall view of the selected executive's career.

- The selected executive will have a significant role in Metro-Financial over the next several years. If you want a role in which you can make a difference, this job will provide that opportunity.

- The executive in this position will gather superb experience and expertise in a strategic role, one that requires analysis, implementation with diverse partners inside and outside the firm, and powerful influence skills across the corporation.

- The combination of the analytical skills and the operational implementation will set this person up for further significant roles at MetroFinancial.

We hope you agree that this section is critical. You have to get into the mind-set of a possible qualified candidate and ask yourself, "Why would I consider this role? Why would I think about leaving my current company, job, and work pals?" This summary makes it easier for candidates to justify first to themselves, and then to their spouse, friends, and, at a certain point, their current boss, why they would make a move. Here your position description begins to mention qualities defining your organization's culture, so that candidates—and eventually you, in interviews—can determine if they would make for a great cultural fit. One study reports that one-third of CEOs surveyed believe that one of the biggest reasons for their hiring mistakes was not evaluating cultural fit (Smart & Street, 2008).

In this section, we again don't assume anything. We don't assume, for example, that readers will acknowledge our client is a well-known firm with a positive image. We tell them outright that this is "a great brand," adding our belief that working for such an organization casts an executive in a positive light as well. If your customers or clients let you know that your firm is awesome, or if your firm is on a positive list of similar companies (e.g., *Inc.*'s "Fastest-Growing Small Businesses," *Forbes*'s "Best Companies to Work For"), explicitly state such points in a position description.

Also don't assume that readers will connect the dots and come automatically to the positive conclusion you want them to reach about the bigger implications of this role for them. That is, spell out for them what this job can mean for their professional development. For example, in the sample, we explicitly say that the person who fills this position will have real impact—he or she will "make a difference."

We also mention some of the valuable skills to be learned in this role—influence

> # A company is only as good as the people it keeps.
>
> MARY KAY ASH

internally and externally, strategic analysis, tactical follow-through—and how that experience can segue into future opportunities. Retention experts Beverly Kaye and Sharon Jordan-Evans (2014) tell us that "exciting, challenging, or meaningful work" and "career growth, learning, and development" are among the top reasons people stay in an organization. (See the full list in the Pull Up a Chair feature in this section.) These same items are what will help attract talent to your organization, so be sure to let prospective candidates know what good things lie ahead—without exaggerating or fibbing, of course.

Defining the Job

8. Primary responsibilities

You have captured readers' attention by painting a compelling portrait of the role and the organization. Now they want to learn more, so describe what the person in this job will primarily be doing, today and in the future:

Primary Responsibilities

- Manage a product development and support team to develop products for Long-Term Investing, including retirement, managed products, fixed income, mutual funds, annuities, ETFs, etc. Product development responsibilities would include both online tools for long-term investing, ownership of investment advice products, and working internally and externally on new strategies to differentiate MetroFinancial.

- Orchestrate all advice on product initiatives, ensuring new products and enhancements meet identified clients' needs within the applicable regulatory framework as well as to meet key profitability and AUM/revenue goals.

- Monitor and be aware of industry trends impacting the product line to identify opportunities to successfully differentiate the MetroFinancial product range and leverage the firm's investment capabilities. Responsible for competitive benchmarking of product offerings.

PULL UP A CHAIR!
Attraction and Retention Work Hand in Hand

The elements of a powerful position description that serve to attract strong candidates to the role and your organization are the same ones that will help retain them once they have taken the job.

Surveying more than 18,000 people around the world, Kaye and Jordan-Evans (2014) have compiled a list of the most common reasons employees remain at an organization. These researchers note, "The items recur throughout every industry and at every level. The differences between functions, levels, genders, geographic regions, and ages are minor" (p. 8). Here are the top 13 responses, listed in order of frequency.

1. Exciting, challenging, or meaningful work
2. Being recognized, valued, and respected
3. Supportive management/good boss
4. Career growth, learning, and development
5. Job location
6. Job security and stability
7. Fair pay
8. Flexible work environment
9. Pride in the organization, its mission, or product
10. Fun, enjoyable work environment
11. Working with great coworkers or clients
12. Good benefits
13. Loyalty and commitment to coworkers or boss

If your organization has these qualities to share, let potential candidates know. The more of these elements you can fold into your discussion of an open role during the recruiting process (including explicitly stating them in position descriptions), the better. You can see the full demographic breakdown of results and take Kaye and Jordan-Evans's "What Kept You?" survey yourself at www.keepem.com.

- Work across functions to organize sales and marketing around customer development programs and initiatives with both product and investing tools. Develop share-of-wallet programs to increase the depth of relationship with our customers via investing tools and product offerings.

- Develop programs for the Sales organization to effectively engage building relationships with current and potential long-term investing-focused clients. Work cross-functionally with Sales, Marketing, Customer Experience, Innovation, and other departments to build broader share-of-wallet programs.

The "Primary Responsibilities" section tells a candidate exactly what the job entails, starting with the core or most important element at the top of the list. This is the meat of the role. If you're lucky, you have a current position description that covers these main responsibilities, and now you can simply confirm them and update them as necessary. Most times, however, you will be relying on your conversations with the hiring manager, the incumbent, and perhaps one or two other people (e.g., the CEO, peers who will be closely collaborating with the new hire).

OUTCOMES

Some position descriptions include a section called "Desired (or Expected) Outcomes." This component is nice to have but, frankly, hard to originate—mainly due to the usual urgency that surrounds a recruiting effort and also the difficulty many hiring managers have in describing performance expectations in great detail.

That said, when it's feasible, do include specific metrics within the responsibilities listed in this section of your PDs. A recruiting position, for example, might include "Decrease time-to-fill rate from 90 days to 45 or less, by end of quarter 2." Our own sample does not go into this level of specificity, because this was a new role in a brand-new space for our client firm, and even the new hire's boss did not know exactly what outcomes would be realistic at the time.

An "Outcomes" section does bring a strong advantage. By including specific expectations that define optimal performance of the job, you are letting applicants know, right off the bat, that they will be held accountable to achieve certain outcomes. Try to glean this level of specificity by asking the hiring manager:

> "If this person winds up hitting it out of the park a year from now, what will he or she have done or accomplished?"

Stating the Job's Requirements, Part 1

9. Necessary qualifications

Every job has "must-have" qualifications in terms of education, experience, skills, and knowledge, as well as specific competencies or soft skills. We will consider both types of qualifications separately.

List the job's required qualifications in some detail, so that many job hunters will self-select out of the recruiting process. Here are the qualification requirements we spelled out in our sample PD:

Requirements

A successful candidate will have:

- 10–15 years of directly related experience in retail financial services, product development and strategy, project management, and synchronization of these products, tools, and services across a corporation while including multiple investment vehicles.

- 5–10 years of team management and leadership experience of mid-size to large product development teams. Proven ability to develop employees and recruit, manage, and build teams effectively.

- Strong experience with diversified products and offerings, including UMAs and SMAs (unified managed accounts and separately managed accounts), mutual funds, ETFs, annuities, insurance, managed products, etc. Proven ability to think creatively and strategically as it relates to investing tools and product development in order to assess and meet clients' needs via both online and off-line channels.

- Exceptional expertise facilitating communications and forming collaborative partnerships firm-wide and with external vendor partners.

- Exceptional project management skills, with a demonstrated ability to identify and implement creative product and business solutions. Strong organizational skills with business development acumen and strategy.

- Experience with both online and off-line distribution channels is ideal.

- The most successful candidate will have a deep background executing programs across Marketing, Sales, Strategy, and Legal/Compliance with diverse teams.

- A bachelor's degree is required.

This section lays the foundation for your engagement with candidates during an initial phone screen and then the full-blown job interview. Chapter 6 discusses interviewing in detail, but we will delve into the topic a bit here to illustrate how a well-crafted position description can help facilitate an effective interview.

To write the "Requirements" or "Necessary Qualifications" section of your PD, imagine an ideal candidate—a person who is currently doing this job or one very similar to it, probably at a competitor firm. Capture a description of what the person is doing in the role: Meeting with current customers to offer additional services? Writing code for Android apps? Assessing quality on a shop floor in Taipei?

Another way to tackle this section is to think in terms of *key accountabilities*—the specific yet concise statements describing a result needed for superior performance. Any job, at any level, should have three to five key accountabilities.

The first item in the sample PD cites these criteria:

- 10–15 years of directly related experience in retail financial services, product development and strategy, project management, and synchronization of these products, tools, and services across a corporation while including multiple investment vehicles.

To determine whether the candidate has this qualification, you could ask the following questions that underscore (literally!) the requirements spelled out in the PD:

1. In your last <u>10 to 15 years of experience</u> in <u>retail financial services,</u> describe what you implemented in <u>product development and strategy.</u> For two projects, please describe the specific situation you faced, the problem or challenge at hand, the actions that you and your team took, and the measurable results.
2. Over the same time period, tell me about your experience with <u>project or program management</u> of investment <u>products, tools, and services.</u>

Answers to questions like these are hard for a candidate to fudge. And talented candidates will be able to tell you compelling stories that clearly illustrate their ability to *do* what the job requires.

Let's turn now to the second part of a job's required qualifications as presented on a position description.

Stating the Job's Requirements, Part 2

10. Critical competencies

Throughout our talent management work, we apply the following definition of *competency*:

> A competency is a measurable characteristic of a person that is related to success at work. It may be a behavioral skill, a technical skill, an attribute (such as intelligence), or an attitude (such as optimism). (Lombardo & Eichinger, 2008, p. 5)

For this part of a position description, "Critical Competencies," however, we are referring particularly to an ideal candidate's behaviors, attitudes, and attributes, because technical skills should be covered in the "Necessary Qualifications" section, as just discussed. Here's what we came up with on our sample position description:

- Very strong emotional and social intelligence
- Motivating others; strong team building
- Negotiating and conflict management
- Managing vision and purpose through systems
- Political/interpersonal savvy with peers, teams
- Presentation skills
- Sizing up people, hiring
- Impeccable integrity, trustworthiness
- Strategic agility
- Process management
- Problem solving
- Setting priorities
- Action oriented; drive for results
- Creativity, innovation

Where do these competencies come from? In some cases, an organization has a competency model that is custom made for the whole organization (e.g., the health care model shown in Figure 4.1). In fact, nearly two-thirds of "best-in-class" organizations use one not just pre-hire but throughout the entire employee life cycle (Lombardi, 2013, p. 20). Sometimes a department or functional area has its own competency model (see, e.g., the competencies for various HR roles in Table 5.2 in the next chapter where we discuss benchmarking). The fact is, a vast number of competency models are available—some generic, some specialized. Type "competency model" into your search engine and see what pops up. We even found one for an HR business partner tucked into a report titled "Business-Driven HR" (Deloitte, 2011, p. 11):

Business Capabilities

- Commercial awareness
- Customer focus
- Business acumen
- Aligning business & HR strategy

HR Capabilities

- Employee relations
- HR subject matter expertise
- Change delivery
- Gets the basics right
- Use of HR metrics

Consulting Capabilities

- Brokering
- Impact & influence
- Leadership
- Trusted advisor
- Facilitation & coaching
- Project delivery

Frankly, we're not convinced a custom-made model is always necessary, because decades of research have shown that the characteristics that define star performance are strikingly similar whether the executives are, for example, general managers, finance professionals, salespeople, or, in the case of our own recent research, chief security officers (Larson, 2012).

Moreover, the attributes marking high performance have remained constant over time. That is, the core qualities of top performance in a work role—such as learning quickly and tolerating ambiguity—have changed very little even in an era of increasing technological development.

Make no mistake: Each of these types of jobs does have some unique aspects, but those are mostly related to the *technical* knowledge necessary for that role—what you have laid out as "Necessary Qualifications" or "Requirements" in the position description. But the *behavioral and attitudinal competencies* it takes to do a job exceptionally well are mostly consistent across roles. Perseverance, for example, means "not giving up" whether you are a chief marketing officer or a computer programmer. Listening means "listening" whether the role is in Chicago or Singapore. Management gurus W. Edwards Deming in the 1950s and Tom Peters

> A common language supports increased alignment between [recruiting] activities and the skills required by business strategy.
>
> MOLLIE LOMBARDI

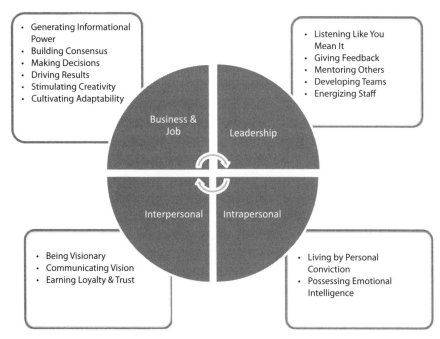

FIGURE 4.1 Health Care Competency Model
Source: Adapted from Dye and Garnman (2006).

and Robert Waterman in the 1980s cited "customer involvement" as one of the competencies marking success in the disparate industries and locations of Sony in Tokyo (Deming) and Disney in Los Angeles (Peters and Waterman).

To sum up, we may not care where your list of competencies or more formal competency model comes from, but we do care that you cite these qualities in your position descriptions. "Having a competency framework really means having a language by which an organization can describe the skills, knowledge and capabilities required for specific roles and at specific levels of the organization" (Lombardi, 2013, p. 8).

When we're beginning to nail down requirements for a position description, we ask the hiring manager to quickly flip through a stack of competency cards. We use the Lominger Leadership Architect® Sort Cards available at www.KornFerry.com, but you could also make your own cards defining each competency; or simply type up a list and ask your colleague to mark each competency 1, 2, or 3 for the following three categories:

1. Absolutely critical
2. Good to have
3. Not sure or not important

This is not a laborious process—you'll be surprised how quickly your colleague can identify what matters most and what does not when you lay out clear options. Just remember not to reduce this exercise to "another HR form to fill out" in the minds of your colleague or an example of "HR as order-taker." Make this exchange a dynamic dialogue, asking good, open-ended questions to help pinpoint what success in this role would look like. With the hiring manager's selection of must-haves, usually 10 to 15 traits, you have the top behaviors, attributes, and attitudes you're looking for in an optimal candidate.

Just as you do for the hard-skill requirements, you can also craft interview questions that will delve into the degree to which a candidate possesses these critical competencies. Visit SHRM's website at www.shrm.org for sample behavioral interview questions (which we discuss at length in Chapter 6), or see the appendix in *Topgrading* (Smart, 2012). You can also tap technology for this purpose: the next chapter will describe some quick, easy-to-use online instruments that measure competencies in validated and EEOC-compliant ways. Many such online tools generate interview questions, too, as part of an individual's results.

Bonus Round: Compensation

We have covered the 10 pieces of a position description that we believe are critical to fleshing out the role in enough detail so that you attract and deliver top talent for your organization. Other data you may also include are things like start date and a salary range. Some candidates' first question to us when we initially approach them about a role is "What's the comp?" Here's how we covered this point in the sample position description for MetroFinancial's SVP:

> **Compensation**: The total compensation will be carefully determined to be very competitive in the New York metro area. The compensation will be composed of a base salary, and both cash and equity performance-based elements.

You notice that we don't cite specific dollar amounts. For some roles, perhaps you do know precisely what the budget allows for the salary, you are confident it won't (or can't) change, and you and your hiring manager are fine with publicizing that information. Our standard view is that compensation is whatever will get a top candidate into the role. Sometimes this amount is less than what the incumbent makes, sometimes it's more, but it's almost always more than what the candidate is currently making—and that's the key.

When we recruited a new CIO for an investment bank, for example, the fellow currently in the role was making about $600,000 as his base salary and cash bonus. The fully qualified candidate who wound up accepting the job, delightedly, started at about $300,000 total first-year cash; he was delighted because this was a 20 percent increase from what he had been earning. In his mind, the deal was more than fair. Even his wife was thrilled! Needless to say, our client was also thrilled, because they just cut 50 percent from a senior executive's salary, saving a few hundred thousand dollars.

> **Pay your people the least possible and you'll get from them the same.**
>
> MALCOLM FORBES

If you follow our cue and use the words "very competitive in the ___ metro area" in your position description, obviously ensure this statement is accurate, because sooner or later, you will have to provide specific numbers to a candidate, and they indeed better be "competitive." Visit Salary.com to make sure a job's compensation is comparable to similar roles in like-sized organizations in your sector. Savvy job hunters will do their research and ensure that the comp is aligned with what they might find at a competitor.

The other issue that can surface while working with candidates is overestimating the actual compensation. You never want to be in a situation in which the candidate, after receiving a verbal offer, comes back and says, "Wait a minute—so-and-so said that the compensation was much higher!" Focus on what the finalist candidate is making today, and work from that number. Many companies may have a target of what they want to pay a candidate, but the laws of supply and demand will eventually play out, as our own experience with the happy CIO illustrates.

PARTING PD ADVICE

When you invest the time up-front to craft a detailed position description, you are really setting yourself up for success in the steps that follow: using online assessment, interviewing, and, ultimately, hiring well. But you also want to do what you can, now, to help set the candidates up for success, too. What do we mean?

Well, we have made the point that a great position description tells *and* sells: it serves as a marketing vehicle not only to describe the role in good detail but also to advance someone's professional growth and promote the entire organization. Set candidates up for success by delivering on what you promise; in other words, be truthful about what the role offers. Some of you work in sectors that are highly competitive. In general, top sales talent is always in high demand, because salespeople drive revenue anywhere they work. It's tempting to lure the best and brightest of the talent pool to your organization by "sweetening the pot" on your position descriptions. If what you say is true, go for it. But the last thing you want is someone to take the job expecting one thing (mentor with the CEO) and discovering quite another after a month or two (supervise interns). That is precisely how seemingly good hires turn bad, fast.

Just as we have suggested you do with your colleagues in other business units, treat candidates, too, almost like customers: think about what you can offer them—for now, on the position description; during the interview, with specific examples from your workplace; and of course, later on the job, in reality. As we mentioned before, the very best position descriptions will not only attract candidates from the cream of the crop but also help you retain those stars after the hire. Strive to exceed your customers' expectations, whether they're candidates or business colleagues.

Online Assessment
The Pre-Hire Gift That Keeps on Giving

"Is this person really going to do what she says she's going to do?"

"Am I going to get a good return on our investment by hiring this person?"

"How do I know this person is 'right' so that I won't screw up and get an earful from my boss?"

"I like what this candidate is saying and the stories he's sharing—but is he telling me the truth?"

"In the end, will this person actually fit in with her new boss and colleagues?"

CAN YOU relate to these sorts of questions? If you're like many of the professionals we've worked with, you probably weigh considerations like these when it comes to critical hiring decisions.

As this chapter's title suggests, we are unabashed fans of using online assessment instruments during the recruiting process. We believe that for a modest financial investment, organizations can include these tools in their selection efforts so that they are more likely to hire well-qualified candidates who will not only do the job but excel in the role and in the culture—in a word, *fit*.

This chapter will discuss the benefits of using assessment instruments pre-hire to help you realize your organization's strategic goals by delivering superb talent. Our examples highlight those instruments that we're most familiar with and that we trust because they've been a regular part of our own recruiting process over the last 10 years. Hundreds of assessment instruments are out there, and you may very well already be using some. Whether you're new to online assessment or not, by the end of this chapter, we hope you'll agree that they're a hiring gift that your organization deserves.

WHY BOTHER WITH ONLINE ASSESSMENTS?

Using reliable, validated instruments helps you address two factors that are always critical no matter where you work: time and risk. Let's start by looking at how they can trim time in your talent selection process.

PULL UP A CHAIR!

This Is Not a Test.
No, Seriously—This Is Not a Test!

As you may have noticed, we're making a distinction between the terms *assessment* and *online assessment/assessment instrument,* and we think it's an important one. We define *assessment* in our work as a multifaceted evaluation process that includes several components: online instruments, behavioral and deep-dive interviews, reference checks, and more. This chapter is really focused on just the single ingredient of assessment that is the Internet-accessible tool we're calling *online assessments* or *assessment instruments,* interchangeably.

And while we're on the topic, please remember that online assessments are not "tests"—no matter what instrument you use, there are no good or bad, right or wrong answers. All online assessments simply provide you with more data points to consider as you prepare for interviews with both candidates and their references (which are discussed in the next chapter).

We return now to our regularly scheduled programming.

Saving Time

Why use online assessments? The short answer is to *quickly* eliminate candidates who are not qualified. By "not qualified," we mean in terms of skills, behaviors, personality, and, potentially, inappropriate behaviors on the job. "Sifting through résumés as a means of identifying capable, vibrant human beings is a very imperfect process," Bill Wray, the COO of a Blue Cross Blue Shield organization, told us. "I need my HR partner to make that process feel less random so I don't miss that one special talent that may not have shown up in the right pile."

You might think that adding one more step into the recruiting process, multiplied by the number of candidates applying for a position, increases your time-to-fill rate rather than decreases it. Not so, in our experience. A basic but important reason to fold assessment instruments into your pre-hire process is to screen out unqualified applicants quickly. If they're like most of the executives we work with, your partners in other business units probably want their open positions filled yesterday. One recent survey reports that 43 percent of its respondents complained that open positions "haven't been filled in the anticipated time frame," with even more noting that it takes over two months to find the right candidate (Li, 2012, p. 3). Time is of the essence, and HR can go a long way toward impressing colleagues and earning their respect by employing a recruitment protocol that delivers great candidates (and ultimately superb hires) fast.

Particularly today, when we have tens of thousands of job seekers in a still-recovering economy, HR professionals are awash in applications. In fact, we suspect that the rise in pre-hire assessment instruments over the last few years has something to do with the corresponding rise in the number of people looking for a job. About 80 percent of Fortune 500 companies use some sort of instrument pre-hire—a number that is up from nearly 50 percent just a few years ago (Dattner, 2008; Mantell, 2011; Metheny, 2011). In its *Assessment 2013* survey, Aberdeen Group notes that 85 percent of best-in-class organizations have "a clearly defined process in place to assess candidates and applicants," with 94 percent of those using "behavioral-based/personality-type assessments" (Lombardi, 2013, p. 14).

Even in the best of economic times, however, open positions at all levels can attract hundreds of interested job hunters. Assessment instruments can help you expedite filling these roles by evaluating, at a minimum, basic skills

(Figure 5.1 summarizes the main reasons organizations use assessments, especially pre-hire). That's not to say these online tools don't have a role to play for high-level positions. They do, in terms of reducing the heightened risk around these positions as well as saving time. Jack once worked on a search in which he was looking for a senior vice president in a Fortune 500 corporation that drew 661 initial applicants. He dutifully reviewed everyone's résumé and cover letter and of the 661 people wound up presenting exactly . . . 1! This example was not unusual before he began using online assessment pre-hire. He still covets the time he might have saved if he had been able to use some sort of screening instrument to separate candidates who met the required qualifications *and* had the critical competencies (see Chapter 4) from those who did not.

As the saying goes, time costs money, and your leadership will always appreciate your doing what you can to operate both time- and cost-efficiently. Risk costs money, too, as you will see in the next section.

FIGURE 5.1   Reasons to Use Pre-Hire Online Assessments
Source: Adapted from Lombardi (2013), p. 4.

PULL UP A CHAIR!

Talk Nerdy to Me: Validity and Reliability

Time-saving tools are great, but not if they sacrifice quality for speed. Critical measures of an assessment instrument's quality are its validity and reliability.

Before you nod off, trust us: these concepts are not so difficult to grasp that only numbers nerds can understand them. Simply put, an instrument is

valid when it measures what it's supposed to measure and

reliable when its results are consistent over time and among different groups of people.

For example, the Hogan Personality Inventory (HPI) has been validated to measure only personality—not IQ, emotional intelligence, leadership style, problem-solving ability, or anything else. The instrument has been researched in deep detail and found to be a reliable and valid measure of this one factor: personality. In addition, whether the person taking the HPI is a female Caucasian HR executive in San Francisco, an Arabic-speaking millionaire in Dubai, or a Chinese CEO in Qingdao, the results are reliable. It's possible that all three of these people, taking the assessment in different cities at different times, could wind up having very similar results— because their personalities are very similar.

As we note later in this chapter, it's important that you debrief a candidate to some level of detail on his or her assessment results and check for "face validity": the degree to which the candidate thinks, "Yes, this sounds like me" or "No, I must disagree with this comment."

Many (but not all) assessment instruments on the market today have been thoroughly researched to be valid and reliable in the scientific sense of these terms, so your job in choosing instruments has been somewhat

(continued on next page)

facilitated. The degree to which an instrument is valid and reliable can vary, however—a point you'll be reading about when we discuss specific instruments (e.g., DISC). In addition, in the sea of instruments being sold, you'll want to choose only those that are measuring what *you* want to measure, or that are *valid* for your specific objectives. The time spent doing a bit of homework is well worth it, and we'll offer other tips as you shop for pre-hire assessments.

Reducing Risk

Risk comes in many forms, but in the context of selecting talent, we see risk manifesting in three ways.

First, some risk is, of course, innate to any hiring decision, whether you use online assessment or not. As scientifically sound as an instrument may be, no results are ever 100 percent accurate. The bottom line is you're always taking a leap of faith that the candidate who wows you during an interview will still wow you 3, 6, or even 12 months from now.

Second is the matter of reputational risk, for you and for your organization. Your most valuable customers—your CEO and the key players in other departments—are relying on you to cast a net into the talent pool and bring highly qualified individuals to the interview table. Your reputation will be dramatically enhanced if

> Few risks are greater than operational risk. And that boils down to people.
>
> ANDY GOODMAN

you deliver great people. Conversely, if you get a rep in the organization for being consistently unable to pick good people, your career prospects will be short-lived. Use online assessment tools so that, ultimately, you can make better talent decisions.

The more senior the role, the more the organization—and especially your boss—is counting on you to help make the best hiring decision possible. No company wants the reputation of making poor hires and subsequently having high turnover. When Laura used to mention the publishing company where she held one of her first jobs, the typical response was "Oh, they've got a lot of people leaving. What's going on?" It didn't matter that the publisher produced high-quality books, making it the largest publisher in the world in its niche. What mattered was that the average person in the community had a negative impression about this company as a place to work. That's not the sort of publicity you want.

Finally, risk can be measured in dollars. You're investing a lot of money in the typical employee—salary, bonuses, health insurance and other benefits, the cost of training and office equipment, and more. If the new hire doesn't work out, the cost of replacing him or her, on average, is about 20 percent of that position's salary. This figure can go as high as *213 percent* of the salary for senior-level executive roles (Boushey & Glynn, 2012).

No matter what the level of the job, however, calculating both the direct and indirect costs of a bad hire is important, though researchers Boushey and Glynn note that "by their very nature indirect costs may be hidden and difficult to ascertain" (p. 6). Table 5.1 lists examples of both types of costs.

Take your best stab at estimating just one single indirect cost—lost opportunities—of hiring a so-so salesperson (X) versus a star (Y). If you're lucky, X won't exasperate existing customers enough to drive them to your competitors. But he probably will settle for simply renewing those current accounts rather than expanding them; he certainly won't be blowing quotas through the roof on new business. Y, the star, will not only meet existing customers' expectations but exceed them, cross-selling and upselling to mine those customers for all they're worth. At the same time, she'll be crushing it in new territories, too. What's the *lifetime* value of just one lost or missed opportunity—one customer—for your firm?

It's not far-fetched to estimate that for some businesses, this *single indirect cost* of just one bad hire equals hundreds of thousands of dollars or more—annually. Missed opportunities multiplied across a team of bad hires might even determine whether a company survives. One of our clients in digital marketing watched its stock price fall from $4.50 per share to about 30 cents while its competitors were riding the wave of popularity that mobile marketing media were enjoying at the time. Understandably frustrated, the CEO told us, "With our technology, we're driving a Rolls-Royce while everyone

TABLE 5.1 Costs of a Bad Hire

DIRECT COSTS	INDIRECT COSTS

• Separation costs
  ○ Exit interviews
  ○ Severance pay
  ○ Increased unemployment taxes
• Additional comp to cover duties (temps, overtime pay for other staff)
• Replacement costs
  ○ Advertising
  ○ Recruiting/search fees
  ○ Screening (physicals, drug test, assessments, background checks, etc.)
  ○ Interviewing and selecting candidates
  ○ Candidate costs (travel, hotel room, relocation expenses)
  ○ Hiring bonuses
	• Decreased productivity of departing employee (e.g., work time diverted toward job-hunting activities; low morale)
	• Reduced morale among colleagues
	• Emotional/physical costs to staff assuming additional duties
	• Heightened risk of losing other employees (to follow departing colleague, to also "get a better deal")
	• Lost institutional knowledge
	• Lost customers and clients
	• Missed opportunities
	• New-employee costs
	  ○ Training
	  ○ Lower quality, errors
	  ○ Waste

Source: Adapted from Boushey and Glynn (2012), p. 5.

else is in Pintos!" He came to understand that the difference in financial performance between his firm and competitors was due not to the technology behind their service but to the widely varying quality and capabilities of his sales team. (The starring role that salespeople, like these, play in executing the most critical part of any organization's strategy—increasing revenues/profits—is why we often use them in our examples, real and fictional.)

This CEO lost the confidence of the board and eventually *his job* because of missed opportunities. His firm lost a lot of money. Its reputation took something of a hit, too, because of harsh scrutiny from market analysts. At least 15 highly qualified executives we approached about an open senior role in the

> The fastest way to improve a company's performance is to improve the talent of the workforce.
>
> JOHN ZILLMER

company declined, citing explicitly these financial and reputational concerns. They were more than happy to stay put at their current jobs in competitive companies.

Are these risks you'd like to avoid? Then read on.

USING ASSESSMENTS TO
ENHANCE TALENT SELECTION

Coauthor Jack has been fascinated with measuring human performance for over 30 years, since his days conducting statistical research at Columbia University and in elite combat infantry units in the U.S. Army. Your selection efforts likely don't have life-or-death implications as Jack's did in the Army, but we bet your colleagues would love to have their own "Special Forces" group of A players. Here are the two basic steps you can take to work toward that goal:

1. **Review the critical competencies** you have listed on your position description (Chapter 4).
2. **Select the assessment instrument(s)** that will best serve this particular search.

In other words, for starters, determine *what* you want to measure. This is what you've started to define by speaking with hiring managers to narrow down the list of must-have qualities in a candidate. In our search/recruiting business, we're most interested in taking a close look at these four areas:

- Personality as it manifests on the job
- Potential derailing behaviors
- Behaviors at work
- Values, or what motivates someone to do his or her work

Therefore, we use instruments that accurately measure these elements (i.e., they're valid for this purpose, as defined earlier), are reasonably priced, and require only about 10 to 20 minutes of the candidate's time to complete.

Why these four elements? We're not fortune-tellers, but we're still trying to get as good an objective sense as possible of *how* these people will behave and emote, not just during the interview phase but well after they're hired. These assessments give us a measure of a candidate's reliability over time. Frankly, our biggest fear is that we'll identify and present a candidate, and then two months later, the client calls and says, "Hey, this executive is like a different person—what gives?"

The Value of 20/20 Hindsight— or a Pre-Hire Assessment

Trust us: the "What gives with this new hire?" question is not the sort you want to have to answer. We've engaged in exactly

> People who don't fit fail on the job, even when they are perfectly talented in all other respects.
>
> GEOFF SMART &
> RANDY STREET

this kind of conversation—but, thank goodness, it was not about an executive we had recruited. Instead, our job centered on coaching this executive's direct reports. In the course of that work, they shared comments like these (and these are their actual words, from e-mail correspondence and 360° feedback):

- "[He] holds things real close."
- "He's a bit reserved. Internally he adheres to 'a chain of command' to communicate, which at times makes him seem unapproachable."
- "I *don't* perceive that he respects that several of us on the senior team have also had successful careers in business and leadership roles for decades."
- "Communicating 'sensitive' topics to him isn't hard—it's nearly impossible."
- "Whether recognized or not, there is a clear double standard at work with regard to departmental treatment [among different business units]."
- "It's clear who he's fond of or not."
- "I get the impression that he listens to everyone in the room but typically has already made his mind up beforehand even on topics which he may have little to no expertise on."
- "He doesn't really listen to his lieutenants."
- "I've heard that he has a very bad temper from numerous employees in the workplace."
- "Morale is pretty low."

A little more than a year earlier, this executive—as a CEO candidate—had completely impressed interviewers with his interpersonal and influence skills, intelligence, thoughtful listening ability, and overall depiction of "servant leadership." He had risen among four other finalists for the job as the hands-down winner. Now, on the job, he struck his team as "unapproachable and stiff." When he was in town, he stayed pretty much in his office, not even sharing a cup of coffee with a direct report in that person's office, let alone lunch. Most important, key operational and budget decisions would be allegedly agreed to at a staff meeting, only to be discarded and reversed later when he would inform (though not always) everyone at the next staff meeting that he had decided on a different course of action. As mere observers at these meetings, even we would look askance at each other: "Where did *that* come from?"

It's no wonder, then, that a key player in hiring this CEO, the chairman of the board—that is, the CEO's boss—was more than a little peeved once he got the real-life feedback on this executive's behaviors and emotions on the job. "What happened to the personable, enthusiastic guy I hired a year ago?" he bellowed over the phone. After taking a deep breath, we delicately suggested that he and the other hiring executives had likely succumbed to the very common phenomenon of "dating behavior" we often observe among candidates during the recruiting process (we discuss dating behavior, and how not to be seduced by it, more in the next chapter). The interviewers had "fallen in love" with a real heartbreaker.

We were compelled to share another tough data point with this angry chairman. When we had given the CEO and his direct reports the DISC instrument, we experienced an unpleasant and historic moment in our assessment work: never had anyone scored lower on the Influence dimension than this fellow. On the 1–100 scale, he scored a 6. The adjectives that described this people-oriented dimension for him were *calculating, skeptical, undemonstrative, suspicious, incisive, pessimistic,* and *moody.* His results summary included statements like these:

- X likes people, but can be seen occasionally as cold and blunt. He may have his mind on project results, and sometimes may not take the time to be empathetic toward others.

- He tends to have a "short fuse" and can display anger or displeasure when he feels that people are taking advantage of him.

- He could improve his communication skills by being patient, listening and displaying genuine care for the people with whom he comes in contact.

- X feels that the convincing of people can only be done within the framework of logical facts presented by totally objective people or machines. He rarely displays emotion when attempting to influence others.

- X will use an undemonstrative approach to influencing others. He prefers to let the facts and figures stand for themselves.

- His trust level is calculated on each interaction.

Compare these assessment results to the real-life comments from staff cited earlier—there are some true parallels. The two of us don't always agree, but this was a case where our professional opinions completely overlapped: *if we had seen results like these on a pre-hire assessment, there is* no way *we would have even presented this person as a candidate.* Instead, here he was, CEO of a global organization, not truly leading but merely coexisting with a team of very unhappy direct reports, casting a shadow of low morale throughout not just headquarters but many branch locations around the world, and spending hundreds of thousands of dollars in ways the board and senior team had not anticipated and, in some cases, did not agree with. The boss/board chairman admitted that he wished he and his co–hiring managers had been tipped off about potential disruptive behaviors and emotions like this *before* they offered this person the CEO job.

Wouldn't you prefer to have information like this, too—before you even meet candidates, let alone hire them? When you do, you're dramatically boosting the likelihood of delivering the talent that can deliver strategic results—and not surprise your boss!

Serving Your Internal Customers

Another consideration with assessment instruments and the outcomes you're trying to measure is the nature of your internal customers—the hiring managers. Frankly, they're likely more interested in the right body, right now, than much of the detail surrounding the hiring process. This point aligns with what we've suggested throughout the book in terms of not inundating your business colleagues with HR-heavy jargon or every bit of data you unearth. Even in the most collaborative of partnerships between HR and business units, hiring managers have probably been mulling over a talent need for some time before they share the specifics of that requirement with you. Now they want things to proceed quickly, in something of a "Just tell me what we need to do" manner. For example, a client once asked us on December 24 to recruit a unique, senior-level executive for a key role so that the person would be *on the job* by January 31. No doubt you've experienced demands like this, too.

Assessment instruments that both meet the reliability/validity criteria and generate easy-to-understand results provide ideal summaries for the typical busy, distracted hiring manager—not to mention for you, who are probably just as busy and distracted! Your colleagues in other departments don't care about an assessment's "statistical significance" or "test validity" because terms like these don't hold much importance in their day-to-day operational world. In contrast, the four elements listed earlier that we evaluate in candidates—workplace behaviors, values, personality, and potential derailers—are understandable to hiring managers because they recognize and engage with these attributes every day with their employees. They know what these four elements look like in a person. By using instruments that provide you with clear, meaningful verbiage, you'll be communicating with powerful relevance to your most valuable customers.

Candidates Are Customers, Too

The previous chapter noted that a well-crafted position description will not only attract highly qualified candidates but also start paving the way to strong retention of the new hire. We suggested that you treat the exceptional candidates you want to attract to the role, and then retain in the role, like ideal target customers.

To help keep top candidates engaged, put yourself in their shoes as you imagine the recruiting process and, specific to our discussion here, the online assessment piece. It doesn't matter how great a pre-hire assessment is if its user end is so complicated that it takes an inordinate amount of time to complete. A SmartRecruiter survey notes that nearly half—47 percent—of job hunters opted not to even apply for a job because the process was "too lengthy or complicated" (Li, 2012, p. 5). As we mentioned in Chapter 2, when we described an imbalanced conversation between a recruiting manager and an SVP in Sales, we suspect that some (not all) of the reasons behind the well-publicized skills shortage can be traced to inefficient recruiting practices, rather than unqualified candidates.

A few years ago, we were shopping around for an online instrument that would (1) quickly measure a few critical competencies and (2) be available in Mandarin, since our client was an organization in the People's Republic of China. We came upon a tool that sounded terrific in terms of what it measures—it was valid and reliable—and the format of its questions. And it was available in Mandarin. So, we asked our clients, James and Ling, to give it a test drive. Here's what they shared with us in separate e-mails:

> Jack, it is a lot of questions. I am doing part 4, then stopped.
> I don't think a CEO will like this too much.
> Also some translation is not correct, I guess.
> I am not sure Ling can finish or not, but I felt it was too much.
> Thanks,
> James

> Hi, Jack and Laura,
> Yes, the volume of the test questions is a little bit too much. Anyway, to understand the process, I finished it. However, I didn't find out where to get the report. Please let me know how to get the report so that I can evaluate whether the results deserve so much time spent on it for CEOs. Thank you.
> Best,
> Ling

Suddenly our buying decision was easy: we sure weren't using *this* instrument!

Many vendors offer a complimentary assessment and debrief. By all means, take advantage of such invitations so that you can put yourself in the candidate's shoes. Judge for yourself whether that instrument is indeed measuring what you want, and does so without taxing your patience and requiring too much time. In our own work, we have a general time criterion of 20 minutes or less for any single online instrument we use.

The Fear Factor

Every once in a while, we bump into a client or an HR executive who wonders about candidates' willingness to take an online assessment due to their fear about what the results might say about them. As the president of a corporation told Jack recently, "It amazes me that no one has ever turned you down!" But it's true: not once in over 10 years has a person refused to take any assessment we've included in our pre-hire selection process. What has happened, many times, is that a candidate asks us where we "hid the cameras" because the results were so accurate. We've even had spouses of candidates ask if they could take the assessment, too!

Most high-performing executives actually are very responsive to our requests about completing online assessments. In our experience, candidates welcome an opportunity to tout their successes and explore areas for development. Top performers are very open to feedback and learning, and are continually reflecting on their performance so that they can become even better at their job. Assessments give them an opportunity to do just that.

For those candidates who might harbor some fear or anxiety at the prospect of taking an assessment, and thus try to respond in ways that cast them in the best light, the specific instruments we use have already nipped that possibility in the bud. "When people try to fake, they try to fake in very characteristic ways, and it's really easy to tell when someone is trying to game the test," Robert Hogan, the president of Hogan Assessment Systems, told the *Wall Street Journal* (Mantrell, 2011, para. 8). Therefore, his company's assessments have built-in measures that prevent any such misrepresentation.

Similarly, the company whose form of DISC we use, discussed later, sends us a separate e-mail when a person's results suggest anything remotely "fishy." We've received exactly two of these over the past decade. For example, we were coaching an individual once whose primary issues were (1) too many leads and too little time; (2) office disorganization like we'd never seen before;

and (3) a strong desire to please the boss despite minimal clear communication between the two; oh, and (4) deep marital uncertainty, (5) chronic insomnia, and (6) profound regret over a career change. The assessment results were prefaced by this note:

> Q's responses to the questionnaire indicate Q may be under pressure to be an overachiever. Have Q look at the demands being placed on Q and set priorities. Q should deal only with those demands that are most critical and put the rest on hold, or seek assistance with the lower priority demands.
>
> Therefore, we recommend that the report be carefully scrutinized to ensure the greatest of accuracy in the information presented about Q. In addition, Q may want to consider retaking the instrument later when comfortable in achieving this balance.

We're compelled to add this postscript: (1) we had strongly urged Q's boss not to make this hire, and (2) Q quit about six months later.

It's a heads-up like this—not to mention insights gleaned from the results themselves—that make us firm believers in the power of assessment instruments. Remember the "bonus round" discussion in Chapter 4 about additional elements to consider including on a position description, such as comp and start date? For us, one of those items that has now become standard is an explicit statement at the end of our PDs that says, "*All* candidates for this critical role will be asked to take the same online assessments as part of a rigorous selection process." This statement makes it clear right off the bat, on the position description, that online instruments are one part among many (the phone screen, the initial interview, the face-to-face interviews at the client site, the background and reference checks, etc.) of the recruiting effort. It helps allay any concerns a candidate might have that he or she has been "flagged" for special attention. It also helps ensure you're being EEOC-compliant, which is explored more fully in the next Pull Up a Chair feature.

PULL UP A CHAIR!

Is This Legal? EEOC Compliance

The short answer to this title's question is yes: all of the assessments and procedures we're describing in Part 2 are in legal compliance with the Equal Employment Opportunity Commission (EEOC) and the Office of Federal Contract Compliance Programs (OFCCP).

The EEOC (2013) has approved its latest strategic enforcement plan, citing as its number-one priority:

> **1. Eliminating Barriers in Recruitment and Hiring.** The EEOC will target class-based recruitment and hiring practices that discriminate against racial, ethnic and religious groups, older workers, women, and people with disabilities. These include exclusionary policies and practices, the channeling/steering of individuals into specific jobs due to their status in a particular group, restrictive application processes, and the use of screening tools (e.g., pre-employment tests, background checks, date-of-birth inquiries). (p. 10)

The three screening tools the EEOC cites here could be problematic under these conditions, for example:

- pre-employment tests that might contain bias if not valid for a given group,
- background checks if they include credit history that would prove exclusionary, and
- date-of-birth inquiries that clearly aim to determine a candidate's age and could amplify age bias or discrimination.

To be fit for use in a workplace, an assessment must not only be valid but also show the absence of so-called adverse or disparate impact. Disparate

(*continued on next page*)

impact occurs when members of the protected groups named in this EEOC quote do not perform as well on it as do members of the majority group. Both of these elements—validity and no adverse impact—are required for an assessment to be considered compliant with the EEOC and OFCCP.

> Under the Disparate Impact rule, an employer may not use an employment practice (e.g., a pre-employment aptitude test) that, even though neutral on its face and applied to all applicants and employees, disproportionately excludes members of a protected category. *An employer can defend its reliance on such an employment practice only if the employer proves the challenged practice is job related for the position in question and consistent with business necessity.* (TTI, 2012c, p. 1, emphasis in original)

Obviously, all recruiting efforts inevitably do eliminate some applicants—that's the goal of the selection process, after all. The EEOC acknowledges this reality and thus advocates the "80 percent rule" to determine when a particular practice has an illegal disparate impact. "If the selection rate of a particular employment practice for a protected category is less than 80 percent of the selection rate to the relevant comparison group, that employment practice has a disparate impact" (TTI, 2013c, p. 1).

We mentioned earlier that we explicitly let candidates know that *all* candidates will be asked to take the *same* assessments. This systematic consistency is what you must build into your recruiting process, to further ensure not just commonsense fairness but, more important, EEOC compliance. We remind candidates, too, that an online assessment is not the only or most important factor in a hiring decision; no assessment has "make-or-break" power. HR executives generally follow the rule of thumb that online assessment results should not account for more than one-third of the final hiring decision.

The matter of compliance is critical as you explore assessments for use not just pre-hire, as we're focusing on in this book, but in any part of your talent management efforts. Stay up-to-date on EEOC issues at www.eeoc.gov.

OUR ASSESSMENT INSTRUMENT TOOLKIT

If there are four areas we specifically want to measure, then there also are just four instruments we use to accomplish that outcome:

- Hogan Personality Inventory (20 minutes)—personality on the job
- Hogan Development Survey (20 minutes)—potential derailers
- TTI's DISC (10 minutes)—behaviors at work
- TTI's PIAV (10 minutes)—values or motivation

There are hundreds of ways to gather useful information about a candidate when it comes to assessment, but we want to share with you our firsthand experience of what has worked well for us, in terms of both reliable results and hiring managers' receptivity to this information (i.e., clear, succinct, and easy to understand). The discussion that follows, therefore, will consider just these four EEOC-compliant instruments. (We encourage you to visit our website www.PremierProfiling.com for more information, or contact us directly at Jack or Laura@CageTalent.com.)

For each of these four sample assessment instruments in our toolkit, you'll read some background information on the instrument and the kind of results it generates. According to Jay Gaines, the CEO of an executive search firm in New York City, "Culture fit is an absolutely critical determinant of longer-term fit, and not easy to discern in an interview. There are some short psychological tests that provide reinforcement and support to observations we might make on candidates" (in Mantell, 2011, para. 4). To that end, we also describe ways online assessment results can be used in interviews. We pull some suggested questions from excerpts of results reports, so that you can see how easy it is to create customized questions. As throughout this book, the examples are real, but we've kept the person's identity anonymous.

Hogan Personality Inventory (HPI): Personality at Work

Defining personality is like defining goodness or leadership. What, exactly, is it? Fortunately, the psychologists at Hogan Assessment Systems have figured this out so you don't have to.

BACKGROUND

Two points make the HPI a valid, useful measure for talent selection. First, it describes five elements of personality that everyone can immediately grasp:

- Extraversion
- Agreeableness
- Conscientiousness
- Emotional stability
- Openness to experience

The Hogan team has taken the extra step to conduct all testing, measurement, and research of the HPI with business people, not college students (who are often the subjects of instrument research studies) or any other group. This approach means that the HPI is directly relevant to personality on the job—precisely the area we want to measure in our candidates.

Nested under each of these five factors are the following scales, which will show up on the HPI results report:

- *Adjustment*—the degree to which a person is calm and even-tempered or, conversely, moody and volatile
- *Ambition*—the degree to which a person seems leaderlike, seeks status, and values achievement
- *Sociability*—the degree to which a person seems talkative and socially self-confident
- *Interpersonal Sensitivity*—social skills, tact, and perceptiveness
- *Prudence*—self-control and conscientiousness
- *Inquisitive*—the degree to which a person seems curious, adventurous, and imaginative
- *Learning Approach*—the degree to which a person enjoys academic activities and values education as an end in itself

Again, these are areas that we all can understand without being clinical psychologists, and we all can readily relate to each one in our place of business.

The second point making HPI a uniquely helpful tool is that it measures these personality variables from *other* people's perspectives, not the person taking the assessment. (This feature elicited a "Holy cow!" from Jack—who has three psychology degrees—when he first heard about it.) In other words, the HPI describes the reputation of the individual who is being assessed. How is this possible? During the R&D phase, while the business people were taking the assessment as human guinea pigs, other people who knew those individuals were serving as "observers," reacting to each response of the test-taker with, in effect, "Yes, that sounds like him" or "No, he isn't like that at all."

We're grossly simplifying, of course, but in a nutshell, the HPI has been validated to an extraordinary degree. The computer program running behind a completed answer set considers what *hundreds of thousands* of people have reflected on someone whose responses were all exactly the same. What the results generate, then, is other people's view of someone who happens to be exactly like your candidate in terms of the HPI personality variables. This unique feature eliminates the self-reporting concerns many have about "personality tests"—that candidates will game the assessment because, naturally, they want to seem as appealing as possible. HPI's results report on the *reputation* of someone who has responded the same way:

> The fact that a person gets a high score on say, submissiveness, means that there's some possibility that the person's *peers* [emphasis added] will describe him or her as timid and unassertive. But the score does not explain why the person behaves so as to be described as timid. Assessment is about prediction, not explanation. (Hogan & Hogan, 2007, p. 13)

RESULTS

You can choose to have HPI results appear in a variety of reports, sharing the same raw data in different ways depending on what you need. All of the reports, however, describe in plain English how a person's personality manifests on the job.

One of the formats, the six-page HoganDevelop Career report, presents the results in a simple bar graph and then discusses them in more detail in three sections: Strengths, Shortcomings, and Tips for Career Development. The verbiage is ideal for using in candidate write-ups: you and your hiring managers can read a few paragraphs and immediately get a solid grasp of and a common way of talking about this candidate. The career development section suggests ways the person might adjust his or her behaviors to be even more effective working with others—areas to confirm with references and to fold into an onboarding plan.

USE IN INTERVIEWS

Take a look at the following excerpts from a candidate's HPI. The superscript numerals highlight points that we explore next in sample interview questions for the candidate and references.

STRENGTHS

You are stable and poised, have a positive attitude, and are usually in a good mood; [1]you can easily handle fast-paced environments and/or heavy work loads, and will rarely be irritable. [2]Coworkers and team members will appreciate your steadiness under pressure; this is particularly important for jobs or tasks where there is a lot of urgency, physical stress, and potential risk, and where it is necessary to keep your emotions under control. [3]In times of stress, your coworkers can count on you being calm, consistent, and upbeat. You are active, hard-working, competitive, and eager to get ahead. You like leadership positions and enjoy being in charge. Generally, you are [4]willing to take initiative in a group and, with the appropriate interpersonal skills, you will be able to assume lead roles on team projects. These tendencies are particularly important in jobs that require taking initiative, being persuasive, and working without supervision.

Interview Questions

[1]Tell me about a time you had a particularly heavy workload or tight deadline. How did you handle that?

[4]On a team project, what role do you typically take?

Reference Questions

For Peer or Direct Report

[2]How does he handle pressure in situations that are especially urgent or stressful, or that involve risk?

For Boss

[3]In times of stress, how does he behave?

SHORTCOMINGS

Because you are very self-confident, you may be [1]hard to coach and too optimistic in your expectations of others. This self-confidence can lead to [1]a tendency to be difficult to coach, overestimating your own contributions, [2]ignoring mistakes, and being [3]unwilling to listen to negative feedback. Because you are strongly motivated to succeed, you may compete with and/or [4]intimidate colleagues without realizing it. You should remember to think about other people's agendas when working jointly on projects. Because you are so energetic and outgoing, you may also tend to be [5]over-committed, distracted, and [6]unable to listen very well. You may dominate meetings, and [7]your need to talk and be recognized may cause you to miss information that could be useful for your projects or organization.

Interview Questions

[1]Think of a time when a boss gave you difficult or critical feedback. What was the situation, what was the specific feedback, how did you react, and what was the result? If I contacted that boss, would she say that you did something with that feedback?

[2]You strike me as self-confident. How does that play out for you on the job, in positive and less positive ways?

[4]On a team project, what role do you typically take?

[5,7]What might your team want you to improve in terms of your work style?

Reference Questions

For Peer

[4]What was your experience with Z when working jointly to drive an agenda?

For Boss

[1,3]How did Z respond to constructive criticism or negative feedback?

[2,3,5,7]What areas were you coaching Z on at the time?

For Boss or Direct Report

[6]What sort of listener is Z?

Hogan Development Survey (HDS): What Can Go Wrong?

In 1984, Jack attended a week-long course at the Center for Creative Leadership (CCL) in Greensboro, North Carolina. The instructors were abuzz at the time in sharing research findings about what characterizes executive success and, especially, failure. Jack was then an Army officer who conducted training using live ammunition, and planned and executed complex, dangerous military operations, so he was already thoroughly familiar with the SOP (that's military-speak for "standard operating procedure") of (1) determining what can go wrong and then (2) devising three ways to address that possibility.

Almost 30 years later, he may be out of the Army, but Jack still prepares for the worst-case scenario in the war for talent—that candidate who seems perfect for the role, gets hired, and then goes off the deep end once on the job. Remember the earlier story about the standoffish CEO with the historically low DISC results? For the team who had hired him, including the chairman of the board, that situation was this recruiting nightmare come to life. We do what we can to avoid such a worst-case scenario by asking *every candidate for every role* to take Hogan's HDS.

BACKGROUND

The HDS measures nothing but a person's "dark side"—self-defeating behaviors that the candidate may not even be aware of. We all have our dark side, but we want to uncover these hidden qualities in a candidate and manage any risk around them before they turn ugly on the job.

In creating the HDS, the Hogan research team didn't use a five-factor model as with the HPI, but they sifted through a vast amount of scientific literature on managerial incompetence—or what "bad managers" do—and on personality dysfunction from clinical psychology. They augmented this material with managers' evaluations by coworkers—people who, as for the HPI, knew them and their performance very well.

Like all assessments used in the workplace, the HDS is *not* a tool to diagnose a psychological condition or personality disorder.

> Because the HDS is intended to be used in everyday contexts for career development, job placement, promotion, and other "people decisions"— as opposed to being used to assess mental health status or as an element of a medical evaluation—the items reflect themes from the world of work; e.g., how one is perceived at work, how one relates to supervisors, co-workers, and friends, attitudes toward competition and success, and the like. . . . The HDS is race/ethnicity-, age-, and gender-neutral, ensuring that it can be used fairly in personnel decision making. (Hogan & Hogan, 2009, p. 8)

Reviewing the Americans with Disabilities Act of 1990 (ADA) and court rulings, Hogan purposely gave the HDS scales labels that do not stigmatize people who score high on any of them. The 11 scales are as follows:

- Excitable
- Skeptical
- Cautious
- Reserved
- Leisurely
- Bold
- Mischievous
- Colorful
- Imaginative
- Diligent
- Dutiful

On first blush, many of these terms do seem benign, even positive: Don't we want imaginative employees? Isn't it good to be diligent? Sure, but these scales can exemplify too much of a good thing being, well, not so good. HDS measures the level of these dimensions from 0 to 100, where the higher the score, the greater the likelihood of behaviors that can damage work relationships, reputation, and careers—and the higher the risk around a candidate.

Figure 5.2 provides the full definitions of these terms as they're used in the HDS context. Let's take a look here at how Robert Hogan and Joyce Hogan (2009), co-creators of the HDS, describe in some detail the good and bad of the Colorful scale. People with high scores on this dimension

> need frequent and varied social contact, preferably while being the center of attention. They develop considerable skill at making dramatic entrances and exits and otherwise cleverly calling attention to themselves. Interpersonally, they are gregarious, flirtatious, and often charming. . . . At their best they are bright, entertaining, flirtatious, and the life of the party. At their worst, they won't listen or plan, they self-nominate and overcommit themselves. Although they are entertaining, they are also easily distracted, hyperactive, and unproductive. (pp. 52–53)

What better example (unfortunately) of a Colorful person cruising along the highway of success only to coast right off a cliff than Bill Clinton: high school delegate to a national youth leadership group (who shook hands with President Kennedy), Rhodes Scholar at Oxford, intern to Senator Fulbright, Arkansas governor, president of the United States . . . and front-page philanderer and only the second president in American history to be impeached on charges of perjury and obstruction of justice. Indeed, Hogan and Hogan (2009) describe Clinton as a "high-functioning example" of this Colorful trait.

> Clinton reports that his mother taught him that, after entering a room full of strangers, he should leave with everyone in the room liking him, a rule he still follows assiduously. He is an astonishingly good campaigner because he seems unable to get enough human contact and this makes him inexhaustible; his demand for attention nearly derailed his wife's presidential bid. His chaotic managerial style is legendary . . . as is his

FIGURE 5.2 Definitions of Hogan Development Survey (HDS) Scales

Excitable	Concerns seeming moody, easily irritated, and hard to please, and dealing with stress by quitting or ending relationships.
Skeptical	Concerns mistrusting others' intentions, being alert for signs of mistreatment, and then challenging or blaming others when it seems to occur.
Cautious	Concerns being overly concerned about making mistakes or being embarrassed, and becoming defensive and conservative when stressed.
Reserved	Concerns seeming independent, uncaring, aloof, uncomfortable with strangers, and dealing with stress by withdrawing and being uncommunicative.
Leisurely	Concerns wanting to work according to one's own pace and standards, and feeling put upon when asked to work faster or differently.
Bold	Concerns the tendency to overevaluate one's talents, not admit mistakes or take advice, and blustering and bluffing when under pressure.
Mischievous	Concerns taking risks, testing limits, making hasty decisions, not learning from experience, and demanding to move on when confronted with mistakes.
Colorful	Concerns expecting to be seen as talented and interesting, ignoring others' requests, and becoming very busy when under pressure.
Imaginative	Concerns being eccentric—acting and thinking in creative and sometimes unusual ways—and becoming unpredictable when stressed.
Diligent	Concerns having high standards of performance for self and others, being meticulous, precise, picky, critical, and stubborn when under pressure.
Dutiful	Concerns being cordial, agreeable, and eager to please, reluctant to take independent action, and conforming when under pressure.

Source: Adapted from Hogan and Hogan (2009).

phenomenal ability to "connect" with strangers and to convey the sense that he "feels their pain." His conversations turn into speeches, and his inability to stay focused on a single topic and analyze it in depth is also well known. . . . He exemplifies the charm and attractiveness of this style, as well as its shortcomings in a managerial role. (p. 53)

Two points are important to highlight about the HDS and the behaviors it spotlights. First, we all have deeply ingrained qualities that can emerge in unproductive behaviors or other unflattering ways, most often during high-pressure situations. In other words, these tendencies are context related, in that they typically surface when a person is stressed, fatigued, or ill. Most of the time, we go about our jobs with no flare-ups at all; however, on a tight deadline, say, we may become distracted, hyperactive, or otherwise "color-ful" in its worst sense. "Awareness of your derailers doesn't mean you have to dwell on how bad you are" (Dotlich & Cairo, 2003, p. xxviii).

> When you learn to manage your self-destructive traits, you allow your strengths to emerge.
>
> DAVID DOTLICH &
> PETER CAIRO

Second, the red flags that the HDS identifies are not necessarily stop signs. They are *potential* derailers, with the *possibility* of disrupting work relationships. A candidate may score in the literal red zone on a dimension yet, when interviewed, admit that yes, he can lose his ability to focus under stress, but he tries to manage this tendency by calling five-minute stand-up meetings every few hours with his team when they're on a tight deadline. As with any other assessment, the results of HDS alone should not eliminate a candidate. Use the results to cue up *neutral, open-ended* questions like the ones we offer in the next sections.

Visit www.HowDoYouDerail.com for 60-second videos dramatizing each of the 11 HDS scales; the videos are not only informative but laugh-out-loud funny. We bet you'll be reminded of someone you know—maybe even yourself!

RESULTS

As with the HPI, the HDS is also available in different report formats, depending on the context in which you're using it. We most often opt for the nine-page HoganDevelop Interpret report, which includes the same list of definitions that appear in Figure 5.2; a bar graph of the scores; and sections on each scale that describe that element in more detail, in what percentile the person has scored, and a brief list of ways that "such people tend to be described" by others.

USE IN INTERVIEWS

In addition to the examples presented here, we use an excerpt from an HDS report in the next chapter, too, to illustrate reference questions. Some candidates, however, don't get that far in the recruiting process—such as the fellow who stars in the Pull Up a Chair feature that concludes this HDS section.

EXCITABLE

Scale Description

This scale is concerned with the tendency to develop [1]strong enthusiasms for people, projects, or organizations, and then become disappointed with them. People with high risk scores tend to [2]let little things bother them, become annoyed easily, and change jobs more frequently than others. Coworkers tend to find people with high risk scores on this scale [3]hard to work with because they seem moody, irritable, and hard to please.

Score = 93rd percentile

Mr. Z received a high risk score on the Excitable scale. Such people tend to:

- be described by others as [4]critical and easily irritated
- be prone to [5]emotional outbursts
- become [6]easily upset with other people or projects
- give up and/or [7]not follow through on commitments if he/she becomes disappointed with people

Interview Questions

[1]What was the biggest disappointment at this job—what happened?

[2,6]What frustrates you?

Reference Questions

For Peer or Direct Report

[3,4]Describe Mr. Z—what was/is he like to work with?

For Boss

[5]What were Mr. Z's less developed areas at that time?

[7]When Mr. Z fell short on expectations, exactly what happened?

 PULL UP A CHAIR!

**Candidate Behaving Badly,
or An "Arrested" Development**

Maybe it's just us, but we sure have bumped into some "interesting" people in the course of our work.

Take, for example, a candidate Jack met recently. We often partner with firms who want to "bolt on" assessment to their recruiting process (see www.PremierProfiling.com for a description of those sorts of services). The demand springs from the fact, as we highlighted at the start of this chapter, that nearly 80 percent of firms in the United States use assessment instruments. In this instance, the recruiter we were working with gave Jack the name and contact information of potential candidates for a multibillion-dollar financial services firm, along with their résumés. Jack's initial review of one person's résumé, in particular, suggested this was a man who had a few too many jobs along his career path. Making mental note of it, Jack e-mailed the candidate, along with the others, to invite him to complete the HPI and HDS and to arrange an interview time.

A few days later, Jack saw that the job-hopping candidate had completed both instruments. Jack read the HPI results suggesting that the candidate was a typical guy with no areas of high risk based on his personality. So far, so good. Then he opened the HDS report, and the job-hopper fell flat on his face. Of the 11 potential derailers, he scored in the literal red zone labeled "high risk" (over 94 on a scale of 1–100) in 4 areas (emphasis added):

Skeptical scale. Such people tend to be described as:
- having *a chip on their shoulder*
- possibly willing to *bend the rules*
- *suspicious* of others' actions and intentions

Leisurely scale. This suggests that he may:
- *feel mistreated* or unappreciated when others make demands on him
- be perceived as procrastinating, *stubborn,* and *not following through*
- *ignore constructive criticism* and complaints

Bold scale. Such people tend to be:
- confident, aggressive, ambitious, and visionary
- impulsive, self-promoting, and *unresponsive to negative feedback*
- competitive and demanding
- *intimidating,* especially to their subordinates

Diligent scale. People with scores in this range tend to be described as:
- reluctant to delegate (extra pressure on him and reduced experience for others)
- *critical, controlling, and inflexible*

The reaction from Jack now was "This candidate presents way too much risk for the client" and "Gee, *this* should be an interesting interview!"—in that order.

Following our own advice about using the position description as an interview guide (see Chapter 4), Jack opened the discussion by clarifying how the candidate's background and skills aligned with the requirements outlined in the PD. The candidate appeared to be directionally qualified, but with a smaller management scope than was desired. Jack then asked questions inspired by the HDS report, with a focus on those four high-risk areas. It didn't take long for the candidate to start engaging in "dating behavior" (see the next chapter on interviewing), dodging direct questions and describing himself in the best possible light. All these factors on top of his narrow management scope led Jack to conclude this candidate was not right for the job. He shared his views, including his heightened concerns around those four

(*continued on next page*)

HDS potential derailers, with our recruiter client—who agreed and pulled this candidate from the search.

The story didn't end there. Two weeks later, the recruiter called Jack with some headline-making news about this high-risk candidate: he was in jail, arrested for shoplifting in Ohio.

For this recruiter client of ours, the HDS could be renamed the HDB: "he dodged a bullet!"

TTI's DISC: Not Just Any Four-Quadrant Model

Students of human nature have been classifying observable behaviors into four main categories since the days of Hippocrates around 4000 B.C.E. Back then, the terminology was *choleric, sanguine, phlegmatic,* and *melancholic.* Originally created in the 1920s by psychologist Carl Jung and Harvard professor Howard Marston, the four categories of modern DISC instruments are

Dominance—how a candidate addresses *problems;*

Influence—how a candidate works with *people;*

Steadiness—how a candidate handles the *pace* of a workplace; and

Compliance—how a candidate regards *policies and procedures.*

Two points are very important to underscore about DISC. First, DISC measures only behaviors that are *observable, neutral,* and *universal* (Bonstetter & Suiter, 2007). That is, it describes what people would see a person do on the job, it makes no value judgments on one style over another, and its results apply to the same behavior no matter where in the world it takes place. "Highly talkative and enthusiastic" *looks* the same pretty much anywhere. You might not understand Portuguese, but we bet if you saw a "highly talkative and enthusiastic" woman at a conference table in São Paolo you would describe her that way. This is an important distinction compared to the HPI, for example, which does include measurement of traits we can't see, such as "ambition."

Second, *DISC* is a generic term, and so there are scores of different forms of DISC available, just like there are many different forms of "car" available. Every form of DISC asks the same 12 questions—just like every car has four wheels and an engine—but the power of the DISC "engine" and the results generated vary widely. The programming—or "engine"—that drives the interpretation of DISC responses is different from one company that provides DISC to another. This means that some companies, having invested more in the R&D behind the instrument, offer a version of DISC that will recognize response patterns with more nuanced sophistication than other versions.

This finer-grained detail, in turn, makes for differences in validity and reliability among different forms of DISC instruments. What you actually see, in the form of written results, also differs widely, which will likely impact whether you actually do something with the results. If you can't understand them, you can't use them to full advantage in your selection process—which is the whole point. We've seen DISC results depicted as complicated line graphs alongside statistical gobbledygook, and we've seen DISC results presented in plain English with colorful bar graphs that are visually pleasing and easy to interpret. Some DISC assessments even generate interview questions for you to use.

BACKGROUND

We use the online DISC assessment developed at Target Training International (TTI) in 1984 and refined, tested, and validated ever since, most recently in 2012. What makes this form of DISC special is the quality of its results. Its response-analyzing program uses over 40,000 variables that ultimately generate 384 profile categories. Placement into 1 of 384 versus 1 of 16 categories, as with the Myers-Briggs Talent Inventory (MBTI), leaves a lot more room for subtle differences among respondents—and, as a result, more room for face validity, too (see the feature on the next page). Nearly every person we debrief on their results shares the unsolicited opinion to the effect of "This was spot-on!"

Like the Hogan assessments we've covered, the TTI instruments in this chapter—DISC and PIAV (described next)—have been designed to be appropriate and nondiscriminatory for all ages, abilities, races, and ethnic groups. TTI has never had one of its assessments challenged in court or been the target of an EEOC complaint, and it has up-to-date technical reports that confirm the lack of adverse or disparate impact (TTI 2012a, 2012b, 2012c).

PULL UP A CHAIR!

Myers-Briggs: Two Million People Can Be Wrong

Two million people a year take the Myers-Briggs Type Indicator (MBTI; Krznaric, 2013). Indeed, many of us can rattle off our MBTI summary profile the way we do our astrological sign: "I'm an ESTJ. What are you?"

The standard MBTI asks 94 questions specifically designed to place a person in 1 of 16 personality types. Each type is a combination of four traits that describes how an individual interacts with the world: introverted or extroverted; intuitive or sensing; feeling or thinking; and perceiving or judging. This is where the shorthand comes from—the first letters of each of these traits.

Hats off to Myers-Briggs for bringing online assessments so prominently into the workplace vernacular, but does it have a place as a pre-hire tool? Probably not. We believe even the creators would agree.

Isabel Briggs Myers, with coauthor Mary McCaulley, writes in the *MBTI Manual*:

> Studies suggest the MBTI is not a useful predictor of job performance. The MBTI measures preference, not ability. The use of the MBTI as a predictor of job success is expressly discouraged in the MBTI manual. It is not designed for this purpose. (1985, p. 78)

MBTI poses two problems. (Psychologists and researchers have been trying to make these points for at least 30 years, but we'll give it our best shot.) First, it's low in that critical criterion of reliability—specifically, "test-retest reliability." This means that if you take the MBTI and then take it again just five weeks later, there's about a 50 percent chance your results will be different from the first time you took the assessment.

Second, as we mentioned parenthetically when we discussed the version of DISC we like, MBTI force-fits people into hard-and-fast categories. "You are *either* an extrovert *or* an introvert, but never a mix of the two. Yet most people fall somewhere in the middle. If the MBTI also measured height, you would be classified as either tall or short, even though the majority of people are within a band of medium height" (Krznaric, 2013, para. 6).

For starting a discussion among people on their general approaches to the work world around them, the MBTI is a very useful tool. For reducing the risk of a bad hire and delivering superb talent to your business partners, we suggest you stick with instruments like the ones we describe in this chapter.

RESULTS

We like TTI's DISC also for its actual presentation of the results, not just its algorithms that produce reliable results. Immediately upon completion, the candidate (and we, the recruiters) receive a nicely formatted 24- to 30-page color report that shares the results as

- a summary (ideal for introducing a candidate in a succinct, clear write-up, as with the HPI);
- tips for managing;
- do's and don'ts on communicating with this individual;
- time wasters;
- value to the organization;

- areas for improvement;
- self-perception as well as others' perceptions during typical times, under moderate stress, and in high-pressure situations;
- adjectives describing this person in all four dimensions; and
- bar graphs of workplace behaviors most typically observed for this person (e.g., competitiveness, urgency, customer service, frequent change, analysis of data, etc.).

We once phoned a client, the owner of a global search firm specializing in senior security roles, and debriefed him on a candidate by reading a few of the adjectives straight from the DISC report. "Those are *exactly* the words his reference just used to describe him to me!" our client said. He now assesses all candidates with this form of DISC before he presents them to *his* clients.

TTI also offers DISC instruments whose results use verbiage for specific roles (e.g., manager/staff, executive) and functional areas (e.g., sales, customer service), and they can be delivered in foreign languages (as can Hogan's, by the way).

USE IN INTERVIEWS

The excerpt here is a page we turn to almost immediately in a candidate's DISC report, to highlight on the printout those points (italicized here) we want to raise in an interview.

AREAS FOR IMPROVEMENT

S has a tendency to:

- Lean on technical achievement.
- Have [1]*difficulty making decisions* because she's mostly concerned about the "right" decision. If precedent does not give direction, her [2]*tendency is to wait for directions.*
- Be overly intense for the situation.
- Be [3]*defensive when threatened* and use the errors and mistakes of others to defend her position.
- [4]*Lean on supervisors if information and direction is not clear.*

- Be [5]*bound by procedures* and methods—especially if she has been rewarded for following these procedures.
- [6]*Prefer not to verbalize feelings* unless in a cooperative and noncompetitive environment.
- Prefer things to people—things don't show emotion or need restraint.

Interview Questions

[2]Describe your ideal boss. How do you like to be managed?

[3]Tell me about a time you had to defend your position—what was the situation, what did you do, and what were the results?

Reference Questions

For Peer or Direct Report

[1]How does she make decisions?

For Boss

[4,5]Sometimes we have to take action even when we don't have complete information. How did S handle that sort of situation when you worked together?

For Direct Report

[6]What's S's managerial style? . . . Can you give me an example?

PIAV: Unlocking Motivation

Whereas DISC measures an individual's observable behaviors and emotions, PIAV measures personal interests, attitudes, and values. Stated differently, DISC considers *how* someone does a job; PIAV considers *whether* someone will do a job. In sum, PIAV looks at a person's values, which in turn will drive behavior, which is what DISC measures.

PIAV helps you answer talent questions like these:

- Will this person be motivated to do this particular job?
- Does this candidate share our corporate values?
- Is this the right position in our organization for this candidate, or would she be more productive in a different role?
- What will the hiring manager need to know to manage this person in the most mutually beneficial way?
- What can I start doing *now* to make sure we keep this star?

BACKGROUND

PIAV illuminates people's values, which is more specifically defined in this context as

> "that which you value." Your experiences lead to beliefs which cluster together into your values (that which you value). Conversely, your beliefs will also cluster together into that which you do not value. You may value dogs but not value religion. Your valuing of life then shapes itself, over time, into a world view, which is called an attitude. (Bonstetter & Bowers, 2004, p. 3)

Put graphically:

Experiences → Beliefs → Values → Attitudes

Assessment developers at TTI took the original six attitudes described by German psychologist Eduard Spranger in his 1928 book *Types of Men: The Psychology and Ethics of Personality,* updating the verbiage to reflect contemporary society. Their PIAV instrument describes six areas that will motivate an individual into action:

Theoretical—a passion to discover, systematize, and analyze; a search for knowledge

Utilitarian—a passion to gain return on investment of time, resources, and money

Aesthetic—a passion to add balance and harmony in one's own life and to protect our natural resources

Social—a passion to eliminate hate and conflict in the world and to assist others

Individualistic—a passion to achieve position and to use that position to influence others

Traditional—a passion to pursue the higher meaning in life through a defined system of living

RESULTS

TTI's PIAV results are presented in a simple 20- to 24-page report that ranks the candidate with a score of 10 to 75 on each of the six attitudes. Each score is compared to the U.S. national mean. The two highest-scoring values are those that will most influence someone's behavior, from "strong" to "passionate" (i.e., well beyond the national mean). The two middle values are "situational," meaning they may kick in as the person shifts into a different context (e.g., he isn't particularly inclined to do research—a Theoretical motivation—unless his boss expressly asks for his help in collecting competitive intelligence to prep for a sales pitch). Finally, the lowest-ranked values suggest the person is "indifferent" in these areas; a disorganized office, for example, is not going to affect someone who scores lowest in the Aesthetic dimension. (Guilty as charged!)

Most people have a few areas in which they're "mainstream," with scores hovering close to the national mean; but individuals who score well off the mean in either direction, "indifferent" or "passionate," can begin to understand why they might do well or prefer working in some roles more than others. A candidate who scores high in Social, for example, will thrive in a customer service role because this dimension values helping people. The same person's performance will likely suffer, however, if the job calls for a high degree of analysis in a policy-driven environment—job characteristics better suited for a high Theoretical/Traditional employee.

For each of the six categories, the PIAV report presents results in bulleted lists that describe

- general characteristics;
- value to the organization;
- tips for managing and motivating;
- training, professional development, and learning insights; and
- continuous quality improvements.

USE IN INTERVIEWS

The results shared here are for this person's highest-scoring dimension—the area that will best motivate him to do a job.

THEORETICAL

- Many may see him as an intellectual.
- T will seek the "truth," yet "truth" is relative and will be defined by his own standards.
- The [1]*process is not as important to him as the results.*
- [2]*Understanding social problems and their ramifications is one of his strengths.*
- T will be comfortable in any position that requires knowledge to excel.
- T will use his [3]*knowledge to sell others on his ideas and beliefs.*
- T never walked by a bookstore or library he didn't want to visit.
- T will spend time and money helping people who have committed their lives to educating themselves and others.
- T is [4]*good at integrating the past, present and future.*

Interview Questions

[2]At this point in your career, what do you regard as your real strengths?

[3]How do you influence colleagues to your point of view?

Reference Questions

For Peer or Direct Report

[1]What role did T typically play on group projects?

For Boss

[4]How does T synthesize information? Please share an example: what was the situation, what actions did he take, and what was the result?

PULL UP A CHAIR!

"Get Your Red-Hot Assessments Here!"
Selecting a Vendor

Hundreds of online assessments are available today, and many are reliable, well-researched instruments. At the same time, however, some of these generate results that aren't easy to put into use or comprehend without a professional psychologist well-schooled in psychological assessment (and who, preferably, knows how to speak in layperson's terms). Conversely, some are *too* easy to use—meaning their distributors sell them to anyone who wants them, and they don't screen users through rigorous training or certification. Too many instruments are sold like online commodities: just throw a dozen in your virtual shopping cart, and you're good to go.

The following checklist will help you shop wisely for an assessment partner. In sum, a quality vendor will

- ❑ Offer *reliable* tools that have been *validated* and updated to be *appropriate* for your candidates (e.g., business people).
- ❑ Provide online assessments that have been shown to be *highly accurate in predicting performance* now and in the future (potential).
- ❑ Provide instruments that have been shown to be *legally defensible, fully compliant with the EEOC, and show no disparate or adverse impact* (i.e., members of certain protected classes do not perform as well on the assessment as do members of the majority group; revisit the Pull Up a Chair feature on compliance earlier in this chapter).
- ❑ Employ highly trained and *experienced analysts* to administer, debrief, and interpret the assessments.
- ❑ Follow a simple *user-friendly* procedure for the person being assessed.

(continued on next page)

❑ Deliver results *quickly* and in an *easy-to-interpret* manner.

❑ *Customize* offerings as necessary, such as assessments delivered in foreign languages or for specific functions such as customer service or sales.

❑ Be available to *train* an organization's HR team and other staff on using the assessments.

❑ Offer strong *customer service* and support pre- and post-hire.

A TIMELESS GIFT

By now you have a good grasp, we hope, of the benefits of using validated and EEOC-compliant assessments in your recruiting efforts:

- You can quickly screen for highly qualified candidates who are truly "interview-worthy."
- You've done your best to reduce the risks around the all-important matter of fit.
- You get a good portrait of candidates' strengths and weaknesses before you even meet them.
- You're not starting with a blank screen when it comes time to write a profile or with a blank stare when a hiring manager asks you, "So tell me about this candidate."
- You've teed up interview questions that are pertinent to the candidate and the role.

What we've described throughout this chapter is the use of online assessments pre-hire. We call them the gift that keeps on giving because the same assessment results you've generated during the recruiting process are equally valuable post-hire. Here's why: they

- facilitate onboarding from both the new hire's and manager's point of view;

- enhance the ongoing performance of an individual (as part of a professional development plan) or of a department (as part of dynamic team-building exercises); and
- lay the foundation for sound promotion and succession planning.

Because our focus in this book is on talent selection, however, let's briefly explore one more way you can leverage assessments pre-hire: as part of a competency model used for benchmarking.

Using Assessments to Create Competency Models and Benchmarks

Recall from Chapter 4 that we define a competency as follows:

> **competency**: a *measurable* characteristic of a person related to success at work; it can be a skill, an attribute, or an attitude.

A competency model, then, is simply a collection of the major competencies that define a job done well. It encompasses both the role (skills, behaviors) and the culture of the organization (values, motivators).

When you benchmark, you see how candidates' assessment results compare to the degree of each element in a competency model. The more overlap, obviously, between a candidate's results and your model or benchmark, the better the fit and the greater the odds are of a great hire. Table 5.2 lists TTI's benchmark data for a few human resources roles, measuring various skills, behaviors, and values that surface on TTI's DISC and PIAV reports.

TTI has honed its approach to benchmarking in a way that earned it a patent. In greatly simplified form, the steps are as follows (Bowers, 2012):

- **Identify subject-matter experts** on the open position: boss, incumbent, top performer in the role—people well informed about the actual *day-to-day* requirements of the role.
- **Define three to five key accountabilities** for the job. These are equivalent to the measurable outcomes we describe in Chapter 4—that is,

TABLE 5.2 Benchmarked Qualities for Select HR Roles

Title	Competencies	Behaviors	Values/Motivators
VP, Human Resources	• Diplomacy and Tact: 9.9 • Empathetic Outlook: 9.9 • Developing Others: 9.7 • Teamwork: 9.7 • Objective Listening: 9.6 • Results Orientation: 9.4 • Conflict Management: 9.3	• Frequent Interaction with Others: 7.0 • Customer Oriented: 6.4 • Versatility: 6.4	• Traditional: 7.5 • Social: 7.5 • Utilitarian: 6.9
Senior Recruiter	• Developing Others: 9.2 • Personal Accountability: 9.1 • Self-Management: 9.1 • Leading Others: 9.0 • Decision Making: 8.7 • Results Orientation: 8.6 • Accountability for Others: 8.6	• Versatility: 6.4 • Urgency: 6.3 • Frequent Interaction with Others: 6.3	• Individualistic: 9.7 • Traditional: 8.6 • Theoretical: 8.6
Benefits Administrator	• Self-Management: 8.9 • Planning and Organization: 8.3 • Diplomacy and Tact: 8.2 • Personal Accountability: 8.2 • Results Orientation: 7.8 • Goal Achievement: 7.8 • Teamwork: 7.8	• Organized Workplace: 5.9 • Customer Oriented: 5.9 • Analysis of Data: 5.8	• Traditional: 9.4 • Theoretical: 8.8 • Utilitarian: 5.6

Note: All benchmark scores are on a 10-point scale. Competencies listed are the top 7 among 23 competencies; behaviors, the top 3 among 10; and values, the top 3 among 6 (see the text for definitions of the values labels).

Source: Job database of Target Training International, available to certified users only. Contact coauthor Laura Larson, a certified user, for more information: Laura@CageTalent.com.

not a mere list of activities and tasks but concise statements of the expected contributions that define success in the role.

- **Prioritize and weight these key accountabilities** (e.g., the most important accountability is 35 percent of the job, the next two are 25 percent each, and the last is 15 percent).
- **The subject-matter experts each take the assessment** chosen for this job, keeping the key accountabilities of the role (and not the person who may currently be in the role) in mind.
- **Review a single report that has combined the experts' assessment results**. This report represents the benchmark, then, against which candidates' results will be compared.
- **Assess each candidate using the same instruments**. Their results will generate a Gap Report that describes strengths and weaknesses of each individual vis-à-vis the job's benchmark. This report also suggests interview questions.

TTI claims a 92 percent retention rate for hires made using this benchmarking process. Whether you follow its protocol or not, using assessments helps eliminate bias as you and your hiring team determine the degree to which a candidate matches a role's requirements. Another piece of the "fit" puzzle will fall into place as you cross-check the face validity of assessment data through interviews with the candidates and references—the topic of the next chapter.

Hiring Interviews
How to Shift from Gut Feel to Real Deal

LET'S BE blunt: most people really are not very good at interviewing. By "most people," we're referring mainly (but not solely) to people who work outside HR—in other words, the hiring managers and other colleagues we've described as your strategic partners and most important customers in Part 1.

Both HR and the key players in business units should focus very strongly on using the position description as an interview outline (thus our focus on this critical component in Chapter 4). The aim is to determine whether and how—in detail—the candidate has *personally* been responsible, in the current and prior jobs, for achieving the outcomes required for this role.

We believe many people stumble in conducting interviews because few executives know how to get a sense of cultural fit at any level of reliability or validity. As Steve Kerr, the former head of GE's learning center, notes, "Otherwise smart people struggle to hire strangers. People unfamiliar with great hiring methods consider the process a mysterious black art" (in Smart & Street, 2008, p. 7). The use of assessment instruments—the topic of the previous chapter—helps address this common weakness in hiring, especially by generating spot-on reports and interview questions.

In this chapter, we hope to give a booster shot to the skill set of all types of interviewers, whether in HR or another department, expert or novice. We discuss all the nuances of conducting effective interviews in greater depth in our forthcoming book on selection, *A Perfect Fit*. Meanwhile, here we'll describe the who, what, why, and how of hiring interviews, as well as tips for managing group interviews and debriefs. Finally, we conclude the chapter by discussing the valuable input from references, elicited in another critical yet often discounted type of interview.

WHO INTERVIEWS?

Step 1 in becoming an expert at managing job interviews is ensuring that everyone who's invited to participate has several excellent reasons for doing so. This tip applies to both interviewees and interviewers. Because the previous chapters in Part 2 have described how to identify optimal candidates, we won't spend as much time here discussing the participants on the interviewees' side of the table. We will share a cautionary tale, however, to underscore the point.

The words of a senior vice president in Operations still ring in our ears as he described the theretofore futile six-month-long recruitment process for one of his direct reports (i.e., a critical role, especially at that time in the organization's global efforts): "I have no idea why I'm meeting these people." Truth be told, this executive already held a low opinion of his fellow SVP in HR—though not of human resources in general, as he'd "seen the job done right" in prior roles. How much do you think this fellow's meeting unqualified candidates enhanced his opinion of his HR colleague? If you said, "Not much," you're close: his opinion was not just reinforced but lowered. And forget about relying on her for strategic counsel in effecting his mission and goals.

At least this tale had a happy ending. We jumped in to complete the search four weeks after hearing the SVP's grumbling about inappropriate candidates. Calling it his dream job, the new hire transformed the group in the region, Southwest Asia (which included a war zone), to the great benefit of his department, the organization, and, most important, its external customers. And the SVP, HR? She was asked to leave within six months.

The moral of this little story: Don't waste candidates' and colleagues' time. Commit the effort up-front in your selection process so that you're confident that only those candidates who really deserve to be interviewed are asked to do so. Our earlier recommendations on creating powerful position descriptions and folding online assessments into the hiring process should help ensure that you and your colleagues are meeting only truly spectacular candidates who can do the job *and* excel in your organization. Respect colleagues' time, and we believe they will respect *you*.

Interviewer ID

So who should interview candidates? This is a critical question, because too many organizations include too many people in the hiring process. This fact alone accounts for why many people don't conduct interviews well: they shouldn't be doing so in the first place!

Typically, once HR has conducted an initial, thorough screening interview to find out which applicants meet the basic job requirements (e.g., years of experience generating the required outcomes, college degree) and express interest, the recruiting team starts the scheduling process among each candidate and the various people who've been slated as interviewers. Then the candidates show up and meet one executive after another—if they're lucky, that is: sometimes a candidate has to return to the site more than once to speak with everyone on the list. Interestingly, the candidates and the interviewers are often wondering the same thing: "Why am I talking with this person?"

Good question. And if there's not a good answer, the interview with many of these executives turns into a combination of pleasantries ("Hey, I own a King Charles spaniel, too!"), vague questions ("So tell me about yourself"), rambling responses ("Well, I grew up in a small town in Nebraska; then when I was 10, we moved to . . ."), punctuated by an awkward silence here and there—all to fill the 30-minute time slot that has been penciled into the agenda. Both the interviewer and the candidate part ways having had a perfectly fine time, but neither one has likely learned anything pertinent to the hiring decision other than leaving with the general impression "What a nice person!" or "I liked him." "Nice" or "I liked him" does not necessarily a good hire make, as we'll see later when we discuss interviewing pitfalls.

Avoid such decidedly unhelpful results by having a one-on-one chat with the hiring manager about who *must* interview candidates. In general, there are three potential types of interviewers: those on the team who

- know the content and processes of the job;
- have a good track record of having an accurate read of the business unit's situation and its people (and therefore are trusted by the hiring manager); and
- may be useful in terms of gaining their buy-in or agreement that a candidate is a good fit (e.g., the manager's boss, a key business partner).

Given these three guidelines, you should be just as discriminating in determining who speaks with candidates as you are in selecting candidates, but here's our shortcut piece of advice: not everyone needs to come to the party. Some people think that the more people involved, the better the hiring decision will be. We're fans of a democracy as much as any other red-blooded Americans, but we believe that this view is taking the "every vote counts" idea too far.

Some people might also think that they'll avoid the risk of offending colleagues if they include them as interviewers. Our counterargument is that you run a greater risk of offending colleagues when you waste their time, as noted a moment ago when we discussed inviting only truly great candidates for face-to-face interviews. This fear of offending people or somehow triggering displeasure is a common one—and thank goodness, otherwise our workplaces would be a lot less civilized, not to mention smelly!

As a leader, you must become comfortable with making uncomfortable choices. It's not prejudicial to note that the majority—over 70 percent—of HR professionals are women (Ramirez, 2012); even at the top levels of VP and CHRO, 69 percent of these human resource positions are held by women (HRxAnalysts, 2011). It's also been well documented by now that women tend to be more inclusive and conflict-avoidant than men. Women HR executives, possibly more so than men, may be likely to err on the side of including too many people in the interview process rather than too few. We strongly encourage you to resist that urge.

Another unintended consequence of asking too many people to interview candidates is the time added to the hiring process. If the complaints we've heard over the years about HR in general have a single theme, it's that the department is too slow: it's too process driven, so things take too long. These are not the sorts of descriptors that executives ever use to describe their strategic partners—those colleagues they can always count on to get tough jobs done in a timely way, over and over again.

Let's boil this down: after your thorough screening interview, guided by a solid position description, if you asked no one but the hiring manager to interview candidates, you'd likely make a very good hiring choice. We've done top-level searches where that has been the case; in fact, after our deep-dive probing of a candidate, only the HR executive managing the search and the new hire's boss-to-be conducted interviews. These hires were successful partly because the heavy lifting (including interpreting assessment results) had been done in selecting candidates *before* they met with the hiring manager.

Depending on the circumstances around the departure of the incumbent, you might invite that person to interview people, too. Who knows the role better than the person doing that job today? If the incumbent is being promoted internally, say, or in some other regard is leaving on good or neutral terms—that is, if you can trust that she will be casting the role, her boss, and the organization in very favorable light—consider asking her to interview candidates along with you and her boss. She'd be very well placed to connect the dots between what a candidate says and what's required in her soon-to-be former role. Having worked shoulder to shoulder with her team members in the department, the incumbent also can share valuable insights into how well a prospective hire would work with those colleagues.

Admittedly, sometimes there's no getting around the fact that more people than two or three must meet candidates. A prospective CEO, for example, will typically meet many members of the board of directors, the general counsel, and the heads of key business units. Another senior executive may interview with people who will be peers, as well as the hiring manager. Even roles lower on the organizational chart may warrant having more than a few people interview candidates. In these cases, give careful thought to who might be grouped together to interview a candidate at the same time. You don't want an interviewee to feel like he or she is being double-teamed or getting the full-court press, but it is possible to coordinate interviewers' questions so that you balance respecting time considerations with gathering valuable information. The later section on "Group Interviews" suggests ways to reach this balance.

WHAT DO WE ASK AND WHY?

We've noted that sometimes executives aren't the best at the interview game. Where we've observed many executives—in and outside HR, to be honest—fall short in conducting a solid outcomes-based interview is in not asking for enough detailed examples of specific performance and skipping the critical "so what?" follow-up questions (see the section later on just this topic) to dig for evidence of real results. This is how you definitively and confidently answer the question "Can this person do the job?"

This section will suggest ways you and your business colleagues can answer that question with confidence, as well as how to overcome "dating behavior" from a candidate, up the odds of accurate responses to interview questions, and sidestep some common interviewer pitfalls.

Fit, Revisited

We've discussed the extreme importance of fit—into the role, the team, and the organization—already in Part 2, but it obviously resurfaces again when it comes time to interview candidates and see "for real" just how well they do fit and will fit months ahead.

SCREEN FOR JOB FIT

Because you as an HR leader are likely the first person to speak with a prospective candidate in a screening interview (i.e., before a person is invited for face-to-face interviews), you are poised as the first person also to answer the fundamental question "Does this person meet the job requirements?" That's the essential first step. If the person doesn't have the right expertise and demonstrated performance in similar on-the-job situations, then there's really nothing else to talk about—and you should end the individual's candidacy. Don't risk damage to your professional reputation as a talent expert by asking key players to

> The ability to make good decisions regarding people represents one of the last reliable sources of competitive advantage, since very few organizations are very good at it.
>
> PETER DRUCKER

meet with people they'll quickly regard as not qualified. By no means do you want one of your valuable internal customers to circle back with "Why am I meeting this person?"

Once candidates have cleared the screening hurdle and are appropriate for face-to-face interviews, delve deeper now about how their firsthand experience aligns with the job's very specific functional requirements and required outcomes as noted in a position description (see the later sections detailing behavioral interviewing). Ensure that you and other interviewers are using the position description as the driver for their respective interviews. The objective here is to ask questions about exactly what's required in the open role (which is why a strong PD is so essential).

Sometimes we even ask candidates to respond in writing, before an interview, to the necessary qualifications of the position description. That way they're describing in detail how their experience aligns with the role, and we get a sense of their written communication skills (an example appears on pages 195–196). This approach also means we've addressed a lot of important points before our discussion with a candidate, so we can cover more ground during the actual interview itself, particularly areas where we're unclear about the exact role the candidate played in attaining the stated outcomes in a previous job. Another valuable by-product is that this approach gets candidates to *do* something, which indicates their level of motivation for the job.

We've never had a candidate complain or resist our request for written responses, by the way. Consider this approach when you're especially keen on respecting the time your business colleagues will be investing in their own conversations with candidates. You can share the written responses with members of the interview team in your write-ups or debriefs about candidates, so that they know you've already covered those key topics, and now they're free to explore other venues in their respective interviews.

SCREEN FOR CULTURAL FIT

Some of your colleagues in other units may believe that it's HR's job to cover what many still regard as the "touchy-feely" stuff around cultural fit. They might think, "I'm a computer guy" or "I'm the numbers gal," and thus "I'll leave all that 'people stuff' to HR." Therefore, they don't dedicate enough time (if any) to the hugely significant topic of fit on the team and in the broader organization.

We agree with this view: It *is* your role as an HR executive to cover this multifaceted area of fit in depth—it's one of the most important parts of your job, in our opinion. As the organization's talent expert, you need to be especially focused around those elements of interpersonal skills and cultural fit. These elements include behaviors, personality, potential derailers, and competencies (see Chapter 5), and what we call "environmental factors" around the role—the nuances around what it will be like working with the hiring manager and other people on the new hire's team, such as the team's own strengths and weaknesses, personalities, and stressors. In other words, you're starting to envision how this person would blend into the organization, on the team, and with the boss.

All this is *not* to say that just because you and others on the HR team "check the box" around fit, your colleagues can skip this area or gloss over it. Again, this is where the value of using assessment instruments can help interviewers dramatically. These tools provide *specific* content about interpersonal skills so that now, during the interview stage, you and your colleagues can ask about the "high" and "low" comments in the assessment results printout. Summarize these sorts of cultural fit questions and assign them to your non-HR colleagues (see "Group Interviews"). We shared several examples in Chapter 5 and will touch on this topic again in the "Mining Assessments for Interview Data" section of this chapter.

Many executives fail in interviewing by not determining—and not knowing *how* to determine—for themselves how a person will fit as a direct report or peer (or sometimes even as a boss) among the particular dynamics of their team within their department. They may be adept at asking the job-fit questions, but in this team- and culture-fit realm, they stumble. Help them improve their interviewing skills in this critical area by giving them explicit instruction, tips, and precise interview questions. After all, they're the ones, not you, who will actually be working day to day with the new hire. No matter how well *you* think a person would fit on a team, no one knows better than the team members themselves, especially their leader—your most important customer, remember.

Dream Date—or Hiring Nightmare?

Coached by recruiters and awash in the ocean of Internet tips, job candidates today are better prepared than ever before to market themselves. They know how to spin their experience to "fit" the job, provide thoughtful answers to the now-expected "tough" questions, and articulate an appropriately motivated reason that they are the best person for the job, being careful to include favorite buzzwords like *team player* and *leader*.

Moreover—let's face it—a job interview is an artificial environment, for the most part. Despite some organizations' attempts to replicate a role's reality by asking candidates to prepare marketing PowerPoint presentations, deliver a sales pitch, actually perform a job-related task, or otherwise jump through a simulation hoop or two, all these contexts are still not the real thing. The fact is, you won't really know how a person will perform in the job until that individual is well into it, months down the road. What you can do, however, is thoughtfully prepare interview questions that will minimize the likelihood of any unpleasant surprises later on.

Hiring mistakes often come about due to the plain fact that everyone is putting their best foot forward during an interview. They're engaged in what we call "dating behavior": just as we all (usually) try to present our best selves when we're getting to know a prospective romantic partner, a candidate is similarly trying to woo you

> Most people can interview well in their sleep.
>
> NANCY PARSONS

and win you over. Unless a candidate is meeting with you to conduct an informational interview to learn more about the role generally or your organization specifically (purposes that you should be fully cognizant of before you interview the person) or simply to practice his or her interviewing techniques (which means you've already been snowed into nothing but a rehearsal for another, "real" interview for a job somewhere else), the interviewee is poised to say and do whatever it takes to get the job. But be forewarned: according to some consultants, "Those who interview best often perform worst" (Parsons, 2011, p. 2). A perfect example is the CEO we described in the last chapter, whose boss vented angrily to us about this "date" gone bad.

TURNING AROUND A BAD DATE BY ASKING "SO WHAT?" QUESTIONS AND KEEPING CONTROL

All candidates, whether playing the dating game or not, obviously aren't entering an interview in hopes of making a *bad* impression. Ideally, the candidate will answer your questions in a direct and data-filled manner. But inevitably you'll encounter a game-playing candidate who's starting to spin an answer, avoid a tough question, or otherwise seize control of the interview.

When that happens, politely raise your hand in the "stop" motion and ask a "so what?" question—a question that will, in effect, force the candidate either (1) to focus, describe explicit actions, and share the real impact of those actions, or (2) to admit the part he or she played was minor, did not bring about the intended (or required) outcomes, or in some other way fell short. Try these:

- What was the result (impact)?
- What did you bring to the table?
- What was your role?
- How would things have been different if you hadn't been there?
- What did you do that others did not or could not?
- What made your role significant?
- What wouldn't have happened without you?

As the HR executive orchestrating the interview process, it's up to you to anticipate challenges during an interview and "outsmart" a candidate by fully preparing for every interview (yours and your colleagues'). This means asking the same questions of each candidate—both to assure all candidates of fair and equitable treatment, as well as to provide yourself and your colleagues with the same broad and deep fact base on each candidate. Remember to inject a few customized questions for each candidate based on the person's online assessment results, so that you can probe into any potential problem areas now, to help sidestep a bad hire.

Strive to keep your interview discussion on point, by avoiding three common interview mistakes:

- *"Suggesting" ways to answer a question*: "I know when *I* have a disagreement with someone, the first thing I do is get my boss's advice. . . ."

- *Rushing to fill an awkward silence* after, say, asking about a candidate's weaknesses: "Maybe a weaker area for you, like for most people, is delivering criticism?"
- *Sharing your own illustrative anecdotes*: "What's your best 'bad boss' story? Boy, I had a doozy boss at my first job out of college. . . ."

Our inelegant but apt advice is to shut up and let the candidate do most of the talking—but not so much that he or she hijacks the interview. If you have to, ignore the manners you learned as a kid and simply interrupt with "I must stop you here. Please answer my question about . . . ." No one's going to be offended by your doing your job with the utmost professionalism.

Interviewing Pitfalls: The Hiring Habits That Can Trip You Up

It's a curious thing in our line of work to observe talented, articulate professionals with years of experience under their belts really have severe trouble when it comes to interviewing job candidates. As Laura's dad used to say about otherwise impressive people when they took a misstep, "So smart in so many ways, not so smart in others."

To be fair, there are often seemingly good reasons that an executive misfires during a hiring interview. As we noted earlier, many people regard the interview process as the domain of HR; they haven't studied hiring best practices the way they've studied and developed expertise in their own field. Thus, they trust that someone else (e.g., you) will do the due diligence required in selection and hiring. Some are simply too busy, too distracted, or too overwhelmed to prepare comprehensively for an interview. Again, they're probably relying on you to ask many of the tough questions. They spend their time "getting to know" the candidate and seeing if the person would "fit" in that vague "I liked him" kind of way described earlier. Remember the high-turnover publishing company where Laura worked? The man who would be her boss, the CEO and founder, asked her exactly two questions in their interview together: "Do you smoke?" (smoking was contra this company's fitness-centered culture) and "Do you play softball?" (to play on the company team).

And finally, some people think they have a handle on how to interview people, but they really don't. Those are folks who actually believe—and therefore put into practice—one or more of the "archetypes" (as we label them) of interviewing. These approaches are so commonplace, in all sorts of organizations at all levels, that they warrant special consideration.

Few people describe what we're calling interviewing pitfalls better than Geoff Smart and Randy Street in their book *Who* (2008). In a section called "Voodoo Hiring," they describe 10 common hiring archetypes that almost guarantee a bad hire. Here are those that we see most often:

- *The Art Critic*—These interviewers judge candidates based on gut feel. In fact, they probably pride themselves on their ability to "read people." These are the folks who generally say they like or dislike a particular candidate, and that's about it. The sad truth is, "Gut instinct is terribly inaccurate when it comes to hiring someone" (p. 7).
- *The Fortune-Teller*—This interviewer archetype likes to ask candidates hypothetical "what if?" questions: "If you had to fire someone, what would you do?" Most people would know how to game their answer to a question like this so that they appear fair and thoughtful. "The answer sounds nice, but we question how many people would actually do those things. Remember, it's the walk that counts, not the talk" (p. 11).
- *The Prosecutor*—Mimicing TV detectives, these interviewers drill candidates with questions—including trick questions like the classic "Why are manhole covers round?" The problem with this interviewing archetype is that it only reveals a candidate's level of intelligence, knowledge base, or ability to think on his or her feet. As Smart and Street note, "knowledge and ability to do the job are not the same thing" (p. 8).
- *The Trickster*—A variation on the Prosecutor, this practice endorses gimmicks to test for certain behaviors (e.g., what will candidates do if you offer them a piece of gum?).
- *The Suitor*—Other interviewers use their time with a candidate to go into an inordinate amount of detail on what a wonderful opportunity this is. Selling a job is certainly integral to the hiring process, but these folks commit the faux pas of talking more than listening.
- *The Chatterbox*—This archetype is another example of an interviewer simply talking too much. Maybe the candidate does, too, but not

about anything particularly relevant. Both parties at the table have a fun conversation, but nothing significant or pertinent to the position is discussed.

Now you know what *not* to do when it comes to the hiring interview. Let's look at additional field-tested recommendations of what we believe you *should* do so that you can practice sound interviewing skills—and coach your colleagues to do the same.

Learning from History: Behavioral Interviewing

A common type of job interview today is the behavioral interview or behavioral event interview. This type of interview is based on the notion that a job candidate's previous behaviors are the best indicators of future performance. Another advantage of this approach is that candidates have a hard time making up action- or event-based stories off the top of their heads, so you're likely to get a more accurate read of their experience and contributions to the outcomes that must be replicated in the open job.

In behavioral interviews, the interviewer asks a candidate to recall specific instances where he or she was faced with a set of circumstances and how, in detail, the candidate reacted. Here are some typical behavioral interview questions (see also SHRM's bank of questions on the Templates & Sample page of www.shrm.org):

- Tell me about a project you worked on where the requirements changed midstream. What did you do?
- When have you taken the lead on a project? What did you do?
- Describe the worst project you worked on.
- Describe a time you had to work with someone you didn't like.
- Tell me about a time when you had to stick by a decision you had made, even though it made you very unpopular.
- Give us an example of something particularly innovative that you have done that made a difference in the workplace.
- What happened the last time you were late with a project?
- Have you ever witnessed a person doing something that you felt was against company policy? What did you do and why?

The key difference between these sorts of questions and the questions that result from the interviewing pitfalls listed earlier is that these focus on two critical points:

- Reality—the situations described in the answers actually occurred in the candidate's career history (and you'll verify that they're real during reference checks).
- The job—the questions and answers reflect relevant skills and competencies necessary to doing *this* job, at *this* time, very well.

Mining Assessments for Questions

Behavioral interviews lend themselves perfectly to addressing anything that caught your eye, in a not-good way, on a candidate's assessment results. Remember the fellow in the "'Arrested' Development" feature of the last chapter? We share another cautionary tale in our later discussion on reference checks. Chapter 5 provided many explicit examples of interview questions derived directly from online assessment results, so here let's look at just one.

Say the DISC report notes that a candidate has a potential problem with procrastination:

Procrastination is the process of delaying action. It is also the inability to begin action.

Possible Causes:

- Priorities have not been set
- Do not see projects or tasks clearly
- Overwhelmed with commitments
- Hope that time will solve or eliminate the problem
- Fear of failure

As we discussed in the previous chapter, your first interview with a candidate should include a debrief of assessment results, so that the candidate can let you know what he or she believes is accurate and inaccurate. If the candidate didn't bring up procrastination in the first interview and has cleared

PULL UP A CHAIR!
Open-ended Questions: A Key to Strong Interviews

In reviewing the many examples of behavioral interview questions in this chapter, you'll probably notice a similarity among all of them: most don't take yes or no for an answer. Questions like these are called *open-ended questions*. We described these briefly in Chapter 3's feature on measurement and specifically discussing strategic workforce planning with your business colleagues, but let's consider them in more detail for a hiring interview.

Open-ended questions imply to the interviewee that there is no right or wrong answer, but rather that the questions are intended to elicit the interviewee's unique point of view. They also lead to far greater detail, befitting a real conversation versus an interrogation. Compare the following questions. Which is going to provide you with more useful—read "honest"—information on a candidate?

- "Are you a team player?" versus "Would you consider yourself an introvert or an extrovert? In what way?"
- "Do you like your boss?" versus "Describe a time you completely disagreed with your boss on a big decision. What happened?"

Additional examples of open-ended questions appear on page 197, designed specifically to help you coax a candidate to be more forthcoming.

Another way to view questions like these is that you're sharpening the focus, going from the broad and more general (e.g., "Do you like your boss?") to the narrow and more specific. Questions cast like this feed off the juicy tidbits that invariably pop up in a candidate's response. Your candidate write-ups will be far richer—and useful—as a result.

Try to phrase most, if not all, of your interview questions (including those you ask of references later on) as open-ended ones. Then capture the responses as best you can by audio recording or comprehensive note taking. No use in asking great questions if their answers fade from your memory as the candidate walks out the door at the end of the interview!

other recruiting hurdles to make it to the next stage of the interview process, now is the time to go deeper on this potential problem area. You might ask:

> "When was a time you missed a key deadline? What led to that, and how did you handle the aftermath?" or

> "We all have a lot of things to do at work. What's your system for managing priorities?"

Remember not to take the candidate's word for it. Always ask references the same questions around potential problem areas as well as self-identified strengths.

Adding a STAR to Your Behavioral Interviews

You might have what you regard as the best set of open-ended, behavior-based questions ever, and the candidate still offers only a succinct response that barely scratches the surface of what you're really trying to better understand—collaborative skills, learning agility, decision-making quality, whatever. Also, along the lines of our previous point that an interview is an artificial situation, a typical candidate isn't skilled at answering these sorts of questions, often offering canned or trite responses.

To set the stage for the sort of detailed answers you're looking for, try structuring your questions with a STAR. That is, pose your question, and ask the person to include these points in the response:

> **S**ituation—what was the context?

> **T**ask—what was the objective or problem at hand?

> **A**ctions—what specifically did the candidate do?

> **R**esults—how did things wind up, and what were the measurable outcomes for the team or organization?

This addition to your core behavioral question helps you to better understand the context (situation) that the candidate is describing as well as to steer the candidate's response to reveal specific behaviors and outcomes that are related to and required for the job.

Not every question warrants the STAR approach—the interview would become absurdly repetitive, not to mention unbearably long! But do employ it with a handful of especially critical job requirements—the ones that really are deal-breakers if not met: specific requirements listed explicitly in the position description (e.g., integrating disparate cultures postmerger, developing a new services market of high-net-worth individuals) or competencies (e.g., learning a new skill quickly, managing a remote team of Millennials).

VARIATION

Sometimes we kill two birds with one stone by asking a candidate to provide STAR-formatted answers in writing. That way, we learn not only the degree to which a person demonstrates the experience or competency we're interested in, but also how well he or she writes—an important competency no matter what the function or level of the role. An overwhelming majority of respondents to a *Wall Street Journal* poll agree: 96.5 percent believe writing skills are important in the corporate world (Middleton, 2011).

Remember the story we shared earlier in this chapter of the unhappy SVP, Operations who was waiting a long time to meet qualified candidates for his regional role? When we stepped in to complete that search, we asked candidates to e-mail us "STAR stories" that would demonstrate some of the key competencies required in this unusually demanding job. For example, because this regional VP would be working largely autonomously and several thousand miles from his boss, the new hire would have to be able to solve problems and get things done quickly and effectively, with limited resources (this was a nonprofit operating globally; the position was in Southwest Asia). The man who wound up with the job sent us the following STAR story, shortened a bit here but otherwise unedited:

> **Situation**: [ABC Technology] was a company of about 100 people, almost all engineers. They had just delivered a new system to the NSA [National Security Agency] called the Secure Network Server (SNS) as a "Proof of Concept." The NSA bought the idea and immediately directed it be installed and implemented. . . . I was just hired as the Post Sales manager. I had no staff and the company had no experience at anything beyond software development.

Task: Conceive and develop a comprehensive product offering of services and technical support to support the large-scale deployment of SNS servers and successfully implement them worldwide.

Actions: I hired and trained the people, developed processes and services to install, integrate and provide continued support for the life cycle of the product. To include:

- Installation/Integration service—I performed the first installs of the SNS. . . . I developed and priced this into a standard product offering.
- Technical Support—I ordered up an 800 number and placed it on my desk. This was the origin of tech support at [ABC Technology]. I worked with engineering to set up escalation processes and with production to develop RMA [return material authorization] processes.

Results: Through successful installation and support [ABC Technology] developed a reputation for excellent product service and support as a product delineator. This resulted in quick vertical growth in the federal space. Starting from $0 in 1993 and 1 person (me), I grew the support and services business to $80M and 170 people in 2008 on corporate earnings of about $240M.

The candidate who authored this story gave us the details he needed to begin to convince us he was right for this position (i.e., he indicated apt firsthand experience plus very high motivation to do this job). He provided a relevant example from his career about solving problems, including specific monetary figures that answered the "so what?" question with clear results. In addition, he demonstrated he clearly could string words together into an articulate, cohesive message—a skill that shone later on the job in his terrific newsletters "from the front."

Finally, it may be old-fashioned, but a paper trail—even a virtual one like the excerpted e-mail here—can become your best friend when it comes to making a strong case for or against a candidate. Tucked into your candidate write-ups, candidate STAR stories reveal someone's proficiency in one or two critical competencies and let the candidate do the "talking" for you.

Getting Past Resistance

Earlier in this chapter we reminded you of how very well prepared most job applicants are today. For example, people know by now to expect the question "What are your weaknesses?" and have the Ol' Faithful of replies at the ready: "Gosh, I guess I struggle with work/life balance and sometimes still work too much." Taken at their word, all job candidates seem to be devoid of weaknesses and perfect executive material.

Even detailed responses like those encouraged by behavioral questions or STAR stories can be slanted to cast too rosy a glow on the candidate. We suggest you use the following variations on the "What are your weaknesses?" question until you uncover a satisfying answer:

> It's a heck of a lot easier to hire the right people to begin with than to try to fix them later.
>
> BRAD SMART

- What would your boss/team say are your weaknesses?
- What effort in this role didn't work out as you'd expected?
- Looking back, what advice would you give yourself back then?
- What didn't you like about this job?
- What skills had you not yet perfected in this role?
- Knowing what you know now, how would you coach your younger self in that role?
- What did your peers do better than you?
- What qualities of your boss do you wish you had?

The point is to not take no—as in "I have no weaknesses"—for an answer. Patiently ask questions until the candidate is forced to share something more real about his or her skill set. Your persistence will pay off. Answers like "Gee, I can't think of any weaknesses" or "I'll have to think about this and get back to you—nothing comes to mind" suggest that either the candidate is not being open with you and is posturing in his or her own form of dating behavior, or the candidate isn't particularly introspective or self-aware. In our view, these types of attributes are show—and interview—stoppers.

GROUP INTERVIEWS

We stated earlier that we typically take a "less is more" view when it comes to the number of people involved in interviewing candidates. That said, we do admit that it's possible to use group interviews effectively, *if* the process is managed well.

We even see advantages to a group interview approach. For one thing, obviously more topics can get covered. If your team members (and the candidates) don't mind a lengthier hiring process due to more interviews, then you can gather highly pertinent, substantive information, in greater detail, to fold into your impressions of candidates and thus make a better-informed hiring decision.

For another thing, if you prepare your fellow interviewers well by providing each of them with different questions (and a reminder about legality; see the next page), then it's unlikely they'll be wasting time by asking the same questions of a candidate. Candidates appreciate this, too: they're not hearing for the umpteenth time, "So tell me about your backpacking trip in Zimbabwe!" or "Describe a time you had to deliver bad news to your boss." Whether relevant (the latter question) or not (the former), repetitive questions break the workplace commandment of "Thou shalt not waste people's time."

Consider, for example, splitting a candidate's career history into segments and then asking each interviewer to cover that chapter of experience in some depth, delving for proof of having met similar requirements, in previous jobs, to what's in your position description. When all of the interviewers debrief together later, you'll integrate the results as best as you can and discuss the themes or patterns of behavior that inevitably reveal themselves. The interviewing team will uncover things like a candidate's persistent unwillingness to challenge authority, say, or a consistent flair for engaging with and influencing different types of people across an organization.

When we discussed some of the interviewing archetypes and pitfalls that characterize many people's interview techniques, we mentioned that a very common mistake is the interviewer talking too much or chatting about topics not relevant to the role. We suspect in many cases like this, the interviewer believes that someone else on the team is asking the "real" interview questions. The problem is, if each interviewer feels that way, then probably no one actually is asking the "real" questions! An Abbott-and-Costello-like

PULL UP A CHAIR!
Legal Review

As an HR professional, *you* know what interview questions are illegal, but does everyone on your interview team know? Don't assume they do. Review this point with everyone who will meet candidates. Sometimes an innocent question asked simply to break the ice can turn into a discrimination complaint. Here's a list of the legal variations of some common interview questions:

Illegal: Are you a U.S. citizen?

Legal: Are you authorized to work in the United States?

Illegal: How old are you?

Legal: Are you over the age of 18? How long have you been working in this industry?

Illegal: Do you have any disabilities?

Legal: Are you able to perform the essential functions of this job?

Illegal: What is your religion?

Legal: Are you able to work on the weekend?

Illegal: Is English your first language?

Legal: What languages can you read, speak, or write fluently?

Illegal: Are you planning to have children or do you already have children?

Legal: Is there anything that will preclude you from working any hours or traveling, if required? Would you be willing to relocate if necessary?

conversation ensues of "I thought *you* were going to do it!" "No, I thought *you* were going to do it!"

Nip the time-wasters and other frustrations in the bud by coordinating your interview team. Before anyone speaks with a candidate, arrange a quick stand-up meeting or conference call to assure your colleagues that you and your HR team have determined this candidate can do the job and is motivated to move into this role. In your own screening interview, you've already asked fundamental questions like these: "Tell me how you think your experience aligns with this role"; "Looking at your résumé, I see that you increased sales from $20 million to $30 million over 18 months; tell me how you pulled that off and what exactly was your role"; and "How do you feel about traveling seven days a month?"

> The discipline of pooling leaders' judgments about other leaders [should be] comprehensive, continuous, and part of the culture.
>
> BILL CONATY & RAM CHARAN

Explain to the interview team that their role now is to verify this information and reduce any perception of risk around a candidate. Every executive is going to have his or her particular concerns about working well with the new hire, depending on the department's mission, and the interview is the time to address those concerns. For example, a CFO may want to know if a candidate can deeply understand an organization's P&L statement so that whoever is hired manages costs prudently. Her colleague in HR may want to ensure the candidate can work well among a strongly diverse workforce of foreign-born technologists and enhance the performance of an underperforming team. The CEO may want to know, simply, if this person can make the numbers in the current economy. What will this candidate do differently than the incumbent? Figure 6.1 presents an example of an interviewing team's set of questions.

The take-away for the interview team is "Let's not have everyone ask the same question." Reiterate the two main advantages of following your coordinated script of questions. First, this approach ensures that the candidate walks away thinking, "This is a first-class organization with people who collaborate

FIGURE 6.1   Sample Group Interview Questions

HR Professional Asking about . . .

Talent Management

- We've had a challenge determining if the right people are in our key seats. Tell me about how you have assessed the strengths and weaknesses of people on your team.
- Describe for me that last interview you conducted. How did you conduct the interview, and what was the sequence of questions you asked? Why did you ask these questions in those ways?
- What's the composition of your current team, in terms of high and low performers? How are you addressing the needs of the lower performers?

SVP, Operations Asking about . . .

Leadership

- People tend to have one of two different styles in managing others: telling or selling. On a continuum with telling at one end and selling at the other, how would you say you work with others to get results?
- Tell me about a time when you created agreement and shared purpose from a situation in which all parties originally *differed* in opinion, approach, and objectives.
- At one time or another, many of us have been a member of a successful team. Tell me about your experience, and the role you played on the team and in its success.

IT Manager Asking about . . .

Problem Solving

- When have you had to set up a project for which there was no organizational precedent to follow—no "rules of the road"? What did you do? (Ask for a STAR story; see the text.)
- Describe a time when a colleague was impeding your progress at work. What happened, and what did you do about it?
- Sometimes emotions run hot. How have you handled an angry customer or vendor? What happened, and what did you do?

CEO Asking about . . .

Career Motivations

- What are you looking for in your next job?
- Let's say that this role didn't work out and you left in less than a year. What would have gone wrong?
- Tell me about a recent accomplishment that you're particularly proud of. What exactly makes you proud about this one?
- What is career all about for you?

---

and communicate well with one another." Second, it allows your colleagues to play a significant role in the hiring process. The interview team collectively is going both broad and deep, gathering more information on more topics for each candidate.

Finally, a coordinated approach—no matter the number of people on the interview team—means that "when [the interviewers] step back and reflect as a group, amazing things happen: preconceived opinions disappear, insights deepen, and matches and mismatches with the non-negotiable criteria become crystal-clear" (Conaty & Charan, 2010, p. 293). During the debrief among members of the interview team, after everyone has interviewed all candidates, each person can describe his or her judgments about how well the candidate can do the job at hand; is motivated to do the job; and will fit in with the boss, team, and overall culture of the organization. Ultimately, a well-coordinated recruiting process helps ensure that the best hiring decision is made.

REFERENCE CHECKS: DON'T HIRE WITHOUT THEM

Travelers' checks may have gone by the wayside nowadays, but the old slogan "Don't leave home without them" applies to another type of check: reference checks. Don't leave the hiring process without them! Too many people regard reference checks as a sort of throwaway step in the recruiting process that isn't very important to the hiring decision; in fact, they're often conducted *after* a hiring decision has already been made! We ardently disagree, and we think a chapter on the interview process would be remiss if we didn't include a discussion of them.

By this stage, you know the candidate pretty well. This person has been screened, assessed, and interviewed—more than once. Moreover, candidates are human and thus self-serving creatures, so they're going to offer references they know will speak positively of them, or at least not slam them. References themselves, in turn, are also human, and we all like to be perceived as pleasant, agreeable, and helpful. Therefore, what new information, let alone red flag, is really going to surface while speaking with references?

Well, that may be a valid point—if you believe unequivocally everything a person tells you. (Living in Brooklyn, we've got a nice bridge you may like to buy, too. . . .) Reference checks provide the opportunity to verify anything and everything that a candidate shared with you during the interview. Remember our discussion about dating behavior: candidates are going to put their best foot forward during the interview because they want the job. Now's your chance to see whether the points shared during the interview are valid. If you regard the hiring process as we do—an exercise in reducing risk—you'll take the additional hour or two to conduct thorough reference checks.

Who to Use as References

Too many people give too much power to the candidate when it comes to reference checks. Take that power back! If we all know by now that candidates will use as references only people they trust to be positive about their skills and experience, then here's an idea: talk to other people. Brad Smart, the author of the best-selling *Topgrading* (2012), believes that a surefire way to, first, screen out undesirable job hunters who have fudged their résumé and, second, ensure that a candidate is telling you the truth during an interview is through the "threat of reference checks." He recommends starting your interview by telling the candidate you'll be speaking to several of the colleagues (especially former bosses) who will invariably get mentioned in your discussion. Candidates will realize that this is not a typical interview situation and that you'll be checking the truthfulness of their responses with the people who *know* what really occurred—not their current friends but their prior bosses!

We applaud this approach, because it means you're not dependent on the candidate for whomever he or she volunteers as a reference. Anyone is fair game who gets mentioned in the interview, and it's up to you to ask the quick follow-up question to get the details you need: "What was the full name of that sales VP in this story?" or "You mentioned some of your peers disagreeing with your approach—could you spell their names for me, please?"

After the interview, simply review your notes and pluck out the names of prior bosses and other key players in the candidate's career history. Plug these references' names and organizations into a system like LinkedIn; then connect with them with an InMail note, or see if they have other contact information at the bottom of their profile.

Even if you don't have a specific name, you can still find references whom the candidate, on good dating behavior, may have preferred you not use and thus didn't mention. Find the candidate's LinkedIn profile. Go down to a prior company where the candidate worked and click on the URL; you'll be taken to a list of people showing when they were at that organization. Look for a few individuals in the same geography and function who were at the firm during the same period as your candidate, and send them an InMail. Or simply call up prospective references' organizations (the main phone number is almost always on the company website on the "Contact Us" page) and ask to speak to the reference.

Another tip: make note of how long it takes for a reference to get back to you. Unless they're traveling on business or vacation, references with great things to say about the candidate will usually respond very quickly.

Understand that we're not suggesting you ignore the candidate's own reference recommendations or, worse, not ask for them at all. By all means, do speak with those folks the candidate names; then follow our recommendations carefully on questions to ask. Inform *all* candidates that you'll be speaking to several people from their past jobs to better understand their work style and skill set, and no one will feel he or she is being subjected to greater scrutiny than other candidates. No one should feel ill at ease about your chatting with anyone—*if* the person has been honest with you in conversations with you and other interviewers.

Between candidate recommendations and your own forthright inquiries, you should now have as references at least one boss, one peer, and one subordinate from the last couple of jobs, and the current one, too, if the candidate's boss and team know about their colleague's impending departure. We've seen suggested reference lists with as many as 8 to 10 names on it. Before you protest, "I don't have that kind of time!" know that an efficient reference interview should take no more than 10 to 15 minutes. Do the math: wouldn't you agree that two hours is a modest investment if it reduces the hugely time-consuming effort, not to mention expense and embarrassment, of a bad hire? (Refer back to Table 5.1 on the direct and indirect costs of a bad hire.) Keep control of a reference interview just as you've done with the hiring interview, and we think you'll agree that this is time very well spent.

What to Ask

Like online assessment results, reference material is the gift that keeps on giving, because this is information that will be tremendously useful in onboarding a new hire. If it's not useful in helping you avoid a hiring disaster, then certainly it will facilitate the transition into a new job and organization. A collection of good reference interview data serves as a mini–360° review of the person. What a valuable thing to have before the person even begins the job!

After introducing yourself and briefly describing the open position, start your reference interview with a couple of context-setting questions like these:

1. How did you first meet X? (organization and respective roles; time frame)
2. What adjectives would you use to describe him/her?

Now start exploring strengths and weaknesses. Begin with the open-ended general questions listed here; you want to see what the references will lead with when they identify pluses and minuses with no prompting (i.e., they've not been led to say anything). Use the same STAR protocol you used during the hiring interviews to get specific behavior-based examples: what was the *s*ituation, what was the *t*ask or problem at hand, what *a*ctions did the person take, and what was the *r*esult? Focus your questions on the exact role that the candidate played in achieving the results.

3. What is X really good at doing in an organization? (strengths)
4. We all have things that we can do better. What do you think X can do better? or Thinking back, what capabilities did you wish X had while working for/with you? (weaknesses)

If a reference gives a lame response to the weaknesses question (much as a candidate often does), try recasting it so that the reference has to admit, indirectly, that the person is not perfect: "'In what area have you seen the most improvement?' . . . This results in a better conversation. It forces the reference to think" (Lee, in Schachter, 2013, para. 4). You may also approach the weaknesses topic by coming at it this way with a former boss: "What things were you working on with X to improve?" A smooth follow-up question that lets you know how the person accepts feedback (i.e., criticism) is "How did X handle the discussion when you pointed out this developmental area?"

Having covered strengths and weaknesses with some solid open-ended questions, now zoom in and dig for valuable insights into how your candidate is likely going to operate within the particular parameters of this role and within your organization. The position may have very specific or demanding requirements for which you'll want the reference's insights regarding the candidate's ability to meet those requirements. For example, when we were looking for a president of a risk management firm that wanted to mine its target market for a dramatic boost in revenue and profits, we followed up with this question:

> 5. Can you tell me about a time when Y was asked to significantly increase the number of new clients and dial up revenue? What did he do, and what were the results?

Sometimes it's a person, not a functional requirement, that's the potential problem. Here's another real-life reference question we used when our client—the candidate's future boss—had proven inordinately difficult to work with, based on not only his direct reports' comments but our own firsthand experience with him as well:

> 6. Describe a time X had to work with an especially demanding, emotional, or unreasonable person. What happened?

Also in the land of potential pitfalls that most reference interviews avoid, perhaps the candidate's assessment results have highlighted a "warning area" you'll want to explore. No assessment is 100 percent accurate, so here's your opportunity to validate any data points that might be red flags. The Pull Up a Chair that closes this chapter shares an example.

When you've confirmed the candidate's strengths and addressed his or her weaker areas, wrap things up with these last three questions:

7. Do you know of anything in X's personal life that may affect his/her performance?
8. [For a boss] Given what you know now about X's strengths and weaker areas, would you hire him/her again?
9. What advice do you have for X's new boss?

Question 7 serves to protect you from any future inquiries in case something goes awry after the hire; you can honestly say you asked all references about any troublesome areas that might surface on the job. Question 8 puts it on the table that the candidate is not perfect, so the boss is likely to respond with more than a polite yes. Finally, the answer to question 9 should serve as a nice summary statement that's also useful for onboarding.

As with the bulk of your questions for the hiring interview, ask the same questions of all of a candidate's references (except those that are clearly pertinent only to bosses, such as question 8). Stay on point, don't rush to fill a pause or silence, and take good notes so that the references are doing much of the "talking," not you, when it comes time for you to share the results with your colleagues.

We hope we've persuaded you to give reference checks the respect they deserve and to polish your interview skills to a new lustre. By tweaking standard questions and folding in a few additional ones that might nudge you, the candidate, or the reference out of the comfort zone, you'll gather additional information that can only improve your hiring record. When you do that, your colleagues can't help but regard you as the ally they want alongside them in the war for talent. Mastering the interview tips described in this chapter will go a long way to help you deliver the best talent to execute your colleagues' strategic agendas.

PULL UP A CHAIR!
Covering Your Ass(essments) with References

As we noted in the previous chapter on online assessments, these tools are the gifts that keep on giving. The results should be employed again at this stage to help you craft atypical (i.e., genuinely useful) reference questions. Reread your finalists' assessment reports to review those bits you highlighted as potential weaknesses or derailers when you were preparing for the hiring interview. Now you have the valuable opportunity to get other people's—the references'—take on the same points.

We thought we struck gold in a candidate who was a strong finalist to become a client's new chief operating officer. Smart, creative, and eloquent, he had worked at a bigger firm in precisely the same space. He met or exceeded every functional requirement, and he got along famously with the man who would be his boss, the CEO. As a bonus, he was very well connected in the investor community and would be extremely valuable in helping raise investor dollars for this private firm. So what's wrong with this picture?

Well, sometimes "smart, creative, and eloquent" can be too much of a good thing. In this fellow's case, he had scored unusually high—in the 93rd percentile—on the "Mischievous" scale of one of the instruments in our toolkit, the Hogan Development Survey (HDS; see Chapter 5). Here's an excerpt from the results summary, including the bits we had highlighted (shown in italics here):

> This scale is concerned with the tendency to appear charming, friendly, fun loving, and insightful, but also to be impulsive, excitement-seeking, and non-conforming. High risk scorers usually make a favorable first impression, but others may find them *hard to work with* because they tend to test the limits, *ignore commitments, and take risks that may be ill-advised.* Although they may seem decisive,

they can make *bad decisions* because they are often motivated by pleasure and *don't fully evaluate the consequences of their choices*.

Mr. Z received a high risk score on the Mischievous scale. Such persons tend to be:

- engaging, interesting, quick witted, and charming
- friendly and fun-loving
- easily bored
- action seeking *without regard for the consequences*

Talk about a reality check! We quickly added a couple questions to our reference interviews:

1. How would you describe X's decision-making style, in terms of evaluating choices and consequences?
2. Describe a time you observed X take a professional risk. What happened?

In this case, all references provided solid, detailed accounts of both well-measured decisions and appropriate risks that panned out well. Sure, we could have skipped these additional questions and saved the 30 minutes they accounted for, across all interviews, and trusted the material already accumulated on this candidate. But we sure slept a lot better knowing half a dozen people had backed us up.

Conclusion

From Words to Action

MANY AUTHORS write a book in hopes of inspiring change among its readers, and we're no different. We sincerely hope that no matter what level in the HR profession you work in, you'll take away at least one idea or set of approaches that will engage you in your firm's core business challenges. When you do that, consistently, HR becomes—and is regarded within your organization as—a powerful force that fully and actively increases the probability that your organization's strategy will be implemented.

To help you make the shift from reading this book to doing at least one thing differently, we share the views of an actual HR executive who, in multiple Fortune 500 firms, has been a key strategic partner. Then we close this chapter, and the book, with a final Pull Up a Chair feature: a brief self-assessment that will help you focus your energies on those HR/business skills described in this book that could use some work. Perhaps your usual self-confidence dips a bit when it comes to asking your business colleagues questions that dig deeper into their operational issues so that you uncover the truly critical competencies for a role. Maybe coordinating interviews with essential (and nonrepetitive) questions has been challenging. The "HR in the Hot Seat Quiz" will make those developmental areas clear.

INSIGHTS FROM AN EXECUTIVE
ALREADY IN HR'S SEAT AT THE TABLE

In an HR career spanning four decades, including more than 20 years at the senior level, Andy Goodman has been, most recently, the executive vice president/chief human resources officer at E*TRADE and the EVP, HR at CA Technologies. He was also a senior HR executive in the technology division at Merrill Lynch, and, prior to these firms, held HR positions at GE Capital, Bankers Trust, and Ernst & Young. Andy is regarded as an innovative yet practical strategic thinker who partners with C-level executives to align HR with business goals so that strategy can be successfully implemented—in other words, a role model who embodies many of our recommendations.

Here's our discussion with Andy:

How do you, the senior HR executive in the organization, get invited to the table to help develop strategy?
To me, it always seems *incredibly* logical that HR is included as part of a strategy development process. I've actually found that to be the case in most of my career. A strategy is ultimately a plan and a story about achieving an objective. Those plans come with the desire to realize the execution of that plan. The execution of business plans only happens through the actions and performance of human beings. So the opportunity is always there for HR to have a logical role to play to ensure and enable that human performance occurs to allow the execution of that plan.

The bigger question that I always tended to have was not about HR getting invited to the table. I think the question has been more, How many HR professionals are prepared to play once they're at the table? Business expects there to be a component of HR as a logical part of the plan. When you're looking at strategies, it's always really looking at the trade-offs and risks, and the largest risk of most strategies is an execution risk. Most of that comes from organizational capability and execution. So again, I think getting invited to the table is not the core question as much as it is that once you're at the table, are you prepared to play?

> The core question is, Once you're at the table, are you prepared to play?

How do you engage with your peers in other business units or departments so that you understand what they need from you?

I think the biggest issue is that, particularly in a lot of the business-supporting groups—and HR being one of those—they tend to communicate with their businesses on an event- and transaction-based basis. That is not a recipe for success. There has to be a constant communication process that's not just driven by a "crisis du jour" or a particular transaction or event. To be effective, you really have to have a sincere curiosity and a sincere desire to understand what others are doing or trying to accomplish, and how they're going about doing it across all the functions of your business. Then you can assess how you can assist and contribute. Once you do that, you find yourself included and much better prepared to add value because you're part of the natural dialogue and part of the natural decision-making process.

The biggest issue is the "1-800-HR" perspective [of business partners] of "I'll call, and HR will be there." That just doesn't get you context, and understanding, and perspective. So the communication process needs to be constant, the curiosity needs to be sincere, and the ability to ask any functional area of an organization to explain more about what they're doing, what they desire to do, and how they're going about it is the only way you can assess how to be able to intervene and interact.

Some business leaders have a sense that HR executives just don't understand their business. How have you, in several industries, taken daily or weekly steps to figure out each part of the business (Finance, Sales, Development, etc.) so that you come off as credible and helpful?

The core, similar to my response to the previous question, is that it's really essential to ask questions. It's essential to connect the dots on how all the functions interoperate. The ultimate outcome of any business is serving the customer and providing value for shareholders. There's a point to being in business, and everybody is a part of that value chain. What I have found is that the real failing is that even if HR does in fact understand the business, they tend to communicate using HR jargon or speech that gives the *impression* that they're disconnected—that they're not connected to the business objective and that they're administratively focused.

The wonderful thing about being in the HR role is that you have a vantage point of the organization that is unique. You really do have a very good opportunity to look at things horizontally, while others are very focused vertically or within their silo. Understanding how things interact and connecting the dots is very important, but then you've got to be able to communicate and put it together in a way that actually gives the impression that you understand. When you throw it back in HR-speak, you actually lose the business people. So you have to communicate in business language and be able to show you understand the market objectives and the financial objectives that we're all here to accomplish.

In many cases, if you've been working across different industries, there is a whole bunch more similarities than differences in what you've seen. Relating similar past challenges that you've assisted in can help build personal credibility because you can relate to the business of functional leaders. You can say to them, for example, "Hey, when I was at GE, I faced a situation just like that." Your internal client will get engaged and ask, "What did you do?"

So, to sum up, you've got to have a personal credibility quotient, and you've got to be able to ask the right questions and be able to connect things. And for goodness sake, when you do, don't go in there and start quoting the HR hymnal and not relate to things in business terms and business objectives.

What have you learned about translating a business partner's needs into a position description that can really enhance the talent management process?

I've worked through this on a number of occasions. The biggest derailer is to allow the business needs to become some kind of generic box on an org chart or some generalization of what they're looking for. The mistaken belief here is that you can look in the back room for talent that's "in stock." It's really important to take the context and understanding of the business and get into the specific, critical attributes and competencies that are going to make for a successful hire and a functional hire within the organization.

> The biggest derailer is to allow the business needs to become some kind of generic box on an org chart.

The other very important thing in terms of context is not only understanding the business needs and objectives, but understanding the rest of the team that this hire will be part of. The ability to understand how this next component of talent is going to complement the other talent around the table, fill voids, and offer diversity of thought is an essential part to making the talent management process effective and optimized.

I think that the important pieces are (1) take the business understanding; (2) drive into the specific and critical attributes that are really required to make this a successful hire; and (3) look at talent as a complementary component around the table, not a box on an org chart or a static plug-in—it's a dynamic scenario. You want talent to be able to offer something to optimize the existing talent, fill gaps, and bring diversity. I think those are the things that are really key.

What have you learned about vetting candidates so that you're not surprised after they're hired?

People always surprise me—sometimes positively, sometimes negatively. The important piece of the vetting process, to me, is really probing for the way people think and act situationally. You've got to go beyond just the chronological "Tell me what you did next." You really need to get into how they've dealt with situations, how they've solved challenges, and then understand the patterns of behavior that will both eliminate surprise but also—and I think this is almost more important—prepare you for the developmental interventions and the assimilation interventions to make sure they're going to be effective when they come onboard. That's one of the most important pieces, in terms of effectively vetting and interviewing a candidate.

What's your approach for conducting an interview? How do you manage the interview process when several people are meeting with the same candidates?

Ultimately, there is a very valuable aspect to planning, preparation, and coordination. A pet peeve of mine in running the hiring process has always been the traditional approach of five people see Bob and, at the end of the day, all they know is his name is Bob! Going back to when I was in the Boy Scouts, I think it starts with being prepared. When you're setting up an interview, do your homework and know the areas of experience and the competencies that you want to have probed or validated.

It's really critical in the interview process for you to optimize the time of each participant and avoid redundancy. So I think it's very important to make sure that every interviewer has an understanding of the role and the area of concern that they're going to be focused on during this process. That way, you come out with a comprehensive and holistic assessment of a candidate. The biggest failure is redundancy. If five people ask the interviewee the same question five times, you're getting a very narrow slice of assessment as opposed to saying [to each interviewer], "Look, you're going to deal with these competencies; you're going to deal with fit; you're going to deal with culture." This way, you're putting together a coordinated program so that at the end, you can actually piece together the results and have an outcome that's useful.

In many cases, you can also use instrumentation to provide additional insight or validation. I tend to like to do that more at the leadership level of positions.

Another key to any interviewing process that must be reinforced with all the interviewers is listen, listen, listen. Get the candidate to do the majority of the talking. Always allow time for you to be questioned as well and for you to add perspective.

What haven't we asked about that you would like to mention?
One point is the whole area of risk management. Risk management is a *huge* part of the world right now, but most people think of it in terms of trading risk, or reputational risk, or the risk to our physical security, like terrorism.

But again, from the risk management perspective in an organization or business, there are few risks greater than operational risk. And that boils down to people. One of the most important roles that HR plays for an organization is really risk mitigation.

> One of the most important roles that HR plays for an organization is really risk mitigation.

Another point I'd mention is that there are so many additional tools and insights that exist to help HR execute on business strategies, particularly data analytics and profiling, and to be able to get into predictive analytics as opposed to just reporting on the current state of human resources.

Understand that you're dealing with the most irrational, most dynamic, and most unpredictable part of the risk of execution—and that's human beings. It takes a very special skill to get everyone in the organization to understand the importance of optimizing, deploying, and engaging hearts, minds, and brains to be able to produce results.

That's the frustrating and exciting part of what the HR role is all about and what it should be doing for organizations. If you're an administrative checker or if you're the "HR police," number one, it's pretty boring; and number two, life's too short to be that shut off. I think that many organizations and executives miss the boat in understanding the value and importance of the role that HR plays in terms of the ability to execute a strategy.

PULL UP A CHAIR!
HR in the Hot Seat: Get Ready to Take Your Place at the Table

Read each of these statements describing an HR practice discussed in this book and make a quick note of how you assess yourself:

1 = "I have to admit, this is a weaker area or something I know little about" *or* "My boss tells me this is an area to work on."

2 = "Although I could improve here, I try to do this" *or* "My non-HR colleagues have noticed my efforts here."

3 = "This is a real strength of mine" *or* "Other business colleagues praise me consistently for my skill in this area."

HR IN THE HOT SEAT QUIZ

Leading Conversations

1. I have read and understand our strategy and key business objectives. ___
2. I can speak in business (not HR) terms about each element of our strategy and associated objectives. ___

(continued on next page)

3. I'm very comfortable discussing business matters with the leaders of business units because I can "connect the dots" among their challenges. ___

4. I keep up-to-date on economic and societal trends, political and legislative changes, and other forces outside our organization that can affect our business. ___

5. I have the personal credibility and professional poise to talk about HR/talent-centric solutions that support our corporate, and business unit, objectives. ___

Delivering Talent

6. I speak one-on-one in some length with the hiring manager in a business unit to discover and comprehend the critical skills and competencies—hard and soft skills—required for an ideal candidate for an open position. ___

7. I describe our organization's culture in distinctive and compelling ways to attract candidates (and retain them once they're hired) and to help ensure fit. ___

8. I mitigate the risk of a bad hire by using appropriate and valid EEOC-compliant assessments from trusted vendors. ___

9. I'm impeccably prepared for interviews, including creating open-ended behavioral questions, coordinating the interview team members' questions, and respecting everyone's time. ___

10. I link interview questions of candidates and references explicitly to the critical requirements for the role. ___

How did you do? If your 1 and 2 scores clump mainly among the first five questions, revisit Part 1 to "crack the code" in talking shop with business colleagues. If they fall primarily among questions 6–10, read Part 2 carefully for recommendations on highly effective practices pre-hire.

And if you scored mainly 3s, congratulations! As a business-savvy professional, you are a superb role model for folks in the human resources field. SHRM (2008) research indicates that 41, 62, and 71 percent of HR professionals in small, medium, and large organizations, respectively, have mentored others about how HR can contribute to business strategy. "Mentoring and/or advising has been cited as an important means through which HR professionals can inform others about HR's role in business strategy as well as gain a better understanding about the organization's business activities and learn how to form strategic connections between HR activities and business results" (SHRM, 2008, p. 31).

By all means, share your knowledge and wisdom with your HR colleagues as a mentor or coach and . . . take your seat at the table!

Additional Resources

Organizations

American Management Association: www.amanet.org; 855.814.6257

Offering more than 140 classroom (in 40 cities around the United States) and online courses on scores of topics, for corporate, nonprofit, and government employees; as well as certificate programs, designed for individuals or entire organizations, the latter as part of AMA's "talent transformation process."

CEB Corporate Leadership Council: www.clc.executiveboard.com; 866.913.6447

Advisory organization offering best practices of thousands of member companies, research, and human capital analytics, to provide "actionable solutions" to senior leaders and their teams.

Center for Creative Leadership: www.ccl.org; 336.545.2810

Top-ranked leadership education, skill development programs, research, assessments—in sum, "unparalleled expertise" in addressing leadership challenges—with locations in Greensboro, NC; Colorado Springs, CO; San Diego, CA; and seven cities in Europe, Asia, and Africa.

The Conference Board: www.conference-board.org; 212.759.0900

An independent source of economic and business research, as well as a host of public and private forums on critical business issues, in four main areas: Corporate Leadership; Economies, Markets, & Value Creation; High-Performing Organizations; and Human Capital.

Human Capital Institute: www.hci.org; 866.538.1909

A global association for strategic talent management and "new economy leadership," and a clearinghouse for best practices and new ideas, in HR design and delivery, technology, flexible and virtual workforces, human capital analytics, performance management, onboarding, and much more.

Human Resources Institute: www.federaltraining.com; 301.749.5600

As its web address indicates, training for federal agencies and contractors only, in topics like leadership development, staffing, interpersonal skills, financial management, and budgeting.

Institute of Leadership & Management: www.i-l-m.com; in London, 44 (0) 1543 266867

Skills training and certification in Great Britain, plus classes, research, and consulting in leadership and management, coaching and mentoring, HR, and enterprise.

Society for Human Resource Management: www.shrm.org; 800.283.7476

The world's largest association for HR professionals, with over 250,000 members in more than 140 countries, offering education, certification, research, customized support, subject-area newsletters and *HR Magazine,* regional and national conferences, and countless other valuable resources for members (PD templates, competency-based interview questions, etc.).

World at Work: www.worldatwork.org; 877.951.9191

A self-described "total rewards" nonprofit for HR professionals and organizations focused on compensation, benefits, work/life effectiveness, and strategies to engage and retain employees, through education, certification programs, advocacy, and research.

Academic Programs

On the Education page of its website at www.shrm.org, SHRM lists MBA programs around the country that have an HR concentration—programs that feature core business courses and typically four HR management courses. HR professionals with an MBA may qualify for a promotion and a bump in salary (Sunoo, 2013). See www.shrm.org/education/hreducation/pages/masterofbusinessadministration.aspx.

International Masters in Practicing Management: www.impm.org; in Montreal, 514.398.7309

Ideal for the HR professional who wants an experiential education on how business works, the IMPM is a uniquely practical take on an MBA or executive MBA, with real-world relevance. Designed by highly esteemed leadership expert Henry Mintzberg (2011, 2013), the creator of the Five *P*s model described in Chapter 1, this program offered by McGill University in Montreal is for experienced managers who want to enhance their management skills. The curriculum is delivered as critical-thinking roundtables, company visits, and classroom lectures led by global experts, in five modules—Managing Self, Organizations, Contexts, Relationships, and Continuity and Change—of no more than two weeks each, around the world: in Beijing, Rio de Janeiro, Montreal, Bangalore, and Lancaster, England.

Training

Cage Talent: www.CageTalent.com

We offer workshops based on the recommendations in this book that can be tailored to fit your audience's needs and time requirements, covering strategy, business communication, position descriptions, online assessment, and interview techniques. Mix and match the topics you like for customized instruction. Contact Jack Cage at Jack@CageTalent.com or 347.240.5350 for more information. Also see Cage Talent in the next section on "Business Partners" for information on our additional training offerings.

SHRM: www.shrm.org/seminars

The Society for Human Resource Management offers a strong suite of training programs for professional certification and continued learning, as both web-based learning and in-person programs in cities around the country. Besides its SHRM Essentials® of HR Management Course, here's just a sampling of topics particularly pertinent to those described in this book and offered as part of SHRM's Business Focus programs:

- Finance for Strategic HR Partners
- HR Metrics and Workforce Analytics
- Strategic Human Resources: Delivering Business Results
- HR Business Partners

Heinz Negotiation Academy for Women: heinz.cmu.edu/negotiation-academy-for-women; 412.336.8504

Based at Heinz College in Carnegie Mellon University in Pittsburgh, this is the first program in the United States to consider critical leadership skills through a negotiation lens and with a focus on the unique issues for women. Classes are held over six months on a consecutive Friday and Saturday once a month. Here's a sample of topics:

- Excel at Negotiating Smarter for You and Your Organization
- Close the Gender Gap
- Ask for What You Need to Succeed
- Negotiate to Enhance Relationships
- Leverage Your Talents and Claim Your Value
- Expand Your Influence: Make a Difference

Sales Performance International: www.spisales.com; 704.227.6500

In Chapter 3, we adapt Solution Selling® to help HR professionals engage with the key players in their organization on business topics like strategy and talent acquisition. If you're interested in actual sales training for your organization, you'll want to contact Sales Performance International (SPI). Owner of the Solution Selling Suite of sales, management, and marketing curriculum, SPI is a global sales performance improvement firm dedicated to helping the world's leading corporations elevate their sales relationships and drive measurable, sustainable revenue growth and operational sales performance improvement. It's been the leader in helping global companies successfully transition from selling products to marketing and selling high-value solutions.

If you'd like to learn more about their services or acquire templates of the tools we describe in Chapter 3, contact the SPI team at info@spisales.com, or purchase *The Solution Selling® Fieldbook* (Eades et al., 2005), which contains sales templates, scripts, and other valuable tools for several industries.

Business Partners

As the authors of this book, we'd be delighted to partner with you on your talent management needs and assist with the execution of your organization's strategy.

Cage Talent: www.CageTalent.com

Cage Talent partners with private and public corporate, government, and nonprofit organizations around the world in three main areas:

- *Executive search and recruiting*—from the president level to managers, for roles in IT, HR, and financial services; RPO services (e.g., position descriptions and scorecards, candidate write-ups, pre-hire assessment, reference reports, background checks, etc.)
- *Training and workshops*—customized offerings for presentations from an hour-long keynote to a two-day workshop, on mission-critical topics like leadership development and performance, selection and assessment of teams, tying talent management to organizational strategy, core management competencies, hiring best practices, powerful presentation skills, workplace effectiveness, and many others
- *Organization-wide talent audits and executive and team assessments*—survey design, 360° reviews, custom-made competency models, and assessments in behaviors, emotional intelligence, decision making, sales skills, communication, personality, motivators, values, and potential trouble spots

Premier Profiling: www.PremierProfiling.com

Premier Profiling picks up where Cage Talent's assessment offerings leave off, by designing and delivering assessment packages for your organization's or team's specific needs. We define "assessment" as far more than online instruments and include deep-dive interviews, career history reviews, and other components created just for your project. From one individual to teams of several hundred, we can provide you with the information you need to make highly effective talent management decisions (e.g., high-potentials, mentor/mentee matches, workforce reduction, gaps analysis, promotion candidates, succession planning, etc.).

For more information on any of our services or to request a complimentary online assessment:

Phone: 347.240.5350 or 646.284.7284
E-mail: Jack@CageTalent.com and Laura@CageTalent.com

You can also find us on LinkedIn and follow us on Twitter, @JackCage and @AntiguaPartners.

Cage Talent and Premier Profiling
are veteran- and woman-owned businesses
of Antigua Partners, Inc.

References

Abrams, R. 2013. Strategies: Women entrepreneurs sizzle. *USA Today Online,* July 8. http://ux-origin.usatoday.com/story/money/columnist/abrams/2013/07/05/small-business-women-entrepreneurs/2490933/

Aon Hewitt. 2009. *HR outsourcing trends and insights 2009.* www.aon.com/attachments/thought-leadership/Hewitt_HR_Outsourcing_Study_2009_Results.pdf.

Aon Hewitt. 2013. *Transforming HR: Becoming a strategic partner.* www.aon.com/human-capital-consulting/thought-leadership/outsourcing/article_transforming_hr.jsp.

Becker, B. E., Huselid, M. A., & Ulrich, D. 2001. *The HR scorecard: Linking people, strategy, and performance.* Boston: Harvard Business School Press.

Berkley, R. A. 2006. *Teaching guide for "Why We Hate HR" by Keith Hammonds.* Fast Company, *August 2005.* Alexandria, VA: Society for Human Resource Management. www.shrm.org/Education/hreducation/Documents/Why_We_Hate_HR_Teaching_Guide_FINAL_4-06.pdf.

Bolla, D. 2012. Out of the ashes: Where HR services have been—and where they're headed. *HRO Today,* September.

Bonstetter, B. J., & Bowers, R. 2004. *Personal Interests, Attitudes, and Values certification home study guide and manual.* Scottsdale, AZ: Target Training International.

Bonstetter, B. J., & Suiter, J. I. 2007. *The universal language DISC: A reference manual.* Scottsdale, AZ: Target Training International.

Boston Consulting Group. 2011. *Creating people advantage 2011.* Boston: Author.

Boushey, H., & Glynn, S. J. 2012, November 16. *There are significant business costs to employee turnover.* Washington, DC: Center for American Progress. www.americanprogress.org/wp-content/uploads/2012/11/CostofTurnover.pdf.

Bowers, A. 2012. If the job could talk, what would it say? *Success Insights* blog, October 10. www.ttisuccessinsights.com/blog/posts/if-the-job-could-talk-what-would-it-say#sthash.8xepY07r.dpuf.

Breitfelder, M. D., & Dowling, D. W. 2008. Why did we ever go into HR? *Harvard Business Review,* July 28. http://hbr.org/2008/07/why-did-we-ever-go-into-hr/ar/pr.

Cappelli, P. 2011. Why companies aren't getting the employees they need. *Wall Street Journal,* October 24. http://online.wsj.com/article/SB10001424052970204422404576596630897409182.html.

Charan, R., Drotter, S., & Noel, J. 2011. *The leadership pipeline: How to build the leadership powered company* (2nd ed.). San Francisco: Jossey-Bass.

Chen, B. X., & Pfanner, E. 2013. Cheaper iPhone will cost more in China. *New York Times,* September 12, p. B3.

Chermack, T. J. 2011. *Scenario planning in organizations: How to create, use, and assess scenarios.* San Francisco: Berrett-Koehler.

Claus, L., & Collison, J. 2005. *The maturing profession of human resources: Worldwide and regional view survey report.* Alexandria, VA: Society for Human Resource Management.

Conaty, B., & Charan, R. 2010. *The talent masters: Why smart leaders put people before numbers.* New York: Crown.

Daily Mail. 2006. Actor Everett labels Starbucks a "cancer." August 18. www.dailymail.co.uk/news/article-401223/Actor-Everett-labels-Starbucks-cancer.html.

Dattner, B. 2008. The use and misuse of personality tests for coaching and development. *Psychology Today* blog, June 13. www.psychologytoday.com/blog/minds-work/200806/the-use-and-misuse-personality-tests.

Deloitte. 2011. *Business driven HR: Unlock the value of HR business partners.* London: Author. www.deloitte.com/assets/Dcom-Ireland/Local%20Assets/Documents/Consulting/01_Deloitte%20Unlocking%20the%20value%20of%20HR%20Business%20Partners%20High%20Res.pdf.

Deming, W. E. 2000. *Out of the crisis.* Cambridge, MA: MIT Press.

Dotlich, D. L., & Cairo, P. C. 2003. *Why CEOs fail: The 11 behaviors that can derail your climb to the top and how to manage them.* San Francisco: Jossey-Bass.

Dye, C. F., & Garnman, A. N. 2006. *Exceptional leadership: 16 critical competencies for healthcare executives.* Chicago: Health Administration Press.

Eades, K. M. 2004. *The new Solution Selling: The revolutionary sales process that is changing the way people sell.* New York: McGraw-Hill.

Eades, K. M., Touchstone, J. N., & Sullivan, T. T. 2005. *The Solution Selling® fieldbook: Practical tools, application exercises, templates, and scripts for effective sales execution.* New York: McGraw-Hill.

Effron, M. 2013. *New Talent Management Network 2013 state of talent managers report.* Available at www.NewTMN.com.

Elmer-DeWitt, P. 2013. Katy Huberty: iPhone 5C could push Apple to no. 1 in China. *CNNMoney,* August 20. http://tech.fortune.cnn.com/2013/08/20/apple-huberty-china-iphone/.

Employee Leasing Options. 2013. *Your online guide to finding the right professional employer organization.* www.employeeleasingoptions.com/peocompany.

Fallaw, S. S., & Kantrowitz, T. M. 2013. *2013 global assessment trends report.* London: SHL. www.shl.com/assets/GATR_2013_US.pdf.

Fombrun, C. J., Tichy, N. M., & Devanna, M. A. 1984. *Strategic human resource management.* New York: Wiley.

Friedman, T. 2013. How to put America back together again. *New York Times,* April 20. www.nytimes.com/2013/04/21/opinion/sunday/friedman-how-to-put-america-back-together-again.html?pagewanted=all&_r=0.

Global Industry Analysts. 2012. *Human resources outsourcing (HRO): A global strategic business report.* Report MCP-1516. San Jose, CA: Author.

Grensing-Pophal, L. 2012. Financial acumen now a "must have" for consultants. SHRM.org, HR Disciplines, February 15. www.shrm.org/hrdisciplines/consultants/articles/pages/financialacumen.aspx.

Hammonds, K. H. 2005. Why we hate HR. *Fast Company,* August. www.fastcompany.com/53319/why-we-hate-hr.

Hanson, J. 2013. 4 Fortune 500 companies with long job applications. *SmartRecruiters* blog, www.smartrecruiters.com/blog/four-fortune-500-companies-with-long-job-applications/.

Harvard Business School Press and the Society for Human Resource Management. 2004. *The essentials of strategy.* Business Literacy for HR Professionals. Boston: Harvard Business School Press.

Haun, L. 2009. Love helping people? Don't go into HR. *Life between the Brackets* blog, June 9. http://lancehaun.com/love-helping-people-dont-go-into-hr/.

Hogan, R., & Hogan, J. 2007. *Hogan Personality Inventory manual* (3rd ed.). Tulsa, OK: Hogan Assessment Systems.

Hogan, R., & Hogan, J. 2009. *Hogan Development Survey manual* (2nd ed.). Tulsa, OK: Hogan Assessment Systems.

HROPlus. 2009. Benefits of outsourcing HR functions. http://mybackoffice.biz/wp-content/uploads/2012/12/HROplusWhitePaperSummer2009.pdf.

HRxAnalysts. 2011. *What HR thinks and feels: The 2011HRxAnalysts Psychographic Survey of HR Professionals.* Bodega Bay, CA: Author.

Hurt, A. 2010. Myers, Briggs, and the world's most popular personality test. *Mental Floss* blog, August 27. www.mentalfloss.com/blogs/archives/65202#ixzz1kJ5ce3yb.

Kaplan, R. S., & Norton, D. P. 2000. Having trouble with your strategy? Then map it. *Harvard Business Review,* September–October, pp. 167–176.

Kaye, B., & Jordan-Evans, S. 2014. *Love 'em or lose 'em: Getting good people to stay* (5th ed.). San Francisco: Berrett-Koehler.

KPMG. 2012. *Rethinking human resources in a changing world.* New York: Author.

Krznaric, R. 2013. Have we all been duped by the Myers-Briggs test? *CNNMoney.com,* May 15. http://management.fortune.cnn.com/2013/05/15/myers-briggs-problems/.

Larson, L. E. 2012. *Identifying high-performance security professionals using a competency model.* White paper, available from author: Laura@CageTalent.com.

Lee, C. 2013. China Mobile confirms Tim Cook met with chairman during recent visit. *iDownload* blog, July 31. www.idownloadblog.com/2013/07/31/ china-mobile-tim-cook-visit/.

Leonard, B. 2011a. Conaty: Strategic HR is being a talent master. SHRM.org, October 6. www.shrm.org/hrdisciplines/businessleadership/articles/Pages/ BeingaTalentMaster.aspx.

Leonard, B. 2011b. Job market improving for HR professionals. SHRM.org, December 19. www.shrm.org/hrdisciplines/technology/articles/pages/hrjobmarket.aspx.

Li, A. 2012. Why jobs remain unfilled even though unemployment is high. Infographic. Mashable.com, September 10. http://mashable.com/2012/09/10/ job-openings-unemployment.

Lombardi, M. 2013. *Assessments 2013: Finding the perfect match.* Boston: Aberdeen Group.

Lombardo, M. M., & Eichinger, R. W. 2008. *The Leadership Machine: Architecture to develop leaders for any future.* Los Angeles: Lominger International, a Korn/Ferry Company.

Lombardo, M. M., & Eichinger, R. W. 2009. *FYI for your improvement™: A guide for development and coaching for learners, managers, mentors, and feedback givers* (5th ed.). Minneapolis: Lominger International, a Korn/Ferry Company.

Luk, L., & Sherr, I. 2013. Supplier to ship two Apple iPhones in September. *Wall Street Journal Online,* August 20. http://online.wsj.com/news/articles/SB1000142412788 7324747104579022993954766508.

Mantell, R. 2011. Job seekers are getting tested. *Wall Street Journal,* September 11. http://online.wsj.com/article/SB10001424053111904836104576566335092 8693850.html.

Maurer, R. 2012. Survey: HR seen as important but fails to deliver. SHRM.org, HR Disciplines, November 16. www.shrm.org/hrdisciplines/businessleadership/articles/ Pages/HR-Fails-Deliver-Value-ROI.aspx.

Middleton, D. 2011. Students struggle for words: Business schools put more emphasis on writing amid employer complaints. *Wall Street Journal,* March 3. http://online .wsj.com/article/SB10001424052748703409904576174651780110970.html.

Miller, C. C. 2011. A changed Starbucks, a changed C.E.O. *New York Times,* March 12, p. BU1.

Miller, S. 2004. Weighing the advantages of total benefits outsourcing. SHRM.org, HR Disciplines, December 22. www.shrm.org/hrdisciplines/benefits/articles/pages/cms_010453.aspx.

MindTools. 2013. Mintzberg's 5 P's of strategy: Developing a better strategy. www.mindtools.com/pages/article/mintzberg-5ps.htm.

Mintzberg, H. 1987. Crafting strategy. *Harvard Business Review,* July–August, pp. 66–75.

Mintzberg, H. 2005. *Managers not MBAs: A hard look at the soft practice of managing and management development.* San Francisco: Berrett-Koehler.

Mintzberg, H. 2013. *Simply managing.* San Francisco: Berrett-Koehler.

Mirza, B. 2012. In strategic workforce planning, questions more important than answers. SHRM.org, Business Leadership & Strategy, March 14. www.shrm.org/hrdisciplines/businessleadership/articles/pages/strategicworkforceplanning.aspx.

Moore, K. 2011. Porter or Mintzberg: Whose view of strategy is the most relevant today? *Forbes,* March 28. www.forbes.com/sites/karlmoore/2011/03/28/porter-or-mintzberg-whose-view-of-strategy-is-the-most-relevant-today/#.

Myers, I. B., & McCaulley, M. H. 1985. *Manual: A guide to the development and use of the Myers-Briggs Type Indicator* (2nd ed.). Palo Alto, CA: Consulting Psychologists Press.

Parsons, N. E. 2011. *How to make successful employee selection decisions easier & less costly.* White paper. Tulsa, OK: CDR Assessment Group.

Peters, T. J., & Waterman Jr., R. J. 1982. *In search of excellence: Lessons from America's best-run companies.* New York: HarperCollins.

Porter, M. E. 1996. What is strategy? *Harvard Business Review,* November–December, pp. 61–78.

Porter, M. E. 1998a. *The competitive advantage of nations.* New York: Free Press.

Porter, M. E. 1998b. *Competitive strategy: Techniques for analyzing industries and competitors.* New York: Free Press.

Porter, M. E. 2008. The five competitive forces that shape strategy. *Harvard Business Review,* January. Reprint Number R0801E. http://hbr.org/2008/01/the-five-competitive-forces-that-shape-strategy/.

PwC. 2012. *The 15th Annual Global CEO Survey.* London: Author.

PwC. 2013. *The 16th Annual Global CEO Survey.* London: Author.

Ramirez, J. C. 2012. The feminization of HR. *Human Resource Executive Online,* March 1. www.hreonline.com/HRE/view/story.jhtml?id=533345673.

Sandberg, S. 2013. *Lean in: Women, work, and the will to lead.* New York: Knopf.

Schachter, H. 2012. Ask the right questions, hire the right staff. *The Globe and Mail* (Toronto), April 28. www.theglobeandmail.com/report-on-business/careers/management/ask-the-right-questions-hire-the-right-staff/article11577465/.

Schramm, J. 2013. What's your top challenge? *HR Magazine,* January.

Senge, P. M. 2006. *The fifth discipline: The art and practice of the learning organization* (Rev. and updated ed.). New York: Doubleday.

Simon, B. 2009. *Everything but the coffee: Learning about America from Starbucks.* Los Angeles: University of California Press.

Smart, B. D. 2012. *Topgrading: The proven hiring and promoting method that turbocharges company performance* (3rd ed.). New York: Penguin Books.

Smart, G., & Street, R. 2008. *Who: The A method for hiring.* New York: Ballantine Books.

Society for Human Resource Management. 2008. *HR's evolving role in organizations and its impact on business strategy: Linking critical HR functions to organizational success.* Alexandria, VA: Author.

Society for Human Resource Management. 2011a. *Future insights: Top trends according to SHRM's HR subject matter expert panels.* Alexandria, VA: Author.

Society for Human Resource Management. 2011b. *SHRM Workplace Forecast: The top workplace trends according to HR professionals.* Alexandria, VA: Author.

Staffing Industry Analysts. 2013. Matching jobs/skills tougher globally, US bucks trend. *StaffingIndustry.com,* "Daily News," May 28. www.staffingindustry.com/site/Research-Publications/Daily-News/Matching-jobs-skills-tougher-globally-US-bucks-trend-25909.

Sunoo, B. P. 2013. MBAs take human resources to a higher level. Monster.com, Career Advice, http://career-advice.monster.com/career-development/education-training/mbas-advance-hr-to-a-higher-level/article.aspx.

Sutherland, E. 2013. Survey: iPhone 5C could give Apple lead in China. *iDownload* blog, August 20. www.idownloadblog.com/2013/08/20/iphone-5c-apple-lead-in-china/?utm_source=feedburner&utm_medium=feed&utm_campaign=Feed%3A+iphonedlb+(iDownloadBlog).

Swanson, R. A., & Chermack, T. J. 2013. *Theory building in applied disciplines.* San Francisco: Berrett-Koehler.

Swanson, R. A., & Holton III, E. F. 2009. *Foundations of human resource development* (2nd ed.). San Francisco: Berrett-Koehler.

Target Training International. 2012a. *Behaviors technical report.* White paper. Tucson, AZ: Author.

Target Training International. 2012b. *Motivators technical report.* White paper. Tucson, AZ: Author.

Target Training International. 2012c. *TTI performance systems on adverse impact.* White paper. Tucson, AZ: Author.

Taylor, B. 2010. Why we (shouldn't) hate HR. *Harvard Business Review* Blog Network, June 10. http://blogs.hbr.org/taylor/2010/06/why-we-shouldnt-hate-hr.html.

Toscano, P. 2013. Howard Schultz: "I'm not losing any sleep over Dunkin' Donuts." *CNBC.com,* July 26. www.cnbc.com/id/100916904.

Ulrich, D., Younger, J., Brockbank, W., & Ulrich, M. 2012. *HR from the outside in: Six competencies for the future of human resources.* New York: McGraw-Hill.

U.S. Equal Employment Opportunity Commission. 2013. *Strategic enforcement plan FY 2013–2016.* Washington, DC: Author. www.eeoc.gov/eeoc/plan/upload/sep.pdf.

Van der Merwe, L. 2008. Scenario-based strategy in practice: A framework. *Advances in Developing Human Resources, 10*(2): 216–239.

Wright, J. 2013. America's skilled trades dilemma: Shortages loom as most-in-demand group of workers ages. *Forbes* blog, March 7. www.forbes.com/sites/emsi/2013/03/07/americas-skilled-trades-dilemma-shortages-loom-as-most-in-demand-group-of-workers-ages.

Wright, P., Stewart, M., & Ozias, M. 2011. *The 2011 CHRO challenge: Building organizational, functional, and personal talent.* Ithaca, NY: Cornell Center for Advanced Human Resource Studies.

Zappe, J. 2013. Survey says helping people, not profits, is primary driver for HR. *ERE.net, TLNT,* May 17. www.tlnt.com/2013/05/17/survey-says-helping-people-not-profits-is-primary-driver-for-hr.

Index

About the Authors

JACK H. CAGE, Ph.D., is president of Cage Talent (www.CageTalent.com), an executive recruiting and management consulting firm; and Premier Profiling (www.PremierProfiling.com), which offers customized, multicomponent solutions to talent challenges pre- and post-hire.

A graduate of the U.S. Military Academy at West Point, Jack served in the U.S. Army for 22 years: as a commander of infantry units; a special assistant to the Army's senior leadership, advising White House/National Security Council, congressional, and Pentagon staffs; and a CIO overseeing large-scale technology migrations. He returned to West Point as an associate professor to teach psychology, leadership, and research methods. A recipient of the Bronze Star, Combat Infantry Badge, and three Legions of Merit, Jack was an Airborne/Ranger infantryman who retired as a colonel.

Jack created Antigua Partners, Inc., and Cage Talent with his wife, Laura Larson, in 2007 and Premier Profiling in 2011. Together they conduct talent-centric work (search, pre-hire assessment, individual/team evaluation and development, management consulting) for both business and nonprofit organizations, as well as for high-net-worth families in the United States. They also design and implement customized programs centered on workplace effectiveness, selection and hiring best practices, and leadership, for the City of New York, the U.S. Department of State, and Chinese CEOs visiting the United States.

Jack has master's degrees in general and social psychology and a doctorate in organizational psychology, all from Columbia University. Upon retirement from the Army in 1997, he worked as a senior client partner for 10 years in executive search in New York City at the two largest publicly traded search firms, Heidrick & Struggles and Korn/Ferry International. At these firms, he specialized in advanced technology and financial services searches, placing senior executives at, among many others, American Express, Cisco, JPMorgan Chase, Legg Mason, McGraw-Hill, Visa, and Wells Fargo.

Jack is on the board of the Pat Tillman Foundation (www.tillmanfoundation.org). He also does extensive pro bono coaching to veterans transitioning to civilian life.

LAURA E. LARSON is co-owner of Antigua Partners, Inc., and the owner-publisher of Leap for Words (www.Leap4words.com). As a managing partner at Cage Talent, Laura recruits and interviews executives for senior roles, including for nonprofit locations in the Middle East and Asia, conducts 360° assessments of top executives, and manages the West Coast recruiting team. For Premier Profiling, she conducts deep-dive interviews and creates in-depth candidate profiles. She is formally trained to conduct Topgrading® interviews and is a certified assessment analyst in instruments measuring behavioral and communication styles, motivation and incentives, and professional competencies: DISC, PIAV, and TTI-DNA by Target Training International and Team Architect/Voices 360° by Lominger. She completed all coursework in 2003–2004 at Coach University, one of the few programs accredited at the time by the International Coaching Federation.

Laura graduated magna cum laude from the University of Illinois–Urbana with a B.S. in journalism, with minors in French, English, and German. She has studied French and contemporary French history in Avignon; Spanish in a four-week immersion program in Guatemala; and Italian and art history during a three-month stay in Florence.

Laura has extensive firsthand experience in nonprofits, having served on the executive committee of the board of StreetWise, an organization serving Chicago's homeless; as an award-winning volunteer hotline counselor and community educator for women's health, rape, and domestic violence groups; and currently as a pro bono résumé writer for Tillman Military Scholars.

This Book Saves Lives!

LEAP FOR WORDS donates a portion of the sales of all of its titles to select nonprofits. Thus,

25% of the proceeds of *HR's Seat at the Table* benefit UNICEF.

The United Nations Children's Fund (www.unicef.org) works globally to provide health care and immunizations, clean water and sanitation, nutrition, education, emergency relief (e.g., after Hurricane Katrina), trauma counseling, protection against trafficking, and more. It's helped save more children's lives than any other humanitarian organization in the world. UNICEF does *not* receive funding from the UN and relies on contributions from people like you. The U.S. Fund for UNICEF is a four-star Charity Navigator nonprofit, using more than 90% of donor dollars on its programming.

Depending on where you buy this book, *$3 to $7.50 will be donated to UNICEF. Your money goes farthest if you purchase books directly from us,* because there are no intermediate distribution fees (see the order form on the next page). Here's what $7.50—or 25% of $29.99—can do (estimated from examples of "Inspired Gifts" at www.unicef.org):

- **Vaccinate 26 children** for measles (600 kids die of measles every day).
- **Protect 2 children with insect-repellant-treated mosquito netting** to prevent mosquito-borne malaria (which is the #1 cause of children death in Africa, killing one child every 30 seconds).
- **Provide 75 oral rehydration salt packets** to prevent diarrhea (the second-largest cause of child death globally).
- **Deliver 264 high-energy protein biscuits** to victims of earthquakes, floods, cyclones, and other disasters.
- **End the misery of 200 children with deworming tablets** (and assure stronger physical and cognitive development of these kids, too).
- **Give 259 children micronutrient powder packets** or **5 children ready-to-eat peanut paste** to ward off malnutrition.
- **Deliver 3 pounds of milk-based powder formula** to emergency centers and refugee camps.
- **Clean about 5,100 liters of contaminated water** with purification tablets.

Every day about 19,000 children die from highly preventable causes, and the supplies listed here can reduce that number. Use the order form on the next page to make your purchase—and *thank you* for helping save a child's life.

ORDER FORM

To inquire about *volume discounts* or the *donations to UNICEF* from the sale of this book (25% of each book sold; see the other side of this form), or if you have any other *questions or comments,* please e-mail the publisher at Leap4words@gmail.com. To order:

- **Phone**: 917.538.9204 (in New York; see payment options below)
- **E-mail**: Leap4words@gmail.com
- **Online** (also available as an e-book for immediate download at these sites):
  HRs-Seat-at-the-Table.com
  CageTalent.com
  Leap4words.com
- **Amazon.com** (also available for Kindle e-readers)
- **iTunes.com**
- **U.S. Mail**: Please complete the form below and mail to
  Leap for Words, 789 E. 17th Street, Brooklyn, NY 11230-2411 USA.

— —

Yes, I'd love a *Seat at the Table*!
___ **@ $29.95 each**
plus
Sales tax *for delivery in New York state only*: See nystax.gov or contact us for your sales tax rate. In New York City, please add 8.875% (i.e., $2.65 for one copy, or $32.60 + shipping).
Shipping: $4 for first copy, $1 for each additional copy, in the United States;
   $10 outside the United States.
Payment:

- Send a *check* made payable to Antigua Partners, Inc. (the parent corporation of Leap for Words) to the mailing address above;
- Via *PayPal* or *Chase QuickPay* to Leap4words@gmail.com; or
- By *credit card*: ❑ Visa ❑ MasterCard ❑ American Express ❑ Discover

Card number: _____ Expiration: _____
Name on card: _____
Signature: _____

Send to:
Name: _____
Address: _____
City: _____   State/province:_____
ZIP/postal code: _____   Country: _____
Phone: _____   E-mail: _____

Thank you for your purchase today!